# Publishing and Readership in Revolutionary France and America

# Publishing and Readership in Revolutionary France and America

*A Symposium at the Library of Congress, Sponsored by the Center for the Book and the European Division*

Edited with an Introduction by
**Carol Armbruster**

Foreword by John Y. Cole

Beta Phi Mu Monograph Series, Number 4
*Wayne Wiegand, Series Editor*

**Greenwood Press**
Westport, Connecticut • London

**Library of Congress Cataloging-in-Publication Data**

Publishing and readership in revolutionary France and America : a
  symposium at the Library of Congress / sponsored by the Center for
  the Book and the European Division ; edited and introduction by Carol
  Armbruster ; foreword by John Y. Cole.
     p.    cm.—(Beta Phi Mu monograph, ISSN 1041-2751 ; no. 4)
  Includes bibliographical references and index.
  ISBN 0-313-28793-7 (alk. paper)
    1. Publishers and publishing—France—History—18th century—
Congresses.  2. Publishers and publishing—United States—
History—18th century—Congresses.  3. Books and reading—France—
History—18th century—Congresses.  4. Books and reading—United
States—History—18th century—Congresses.  5. France—History—
Revolution, 1789-1799—Congresses.  6. United States—History—
Revolution, 1775-1783—Congresses.  7. France—Intellectual
life—18th century—Congresses.  8. United States—Intellectual
life—18th century—Congresses.    I. Armbruster, Carol.  II. Center
for the Book.  III. Library of Congress. European Division.
IV. Series.
Z305.P78   1993
070.5'0944—dc20        92-38070

British Library Cataloguing in Publication Data is available.

Library of Congress Catalog Card Number: 92-38070
ISBN: 0-313-28793-7
ISSN: 1041-2751

First published in 1993

Greenwood Press, 88 Post Road West, Westport, CT 06881
An imprint of Greenwood Publishing Group, Inc.

Printed in the United States of America

The paper used in this book complies with the
Permanent Paper Standard issued by the National
Information Standards Organization (Z39.48-1984).

10 9 8 7 6 5 4 3 2 1

# CONTENTS

## READING

## COLLECTING AND USING MATERIALS

# FOREWORD

The Library of Congress established its Center for the Book in 1977 to stimulate public interest in books, reading, and libraries and to encourage the study of books and print culture. The Center is a catalyst for promoting and exploring the vital role of books, reading, and libraries--nationally and internationally. As a partnership between the government and the private sector, the Center for the Book depends on tax-deductible contributions from individuals and corporations to support its program.

The success of the symposium and the publishing of these proceedings has also depended on a number of people. We would like first to recognize the generous support of the Embassy of France and the French Ministry of Foreign Affairs in providing assistance to assure the participation of French scholars. We would like to recognize, in particular, His Excellency the former Emmanuel de Margerie, then ambassador of France to the United States, and Jean-Pierre Angrémy, then head of Technical, Scientific, and Cultural Relations of the French Ministry of Foreign Affairs, currently French Ambassador to UNESCO.

Historians of France in the greater Washington area, a constant source of reliable support for any number of French projects at the Library of Congress, were especially helpful during the very busy bicentennial year. We would like to recognize in particular Jack Censer, Robert Forster, Sandra Horvath-Peterson, Emmet Kennedy, and Donald M. G. Sutherland. The American Antiquarian Society, especially Marcus McCorison and John Hench, were also, as usual, invaluable and generous with their support.

Finally, among our many colleagues at the Library of Congress who assisted in numerous ways, we would like to recognize the register of copyrights, Ralph Oman, and, also of the Copyright Office, Lewis Flacks, both for their participation and helpful suggestions. As well, we wish to note with appreciation Anne Boni of the Center for the Book for helping to organize the conference; Janie Ricks, of the European Division, for extensive and reliable editorial assistance; and Stephen C. Cranton, also of the European Division, for technically transforming texts into print.

Carol Armbruster
French/Italian Area Specialist
European Division

John Y. Cole
Director, Center for the Book

# INTRODUCTION

*Carol Armbruster*

> Representation, or representative government, may be
> considered as a new invention, unknown in Montesquieu's
> time; it was almost impossible to put into practice before the
> invention of printing.
>
> *A Commentary and review of Montesquieu's "Spirit of
> Laws"*--Comte Antoine Louis Claude Destutt de Tracy. [1]

Throughout the eighteenth century the international exchange of ideas,
ideologies, and even personalities took place with relative ease among the
countries of Europe and the Americas. Communication in the medium of print
between France and colonial and early republican America was a vital factor
in the events within each country as well as between them. Their struggles for
representative government took place an ocean apart and in different political
and social contexts, but their shared interest and participation in each other's
revolution epitomized a new sense of change and opportunity for the future of
humanity.

The French and the American revolutions were understood as acts of
political will directed by enlightened populations. This kind of revolution,
unlike any previous, had implications far beyond the borders of any one
country. Fundamental to this enlightened political activity was the role of
information and education, a large proportion of which was circulated in print
media. Print media were thus directly related to the mobilization of a
population in their revolutionary efforts to establish representative government.

Thomas Jefferson, a significant figure in both the French and
American struggles for liberty and constitutional government, was well known
during his lifetime for his extensive acquisition and voracious reading of books

---

[1] Philadelphia: Printed by William Duane, 1811, p. 19. Originally written
in French about 1807.

and other publications in several European languages--notably French--as well as in classical Greek and Latin. Jefferson believed in the primary importance of the knowledge acquired from books to meet the local, national, and international challenges of his day. He bought for himself, for friends and relatives, and even for public use books he thought necessary in every field from applied science to abstract philosophy. Many of Jefferson's purchases were published in France or written in French. While he was in Paris as America's minister, from 1784 to 1789, he nearly doubled his already notable library. It is the library he established during his years as governor of Virginia, minister to France, secretary of state, and president of the United States--years of national and international importance--that is of particular significance to the Library of Congress.

In 1814 the Congress of the United States lost its library in the burning of the Capitol Building by British soldiers. Jefferson, then a former president living in retirement at Monticello, offered to replace the lost collections by selling his own books to Congress--a library known as the richest private collection in America. He strongly believed that Congress, which would inevitably be involved in both national and international affairs, would benefit substantially from the range of subjects and languages it contained. The legislators, however, challenged the need for such a variety of materials and questioned especially the extraordinary profusion and scope of French books; and they objected to the French material on both political and moral grounds:

> "It might be inferred," said Cyrus King, one of the principal
> antagonists, "from the character of the man who collected it,
> and France, where the collection was made, that the library
> contained irreligious and immoral books, works of the
> French philosophers, who caused and influenced the volcano
> of the French Revolution which had desolated Europe and
> extended to this country." Jefferson's books, which would
> help disseminate his "infidel philosophy," were "good, bad,
> and indifferent, old, new, and worthless, in languages which
> many can not read, and most ought not." (Cited in paper
> delivered by Douglas Wilson but not included in this volume
> and in William Dawson Johnston's *History of the Library of
> Congress: Volume 1, 1800-1864*, Washington, 1904, p. 86).

Jefferson, however, succeeded in persuading them that such a library was necessary to the long-term work of the Congress, even though it contained so wide a range of subjects and languages, some of which may have appeared irrelevant to a legislature, or even objectionable to it. "There is, in fact," Jefferson wrote, "no subject to which a member of Congress may not have occasion to refer. " The legislature finally agreed and thus acquired a collection that was much larger, much broader in focus, and far richer in all fields than the original library lost in the fire. This acquisition became the foundation and principal inspiration of the collections of the Library of Congress.

The range and depth of international collections at the Library of Congress have increased greatly since the early nineteenth century. The basic focus on the need for extensive international, as well as American, collections for the work of Congress and other branches of government has widened to include a much fuller range of constituencies, such as the national and international library communities, publishers, the media, scholars and researchers in need of print, image, and sound materials, and private citizens looking for information. Throughout this expansion the Library of Congress has continued and extended Jefferson's interest in acquiring French materials.

The importance of Thomas Jefferson in the events of revolutionary France and America and in the founding of the Library of Congress, and the Library's long tradition of strong French collections thus made the Library an appropriate location to discuss, in the bicentennial year of the French Revolution, a primary medium of national and international communication during the eighteenth century.    The publishing and reading of books, newspapers, pamphlets, and other printed materials during the revolutionary years of France and America were topics examined at a symposium at the Library of Congress on May 2-3, 1989. The symposium was organized to commemorate the bicentennial of the French Revolution, to recognize the work of scholars and other specialists in the fields of publishing and reading in France and the United States, and to contribute to the development of a comparative methodology in the international study of publishing and reading. The symposium brought together both French and American specialists.

During the last several decades the study of publishing and reading in France has been best known for the development of *l'histoire du livre*, the study of the production and consumption in society of printed materials--especially books--in French history. Historians of printed materials in France--predominantly social and economic historians--have been among the forefront both in developing a contextual approach to the study of communication by print and in exploiting a wide range of documentary sources other than the printed materials themselves. The focus, methodology, and source materials of these historians contrast with those of other specialists and traditions of the history of print both in France itself and in other countries. *L'histoire du livre* stands in strong contrast especially to the Anglo-American tradition of physical bibliography and its analytical, textual approach to the history of books.

The existence of an important English-speaking community working on the history of printed materials in France and the translation of French historical works into English have both led to a broader dissemination among American and other English-speaking historians of the *histoire du livre* tradition. In contrast, dissemination of the work on the history of printed materials in American culture, especially the book, is much more limited in France. Most work on the history of printed materials remains focused on national histories of publishing and reading rather than on broader, more international themes, and much work remains to be done in the international history of publishing and reading as it affected both Europe and the Americas.

The Library of Congress symposium brought together specialists working on a historical period, the national and international political importance of which is well recognized for both France and the United States. It was a period of intense international exchange of publications. Publishing and reading played significant roles in the mobilization of the populations of both countries in breaking with traditional political orders and establishing new ones. What those roles were, how they developed, and how we can understand them within the historical and cultural contexts of the French and American revolutions were among the themes of the papers presented during the symposium. Broad subjects such as publishing as a profession, publishing and the law, readership, collecting and using materials, as well as methodologies and sources, were the subject of investigation. In presenting those findings, symposium participants not only contributed to the study of the medium of print in the eighteenth century but also experienced themselves and revived the international exchange of ideas that took place throughout this period.

## PUBLISHING AS A PROFESSION

From the seventeenth to the nineteenth century, no significant technological developments occurred in the printing profession. Yet, major changes occurred in publishing as a profession in late eighteenth century France and America. In his review of historical problems related to the study of the French Revolution, Daniel Roche states the need to examine the vital contributions of the publishing industry to the creation of a new political culture. In the growing and more diversified production of printed products, we need to study printed products not only as part of a general information system in a predominantly oral culture, but we also need to measure the impact of these publications as new products. Robert Darnton reconstructs from account books of the Société Typographique de Neuchâtel the labor and economic history of the 1770 edition of the baron d'Holbach's *Système de la nature*, a major Enlightenment text. He uses it as a case study to describe the clandestine publishing of French books in countries on the periphery of the kingdom of France and the role of such activity in the diffusion of the critical ideas of the Enlightenment within the controlled literary market of France. The way in which print culture spread through America, according to Larzer Ziff, was related to issues of political representation in a republic; and a printer as astute as Benjamin Franklin knew how to take advantage of it. Ziff describes how Franklin purposely shifted away from a manner of writing that implied the author as an "immanent" authority figure speaking to a particular community of readers toward a manner that implied the author as a representative of a more indeterminate community of readers, "a common reader."

## PUBLISHING AND THE LAW

The legal controls governing publishing differed in prerevolutionary France and America. The success of the revolutions and of revolutionary programs--especially the efforts to establish constitutional government--involved the relationship between publishing and the law. Carla Hesse examines the effects of the deregulation by the French revolutionaries of the printing and publishing world of Old Regime France and focuses on the "most treasured cultural invention of the early modern period," that is, books. The serious disruption of book production called into question the means by which the revolutionary ideal of a free and enlightened republic might best be achieved. James Gilreath describes the growth of the role of public opinion in eighteenth-century America as a factor in the transformation of printed public information from official government publication of citizens' responsibilities to citizens' use of print as a medium of mass communication in which to debate political and social issues free of government influence. Focusing on both the rhetoric and policy of the first French and U.S. copyright laws (1790), Jane Ginsburg questions traditional interpretations that they had different principles and goals. She describes how the concept of the natural right of creators, which emphasizes protection of the creators' property right, and the utilitarian ethic, which seeks to protect authors' rights in order to stimulate production of intellectual creations for a public benefit, affected the writing of the first French and U.S. copyright laws.

## FORMS OF READERSHIP

Marked changes occurred in readership during the revolutionary eras on both sides of the Atlantic. Roger Chartier discusses the question of whether the origins of the French Revolution can be attributed to the distribution of "philosophical texts" during the eighteenth century. This would assume, he states, that the act of reading was a passive reception of the messages of a text rather than a free and creative activity that varied with individual readers or groups of readers. He calls for a wider cultural context in which to understand the importance of the large-scale circulation of all printed materials and changing reading habits that may have contributed to making the radical break with the older order possible. Lynn Hunt expands the scope of the discussion to consider the relationship between visual and verbal forms of representation. She describes how French authorities, unlike the Americans, devoted considerable energy to revolutionary propaganda through signs and symbols yet tended to value the verbal (printed) over the visual as a more reliable conveyer of messages. She also considers the role that gender may have played in this preference of the verbal over the visual. David Hall, in his discussion of the politics of culture in eighteenth-century America, describes the opposition between an exclusive, learned, and cosmopolitan literary culture and a more inclusive one related to the religious culture of the Reformation premised on broad access to the Word. He also describes how a more democratic world of print may have helped lead to revolution in America rather than to have followed from it as in France. Michael Warner relates the assumption of an intrinsically critical reading public and the understanding of print as impersonal discourse to the Anglo-American strand of republicanism. Within this social and political context, he shows how the mediation of print enabled, indeed obliged, the public to enter into a debate and thereby assume the rights and duties of active citizenship.

## COLLECTING AND USING MATERIALS

By the eighteenth century there were well-established traditions of collecting books and establishing libraries in Europe. The Enlightenment, the revolutions, and the efforts to establish new governments affected and were affected by collections of materials and the access or lack of access to them. Henri-Jean Martin qualifies the French Revolution as the revolution of books par excellence and describes the major commitments made by revolutionaries to collect and preserve the books that made up the cultural heritage of France. He shows how the commitment to establishing a national collection and a national bibliography involved the confiscation of over 10 million volumes from libraries throughout France, an event that resulted in strong collections of France's literary heritage to be housed in a few libraries in Paris, including the Bibliothèque Nationale, and caused major losses of that same heritage in the provinces. Marcus McCorison focuses on the libraries of several major figures from a variety of professional communities and regions of colonial, revolutionary, and early republican America. He shows how Americans continued a tradition of collecting books and other materials based on European cultural traditions but also adapted their collecting to deal with a new world and a new nation.

The symposium also featured several outstanding papers on non-book modes of communication in the eighteenth century, particularly the press studies, that lie beyond the scope of the present volume. The Library is most grateful to all of the symposium participants for providing two full days of very lively discussions. All the speakers and participants in the 1989 conference contributed to its success, and their comments and conversation have informed the papers included in this volume.

# PUBLISHING AS A PROFESSION

# PRINTING, BOOKS AND REVOLUTION

*Daniel Roche*

(Translated by David Skelly and Carol Armbruster)

It is as a historian of Old Regime society and culture--rather than as a historian of books, printing, or reading or as a historian of the French Revolution--that I welcome the opportunity to discuss the role of printed materials and their reception in revolutionary France. I welcome the opportunity of the internationally comparative context to advance our understanding of the cultural origins of the French Revolution, to assess the political and social intelligibility of its development, and to see what sort of information can be obtained from it as regards its major consequences, consequences that underpin our culture to this day.

## HISTORY OF BOOKS, SOCIAL HISTORY, CULTURAL HISTORY

Historians of my intellectual generation are the heirs of a tradition that is based on four major postulates. First, reading is understood as a powerful factor in social change. Reading affected history, and it is thus necessary to understand the diffusion of reading within a society in order to understand the symbiotic relationship between culture and politics so characteristic of Western civilization. The second postulate emphasizes the role played by the Enlightenment in the Revolution. The anti-establishment activities of the Enlightenment were seen within an immediately teleological worldview. The third postulate relates the chronology of intellectual breaks, that is, the development of an anti-establishment mentality, to the traditional breaks of political periodicity: 1685, crisis of conscience; 1715, liberation of the Regency; 1775, failure of reforms; 1785-1789, prerevolutionary explosion. Cultural history--indeed, the study of cultural production--must deal with these major shifts in political history. Finally, the Revolution, which was above all a political break of a social order, generated a revolution in mentality that has even been called a *cultural revolution*. There was a major break in the system of cultural production and diffusion.[1]

The role played by quantitative and statistical methods of inquiry has been considerable. These methods have, in fact, reopened the whole debate about the meaning of the Enlightenment and the Revolution. We have learned that the quantitative approach can be applied to cultural objects as well as to all other human creations. We need to recognize, however, which questions will lend themselves to the statistical method and remember that, like all historical interpretation, that derived from these methods is relative. The statistical method teaches us to read differently by forcing us to make comparisons on the basis of a reconstructed historical object, one with which we are already partially acquainted. It has never postulated that the books themselves should not be consulted, as some critics of the method claim. Its chief merit, on the other hand, is that it helps us to read better by putting our reading back into an overall framework, where the discontinuities, discordances, and disparities are problematic, and by giving us an immediate understanding of what brings us close to, or distances us from, social groups or distinguishes individuals. It has been on the basis of several works of this nature that we have been able to question generally assumed classifications and contrasts: innovation and tradition, break and continuity, production and consumption. In short, using numbers permits us to become better aware of the status of our texts, to inquire as to how they were diffused and what social reception they had, and to identify the scope of their applicability. Their chief advantage has been to raise more questions than they can solve and to complicate problems rather than simplify them.

Today it is possible to look at the cultural origins of the Revolution from a different viewpoint. The use of the word *Revolution* for the cultural, as well as for the intellectual, sphere is a sign of widening perspective. These origins can be studied from the viewpoint of the printed product. We can study how the printed product contributed to a new interpretation of social and political issues. We can also measure the extent to which the circulation of printed matter induced certain effects in a society firmly rooted in orality. Finally, in studying continuities and discontinuities, we can examine the results of the efforts made by the publishing industry as a constituent element in a new political culture.[2]

## PRODUCTION OF PRINTED MATERIALS

Books did not exist in isolation in the past anymore than they do today, not in the printing shop, nor on the bookstore shelves, nor in the peddler's pack. The publishing industry has always marketed a very diverse production and one that is capable of delivering many disparate messages. Production is driven by economic considerations, which do not necessarily correspond exactly to the demands for the printed product. Publishing controls do not even fully explain production. Efforts to subject publishers and booksellers to censorship can produce contrary results. Diderot once exclaimed: "Sirs, please, just a small decree sentencing me to be torn and burned at the foot of your grand staircase."[3]

A growing and more diversified production characterizes the period between the seventeenth and the nineteenth centuries, one unmarked by any major technological change. Books, newspapers, pamphlets, pictures--with or without accompanying text, songs, playing cards, tickets, and administrative material--were all increasingly abundant. An increasing number of books was produced with practically the same technology, a technology capable of printing runs of approximately 1,000 to 1,500 copies. From a variety of sources--bibliographies such as *France Littéraire*, chancellory registers, or library collection surveys--we have charted the increase in the number of book titles available to the public. Around 1700 there were 300 to 400 titles, 1,000 around 1775, and 2,000 in 1789. There was subsequently a decline in book production. This decline is still poorly understood, but it coincided with an increase in the potential of other forms of publication--newspapers, pamphlets, bulletins, and posters, to take the place of book publication.

The demand for an increasingly diversified production was remarkable. The increased production of small formats, more affordable and easier to use, attests to such a demand. So does the success of periodicals, which at first took the place of books but then became more and more a medium of exchange and influence on their own. Finally, it can be seen in the increase of printed formats that included both the written word and images, among them manuals, treatises, almanacs, and chapbooks of the greatest variety and number.

Obviously the circulation of an increasing amount of all kinds of printed material reflected a demand for the materials. We can also see in the variety and distribution of materials elements of constraint and freedom affecting the different kinds of publishing and the publishers. It is clear that everything was contrived to strengthen the grip of the already-existing monopoly of publishers in Paris. The surveys of the chancellory in 1666, 1701, and 1777 prove that this Colbertism of the book adapted quite well to the Enlightenment and vice versa. In mapping out the printshops, however, we see something else.

First of all, we see that the number of printshops declined more in the great urban centers than in the small towns. The decreasing number of shops in the densely populated Paris region thus required a higher production rate of those shops. We also see that the traditional cultural split between the North and South of France was drawn sharply in the mapping of printshops, indicating an indirect ratio between literacy and consumption. Fewer presses existed in those places where a growing population of readers demanded they be developed.   Other major factors affecting the distribution of printshops include multilingualism and the pressure of schools.

Finally, confirming the results of production analysis, we can see two kinds of printing on the maps.   First, throughout France there were the requirements of urban administration, which corresponded to the growing needs of Church and school administrations.   The revolutionary period was to ensure the strength of this kind of publishing.   Second, more dispersed, there was book and newspaper publishing.   This kind of publishing was more subject to business competition, and the provinces could compete with Paris only with great difficulty.   The major printers in the capital had the advantages of proximity and easier access to licenses and *privilèges tacites*, close ties with the literary circles, and a large, immediate, buying public.   In addition, these printers benefitted from the fact that whether they were innovators or conservatives, their activities and their choices generated a widespread habit of consumption throughout France, a fact that guaranteed them even greater profits and a greater control of the market.

The 1777 Council decree, which was intended to readjust the balance between provincial and Parisian production, occurred too late to undo what had become established activities in both Paris and the provinces.   The immediate consequence of this decree was to encourage copyright infringement, which capitalized on proven success and obvious demand.   For the provinces clandestine publishing was an attempt to compete economically with Paris.   Clandestine publishing was also the means by which foreign French-language editions got a foothold in the French market.[4]

The way clandestine publishing worked is well understood today, thanks to the work of Robert Darnton.[5]   Widespread circulation of prohibited books influenced a growing number of readers, mainly in the cities.   These materials were produced and distributed by publishers located in Amsterdam, Bouillon, Liège, Maastricht, Cologne, Neuchâtel, Geneva, and Avignon.   They published and sold books at lower prices and reprinted books that were already in demand, thus guaranteeing profits.   They published something for everyone, from theology to the latest fad in philosophical thought.

The legitimate and the clandestine markets more or less intersected. It was, however, the entry into the market of a flood tide of critical works, broadsides, and pamphlets that accelerated changes in customs and mores. Censorship and surveillance were helpless against them.

The collapse of the French state surveillance apparatus has never been sufficiently emphasized.   The system's activities were dictated simultaneously by the economic interests of the producers and the ideological watch of the three major taboos: the *king*, *God*, and *morals*.   It had been vigilant throughout the century, but people had also grown accustomed to its alternating bouts of moderation and repression, as well as uneven enforcement thereof.   Legal proceedings always came down harder on the small people in the printshops than on the heavyweights in commerce and the academies.  During the Old Regime this system was adaptable enough to encourage free trade and check the spread of licentiousness at the same time.  Tolerance alternated with harshness as a function of the pressures being exerted on agencies that only wanted--and this is a major law in the history of governments--to attend to their administrative duties in peace.  Faced with both a domestic and a foreign production of dangerous publications, the censors and the police, working without a firm and consistent policy or directives, may have often only worked to limit the degree of advertising their feeble measures provided for these inflammatory writings.[6]  The twenty or thirty final years before the Revolution are stamped with the uncertainty of the control system.  Consumer demands, which increased with the century, ended by carrying the system away.

As we reconstruct the production of printed materials we are forced to conclude that the boundary between legal and illegal publications was never absolute nor permanent.  Many books moved from one category to another; many publishers made a profit by publishing without too much trouble what had been forbidden only the day before.  This is why it is so difficult to interpret the meaning of thematic changes in printed materials.

In official and unofficial, legal as well as pirated, production, one fact is highly suggestive of a profound intellectual transformation: the drop in the production of religious books and religious pictures.  Between the seventeenth and eighteenth century writing and painting became secular in France.  Around 1700 religious books accounted for 50 percent of production; around 1780 they accounted for only 10 percent.  There are three problems, however, which analysis of official registers or surveys of local production have never solved.  First is the problem of the ratio of printing to title.  In those registers which include provincial publishers after 1777, religious titles continue to figure prominently.  Fifty percent of 400 titles is 200 works, but 10 percent of 2,000 is still 200.  Thus, even if the *Ange conducteur* did not contribute directly to the making of the Revolution, its remarkable distribution raises direct questions about the connection between production, consumption, and transformation.[7]  Second, what kind of religious production are we talking about?  This problem has not yet been sufficiently studied, especially with quantitative studies of the production.  Studies based on sectorial analysis, however, suggest that religious production consisted mostly of unaltered Tridentine production, with a minority of apologetics alongside the ideas of the Enlightenment.  The basic essentials in the religious domain, however, as Bernard Groethuysen perceived, were played out between the oral and the written, between the sermon and reading.  By its ability to shape a more practical, more nimble, more individualistic way of thinking between exterior discipline and interior religion, the whole religious production was in a position to help mold collective religious feelings differently.

The category of "arts and sciences" benefitted the most from the decline in strength of religious topics in the increasing volume of publications. This shift suggests a new relationship between the individual, society, and nature. Arts and sciences gained followers everywhere and benefitted from a maximum of publicity in the press. It was nonetheless, in all its heterogeneity, a locus privileged by the way in which an extremely diversified production was distributed and received. Studies of the clandestine trade have complicated more than clarified our understanding of the situation. The French survey of the list of administrative interdictions between 1678 and 1776 shows a predominance of religion in art and literature until 1750-60, after which the same reversal can be seen there, as was observed in the book trade catalogs. We can see in the 300 to 500 titles put out by the Société typographique de Neuchâtel and in the inventories from other publishers outside France between 1770 and 1789 the prevalence and large-scale distribution of secular publications. What is evident is not so much a different reading public as a new product taking the market by storm. Scandal played a role in market growth and from time to time made a success of books that were largely critical, satirical, political, and pornographic. We need to measure the full impact of these publications as new products. The formulas of their contents, for example, political pornography, were not new, and had, in fact, existed since the beginning of the century. The transformation that these publications dictated remains to be explained and will necessitate new research into the sociology of the readers and into the "ways of reading and doing." We need, through inventories, to establish the type of production and models of consumption. The interpenetration of official, unofficial, and clandestine markets and the crisis in a state surveillance system confronted with increasing production attest to the strength of the demand. We need to understand the market demand in order to see how it was related to the creation of a new public spirit in which reading and readers constitute the principal factors for change.


## FROM PRODUCTION TO CONSUMPTION

As early as 1766 Voltaire, in a letter to d'Alembert, rightly perceived the problem of book consumption: "I would like to know what harm a book costing a hundred crowns could do. Twenty folio volumes are never going to cause a revolution; those little portable books are the ones to fear."[8] Historical studies that have shifted their focus from the production of the book to its consumption have taken off in three directions. First, there has been an effort to determine the potential number of readers and the different reading traditions that organized public consumption. Second, there is an effort to interpret the act of reading a book in relation to other modes of access to reading. Third is the study of individual and collective use or ways of reading. In spite of regional differences and sexual or social inequalities, literacy increased throughout France. The printed word became more familiar and widespread, as did a number of reading traditions.

The first tradition is the reading done by illiterates, as paradoxical as this may seem. The opportunity to learn to read or write was determined by economics. Numerous peasants and hordes of urbanized migrants remained illiterate and made easy prey for the literate, that is, the boss, the tax collector, the landlord, customs officials, the vicar, the curate, and the nobleman. Although the illiterate groups were predominantly oral cultures, these groups were forced to participate in the literate world. They were often obligated to sign papers. More and more often, they needed to know how to count, usually for the purposes of a receipt. These groups resisted this forced "literacy" in both passive and active ways. Their oral traditions, as well as written hagiography and local stories, were storehouses of ruses that were sometimes adapted for the situation.

Just above this cultural level was that of those who knew how to read, write, and count. There was some mobility between these two groups; people could either climb out of the lower one or fall back into it. Shop foremen; middle-class tradesmen; master craftsmen; masters' widows; wives, sons, and daughters of master craftsmen; farmers; laborers; tithe holders; and small businessmen all had to be able to read on a day-to-day basis. They needed to be able to verify a lease or an order, read and write letters, consult price lists, accounts, and so on. Books were present in this group, often as lone items, sometimes constituting tiny collections of religious and practical books. The New Testament and the tax schedule were emblematic in this environment. The predominance of religious pictures is an index of their integration into high culture. But there were signs of change among these common folk living in either the country or an urban environment. In writing their autobiographies, Jacques Louis Ménétra in Paris and Louis Simon in Fontaine near Le Mans showed what an impact reading could have. Reading led to introspection, which in turn led to unauthorized writing. It was from this very fermentation that cities and villages alike, with their minor littérateurs, derived their potential for mobilization and political action.

The next level, no more sharply distinguished from the second than the second was from the first, consisted of the genuine merchant, the large manufacturer, the large entrepreneur, who all needed numbers and letters. Their personal culture depended on many things, most especially the kind and extent of their education, but also on the scale of their business, their involvement in monetary abstractions, and, finally, their discovery of political economy. Several ledgers, a good arithmetic book, and maybe one or two conversion tables would be all they needed for a long time. These basic needs could be easily taken care of by the local bookstore. Business correspondence would be a daily necessity. The reading and writing habits of local judges, medical practitioners, persons of independent means, and property owners would rarely require more than the specific needs of their professions, their devotional habits, or the demands of the small social life of provincial cities. But it is precisely at this cultural level that the greatest changes came into play and where the study of books reveals a growing appreciation for high culture between the seventeenth and eighteenth centuries. Reading books was both of primary and secondary importance in these groups. Professional interests became more diversified and led to the publication of greater in-depth information. Savary's *Parfait négociant* and travellers' tales are part of this kind of reading. Social life and leisure led to less formal reading. Belles lettres, the theater, and especially novels predominate in this category. Exoticism and sensibility were enormously popular. The catalog of the Bordeaux Museum library gives ample, if purely nominal, evidence of this. Politics is slipped in under many guises, in poetry, reformist articles, plays, and philanthropic pamphlets. Overall, reading habits at this cultural level were less indicative of ideology than of the mobilization of prominent citizens vis-à-vis the circumstances of the time. Intellectual debate was only indirectly connected with reading.

Finally, at the top, there were the scholars and intellectuals, who read and wrote perfectly both French and Latin. Educated at the *collèges* and the universities, they were full of confidence in themselves and in others. It is in this milieu that the great social dramas of knowledge and power were played out. Here was the booksellers' regular clientele; they were habitués of bookshops by profession and inclination. Around 1650 there were 60,000 students in the *collèges*; around 1789 there were an additional 50,000, plus all those who attended numerous new-style institutions. They made up the great bulk of pedants and real intellectuals. Only 12,000 to 15,000 of these ever made it to the universities. All in all, most readers fell between two figures: the literate and the well-read, between 40 percent and less than 1 percent. This stark contrast was the source of the prestige conferred upon regular readers. Four words of caution are in order here.

First of all, the use of books and printed materials cannot be related only to literacy and book ownership. Reading habits progressed in degrees, from occasional to regular readers, and in various ways, all readers could have been reading differently and for different purposes. Reading for any of them could have been efforts to decode written signs and letters, looking for information or escape, or reading for pleasure. Second, access to books and reading presupposed for most of these people a major change in their way of life. As with writing, reading was first and foremost an option. Popular leisure activities and other habits of consumption competed with reading. An everyday use of books assumes an increase in individualization in the general population. In the same way as other kinds of consumption, such as clothing, reading contributed to the development of modern individualism.  Individualism is understood as that tendency either to become identified with or to withdraw from a universe of belonging, and, as Georg Simmel has shown, to demand that liberty and equality be related.[9]

In the third place, we must rewrite the history of the various reading pedagogies, which will provide the key to reading habits.  In writing "barely twelve years old, Emile knew what a book was," Rousseau powerfully expressed the union of the two concepts of individualization.  Reading was a secret domain discovered only after most children completed elementary school.  It expressed the taking on of an exclusive activity.  And, finally, we cannot ignore the roles of the state and fortune.  In any kind of study, they determine access without actually imposing or enforcing laws.  They weave the web of possibilities between basic needs and a taste for culture.  If we follow the scale of reading levels, we will also notice consistences related to reading traditions in families, in various social milieus, and in cultural groups.  Pious, devotional reading generally coincides with the single book owned by the poor man, the bachelor, the adult woman, and the widow.  The average collections of a Parisian shopkeeper or artisan, or of a merchant in one of the cities in western France are already indicative of a more powerful creative capacity: it is less the number of books that is important than the way in which a variety of interests are brought together.  Access at the library level presupposes accumulation and inheritance.  Whatever the tradition--aristocratic, legal, ecclesiastical--there are always different kinds of reading, a variety of cultural tastes.

Nevertheless, it was probably in the different ways of dealing with books that the eighteenth century underwent the most profound and far-reaching changes.  Printed materials were integrated into otherwise nonliterate situations such as population migrations, markets, fairs, and the theater, especially in the cities.  Items such as placards, posters, hymns, songs, libretti, the cheap press, and jokes were part of these social events.  Shop signs, street signs, and house numbers structured perceptions of the streets and established order where disorder had prevailed.  All these kinds of reading were open to everyone, providing both collective and individual activities.  Reading contributed to freeing individuality and encouraged the articulation of private lives and collective culture.  Future research should promote the study of the cultural roles of domestic servants, employees, shop clerks, and soldiers.  They were at the intersection where the dominant cultural values take on meaning because they have to call upon both heritage and acquisition for change, because they move the norms from one point to another in the social space.

One should emphasize the common faces of reading, because there again are entwined individual independence and common assimilation of personal differences.  Reading was no longer identified with possession of a book or with a particularized activity, but, simultaneously, multiple readings were making differentiated abilities universal, were facilitating the transition from a rare gesture generally linked to the possession of a single book to extensive, more varied, habits, whether these hastened the indirect occasions for familiarity with reading or whether they concentrated and broadened direct diffusion.  The workshop and the shop, the religious assembly, festive confraternities, cabarets, and theaters were by way of being common meeting places places where exchanges took place between non-readers and habitual readers.  In these places were circulated the productions least visible to learned perspectives:  they have not held scholars' attention, being ephemeral, economic, with no aesthetic value according to recognized canons.  There we must search for and find pattern books, treatises of weights and measures, booklets of prayers and hymns, ludic material, printed texts of plays and songs.  Those two powerful points of strain, faith and religion on the one hand, and work and leisure on the other, confers on them the value of exemplary relations and fashions a common personality based on multiple personal victories whose benefits are then shared.  The booklets that peddlers sold from house to house and the printed materials of all kinds circulating everywhere played only a marginal role in the enculturation of the poor:  the appropriation of these was, on the contrary, liberating to individuals, and it paved the way for other reading.  The process of diffusion of printed materials obscures things everywhere.  No longer a rare item, reading became a commodity, rarely enough still in rural areas, but massively in the city; from there, the sought-after effects to distinguish oneself by reading, which would enhance one's standing in isolation and seriousness.  The circulation of printed materials and books did not stifle the multiplicity of kind of readers, anymore than it was satisfied with inculcating the discipline of religion or of morality.  As a commodity generating new habits, it sanctioned the unlocking of minds.

The same for direct access.  It could be by way of borrowing, giving, or stealing, evading market constraints in this way.  It could follow commercial routes from the capillary diffusion of large-scale peddling to the clientele relations that spring up between a bookstore and its customers in town.  Onto these tracks are grafted others, such as those of the privileged places of ancient and modern institutions that mobilize printed materials and reading.  To the shop was linked book lending and the paying lending library, which enhanced profits in direct proportion to the speed of turnover of reading materials.  On the practices of sociability and meeting were built the networks of lending libraries and literary societies.  Whatever the printed materials, they turned into immediate material for discussion for those who could pay the subscription. It is not immaterial to see these institutions proliferate either too loosely meshed, as in the case of academic regroupings, or where business and the culture of business called for other resources than those of the academic elites. Reading was no longer characteristic of the private sector, but a factor in the social cohesion of those milieus that have the means to match their culture.

Finally, with the libraries were created simultaneously a tradition of collective access to the treasures of an amassed heritage and that of the sense of civic responsibility among the elites and notables, religious or lay, who unlock them and protect them from the perspective of collective patronage and progress in the service of the city. With that, we have reached the cultural and social limits of their way of doing things. These limits were traced by the increased number of readers, by the inventiveness and suppleness of new resources and new institutions, in the discussions provoked by the overwhelming success of printed matter.     The opposition of reading as a medium, reality or representation, and interiorized, secret reading, the antagonism between a vision of progress supported by reading and negative utopia reveal the sociocultural stakes.[10] But one can also find there the very techniques, the principles of modern life as it is lived chiefly in our great cities:  increasing intellectualism, abstraction of trade created by extensive marketing and production, tension between the individual and the community, and, due to highly developed habits of consumption, between appearances and being.


## READING, TALKING, WRITING

Henceforth it would seem possible to reread the sociopolitical integration sustained by printing.[11] It has something of the nature of the constitution of the public space where, to speak like Kant, all those gather in the free exercise of reason, who consider themselves equals and manifest their critical interest in matters constitutive of society and the state.  Sociability and reading have reinforced each other, calling on books and newspapers, and also on unprinted forms of writing: articles and correspondence.  This is a trait common to all the gatherings going on everywhere just before 1789: salons, cafés, lending libraries, literary societies, museums, schools, Masonic lodges, academies in Paris and in the provinces.  More or less intellectualized, the practice of meeting together, where the equality of the participants is always affirmed, no matter what their social origin (at least in principle), mingled reading and conversation, discussion and reporting; but printed matter serves everywhere as a point of reference for critical reasoning and causes it to penetrate realms prohibited to public debate until then.  It was printing and writing in all their forms that brought public opinion into being by setting into motion a society in which texts were produced, in which there was occasion to read and write. The phenomena of competition are decisive from this point of view.  First of all, they provoked discussion, correspondence, and then publicity, via the press.  They generated manuscripts in response, which then produced renewed debate on the reading material; questions in committee; reports in assembly; voting; publication of the results; and, in various guises, summarized, complete, synthesized, texts applauded or rejected.  It was by

way of this routine, tried out throughout the whole century everywhere in
Europe, that those habits of intervention were built up which would become the
new politics. Paris set the fashion, but in a permanent dialogue with the
provinces in which can be read the formation of the references that constitute
the new use of printing. The developing Revolution was to bring the collective
practices of these closed and shuttered circles where the men of the
Enlightenment disputed under the watchful eye of the establishment and in
abstract confrontation into the realm of real confrontation. From an impulse
connected with the cultural definition of the role of the state giving way to all
the possible readings by the Enlightenment, from the most extreme radicalism
to moderate reformism to enlightened conservatism, where to amuse, instruct,
and administer are taken up in a single perspective of acknowledgment of
identity, one comes to a political sociability gathering together a community of
readers and users who admit of debate and the possibility of exchanges.

Two phenomena contributed mightily to this fundamental
transformation. The first could be interpreted in terms of intellectual
generation and reopen the study of those groups of new intellectuals issuing
from the growth of academia and eager to make themselves heard in the name
of new technological and political skills; stopped at the gates of the academic
institutions without, however, becoming totally alienated, they are proof of,
and they are aware of it, the inability of ancien régime society to integrate the
very ones it had caused to rise culturally. Second, the march of events
underscored the background rupture and exposed the division in the public
sphere, whose institutions first entered into purgatory, lacerated each other,
and finally became suspect. It was because the associative political fever had
remodeled the entire edifice on a national scale and that representatives of
groups which until then had been excluded from cultural sociability burst in on
the network of clubs and popular societies. It remains to see how printed
materials were mobilized on this terrain to nourish communication and, above
all, to inquire into how they were put into operation. This is one of the ways
in which one could recapture concretely the social forms of the cultural
transformation established before and during the Revolution.

One other possible way is to return to the political readers and
principally to those many who spoke up at the time: autobiographers, those
under indictment and writing accounts of their lives, victors of the Bastille,
soldiers mobilized into the army.[12] Work on these texts could, first of all,
elicit explicit references--there are enough of them here and there--and thus
take the indices of diffusion. One might also bring out how the printed culture
was used, the ways of reading and memorizing, reusing and transforming. The
event granted a possibility and gave an incentive to all those who had been
excluded from the old circuits of expression. One might then be able to
understand by reviewing these speeches what relations were set up among the

various resources, the power of the printed word in relation to various forms of reading.

"We owe the Revolution to books!" shouted Marie Joseph Chénier during a debate on the future of the Bibliothèque Nationale, until then the Bibliothèque Royale. Today we are in a position to understand better the changes that both the players and spectators of the Revolution were aware of. Explanations using economic and social history have distended the link traditionally permitted between the event and ideas. The market for and the consumption of printed materials are means of access to the cultural transformations; they are a simultaneous introduction to the articulation of the individual and the collectivity. It remains to better perceive how from the Old Regime to the Revolution, the needs they called forth or satisfied were variously recognized, in short, how the activities and operations connected to the existence of increased printing were linked between the imaginary and the material.

## NOTES

1. These four postulates were laid down by the historian Daniel Mornet in *Les Origines intellectuelles de la Révolution française (1715-1787)* (Paris: Armand Colin, 1933).

2. This all assumes that one is willing to abandon certain habitual and comfortable metaphors, *the cellar and the attic* for example, in order to visualize cultural practices through relations and exchanges, temporal simultaneities, and acculturation. See Michel Vovelle, *De la Cave au grenier. Un itinéraire en Provence au XVIIIe siècle. De l'histoire sociale à l'histoire des mentalités* (Québec: Serge Fleury, 1980).

3. Denis Diderot, *Lettre sur le commerce de la librairie* (1763; Paris: Fontaine, 1984), p. 124.

4. See Julien Brancolini and Marie-Thérèse Bouyssy, "La Vie provinciale du livre à la fin de l'Ancien Régime," in *Livre et société dans la France du XVIIIe siècle*, ed. Geneviève Bollème (Paris and The Hague: Mouton, 1970), pp. 3-38.

5. Robert Darnton, *The Business of Enlightenment: A Publishing History of the "Encyclopédie," 1775-1800* (Cambridge, Mass.: Harvard University Press, 1979); and his *Literary Underground of the Old Régime* (Cambridge, Mass.: Harvard University Press, 1982).

6. Daniel Roche, "Censorship and the Publishing Industry," in *Revolution in Print: The Press in France, 1775-1800*, ed. Robert Darnton and Daniel Roche (Berkeley: University of California Press with the New York Public Library, 1989).

7. See Furio Díaz, *Per una storia illuministica* (Naples: Guida, 1973); and Marina Cedronio, Furio Díaz, and Carla Russo, *Storiografia francese di ieri e di oggi* (Naples: Guida, 1977).

8. Voltaire, *Correspondance,* ed. Theodore Besterman, 8 (April 1765-June 1767) (Paris: Gallimard, 1983), p. 427.

9. See Georg Simmel, *Brücke und Tür: Essays des Philosophen zür Geschicte, Religion, Kunst und Gesellschaft,* ed. Michael Landmann and Margarete Susman (Stuttgart: Koehler, 1957).

10. See Roger Chartier, *Lectures et lecteurs dans la France d'Ancien Régime* (Paris: Seuil, 1987).

11. See Pierre Goubert and Daniel Roche, *Les Français et l'Ancien Régime,* vol. 2 of *Culture et société* (Paris: Colin, 1985).

12. See "Beschleunigung und Mutation von Akkulturationsprozessen an Hand autoriographischer Quellen," in *Die Französische Revolution als Bruch des gesellschaftlichen Bewußtseins, Vorlagen und Diskussionen der internationalen Arbeitstagung zum Zentrum für interdisziplinäre Forschung der Universität Bielefeld, 28. Mai-1. Juni 1985,* ed. Reinhart Koselleck and Rolf Reichardt (Munich: Oldenbourg, 1988), pp. 319-418 (chap. 6).

# THE LIFE CYCLE OF A BOOK: A PUBLISHING HISTORY OF D'HOLBACH'S *SYSTÈME DE LA NATURE*

*Robert Darnton*

In grappling with intellectual history, one sometimes feels like a child trying to catch smoke: it seeps through the fingers and floats off into a cloudy climate of opinion. *Was ist Aufklärung*? We are still groping for an answer. But we can get a grip on more manageable questions, such as: What was the Enlightenment as a campaign for spreading light (*Lumières*)? Or, more concretely still, how did the *philosophes* get their message across to the public? How did their books reach readers? To be sure, a great deal will be lost in transliterating from philosophy to something that smacks of sociology, and a shift in the way of putting questions will not provide an answer to Kant's original query. But something may be gained--if not a new notion of the spirit of the age, at least some knowledge of the social history of ideas and of the Enlightenment as a process of idea diffusion.

In order to illustrate this proposition, I would like to trace the life cycle of an edition of a key Enlightenment text, *Le Système de la nature* by Paul-Henri Dietrich, baron d'Holbach.[1] When the book first appeared in 1770, it created a sensation: here was bold-faced atheism, illegal and unashamed, shouldering its way past the police and onto the literary marketplace. The *succès de scandale* fired appetites everywhere in the book trade. As soon as the work's original publisher, Marc-Michel Rey of Amsterdam, saw that the first edition was being snapped up, he started setting type for a new one, and a dozen other publishers raced to get out pirated editions.[2]

"Piracy" hardly describes their assault on the market, however. Atheistic tracts could not be published openly anywhere, least of all in France, where the censors, the booksellers' guild, and the police set limits to the legal book trade. No one dared claim ownership of a work like *Le Système de la nature*, so everyone felt free to reprint it. By 1770, the reprint trade was

booming, especially in the publishing houses located across France's
boundaries in a great arc that stretched from Amsterdam to Avignon.  No
international copyright agreement restrained the scramble for business in this
border territory, and local authorities--the duke of Bouillon, the prince-bishop
of Liège, the prince of Trévoux, the legate of Avignon, and the burgher
councils of the Dutch and Swiss cities--actively encouraged it.  In the eighteenth century, best-sellers reached readers by a process that differed fundamentally
from what exists today.  Instead of being produced in huge numbers by a
single publisher, who might auction rights to a paperback house, they appeared
in many small editions put out simultaneously by competing firms, which
tumbled over one another in the general rush to get to the market first.

Something of the flavor of this business can be appreciated from a
report sent to one of those publishers, the Société Typographique de Neuchâtel
(STN), from its agent at the book fair of Bern in November, 1770:

> It has been impossible for me to get my hands on the
> *Système*.  M. Syrini [a bookseller from Basel] did everything
> in his power ten days ago to find it for a French officer, who
> had offered him 10 louis [240 livres, a spectacular price];
> and he wasn't able to obtain it. . . . The fair is turning out
> to be terrible, and it looks as though I won't sell much at all.
> . . . The place is full of spies, who keep their eye on
> everything transacted on the market.[3]

Police spies, market reports, secret shoptalk about fabulous
profits--everything pointed to the possibility of a coup, if only the STN could
find a copy of the text in time to put out a quick reprint from its shop in
Neuchâtel, Switzerland.  Then, just when the time seemed ripest, a copy
materialized in the printing shop itself.  It came in the baggage of Jean Louis
de Boubers, a publisher from Brussels, and Boubers arrived on business.  He
was a specialist in illegal literature, one of the boldest in the book trade.
Having invested heavily in a pirated edition of Paul-François Velly's *Histoire
de France*, an eight-volume work then being extended to sixteen volumes by
its Parisian publisher, he had learned that the STN was planning to
counterpirate him from Neuchâtel.  Instead of undercutting one another, he
proposed that they cooperate.  He would supply the STN with 100 copies of
his duodecimo edition and 25 of his quarto in exchange for an assortment of
books from its stock.  Meanwhile, it could occupy its presses with the *Système
de la nature*, printing from his copy, an octavo in two volumes.  To sweeten
the deal, he would place an advance order for 500 copies, but he wanted them
at a reduced price, one sou per sheet, and he wanted them fast--by February
1771 at the latest.

Such were the terms of the agreement as far as one can tell from the subsequent correspondence of the two publishers.[4] They never signed a contract, perhaps because the STN did not want to keep any compromising documents among its papers. In its account books it always referred to the *Système* by a code name, *Ouvrage de Boubers*. Its principal director, Frédéric-Samuel Ostervald, received permission from the local censors to produce the book on the grounds that the entire edition would be sold outside the principality, but he knew that he could get in trouble if Neuchâtel's ministers, organized in the Vénérable Classe des Pasteurs, got wind of the business. Still, Ostervald had considerable influence himself. As banneret, or head of the local militia, he occupied an important place in the governing Conseil de ville, and he knew that he could always appeal above the Conseil to the ultimate sovereign of the principality, Frederick II of Prussia, who could not have cared less if some atheism came off the presses of his Swiss subjects.

So the STN set to work, printing the *Ouvrage de Boubers*. Its progress can be followed, sheet by sheet and week by week, in several account books of the firm. We can study the printing of volume I as a model of the production process -- its rhythm, costs, and labor. This involves a certain amount of esoteric detail, but the detail is worth studying, because we still know relatively little about how books were produced and distributed in the era of the common press.

By way of background information, it should be noted that the STN's *Système de la nature* was published under the false address "Londres, 1771" in two octavo volumes printed at a pressrun of 2,000. Volume I contained 26 sheets (416 pages). The accounts were kept primarily in French livres tournois (1 livre = 20 sous; 1 sou = 12 deniers) but also in Neuchâtel livres (4 livres tournois = 3 Neuchâtel livres). In accounting for paper, the STN reckoned in reams (*rames*), quires (*mains*), and sheets (*feuilles*) -- 1 ream = 500 sheets or 20 quires; 1 quire = 25 sheets. But the basic unit of production was the sheet, or strictly speaking the *feuille d'édition*--that is, the total output for each sheet, a sheet corresponding to a signature of the gathered volume and to the two formes of type used in the printing.

Because it aimed its edition at a public of *curieux*, or free spirits who wanted to read something scandalous, the STN did not attempt to produce a luxurious book. It bought an ordinary grade of paper--*bâtard mi-fin petit format*--from an obscure paper-miller named Monnier in Sirod, a small bourg in the Franche-Comté. The *Registre de papier délivré* reveals the overall size of the pressrun: four reams (2,000 sheets) with four quires (100 sheets) as *chaperon* to cover spoilage. The accounts also show precisely how many perfected sheets were produced by the teams working at each press.

For example, the first and last sheets of Volume I appear as follows (the columns on the right refer to *rames*, *mains*, and *feuilles*):

| | | | No. des presses | Papiers blanc | | | Papier imprimé | | |
|---|---|---|---|---|---|---|---|---|---|
| | | | | R | M | F | R | M | F |
| Déc. 7 | pour Ouvrage f. | A..... | 3 | 4 | 4 | - | 4 | 3 | 23 |
| Déc. 8 | pour............ | B..... | 3 | 4 | 4 | - | 4 | 3 | 7 |
| Déc. 13 | .................. | C..... | 3 | 4 | 4 | - | 4 | 3 | 8 |
| [Then skipping to the end of the volume:] | | | | | | | | | |
| Jan. 31 | .................. | X..... | | 4 | 4 | - | 4 | 2 | 21 |
| Fév. 4 | .................. | Y..... | | 4 | 4 | - | 4 | 3 | 21 |
| Fév. 5 | .................. | Z..... | | 4 | 4 | - | 4 | 3 | 17 |
| Fév. 7 | .................. | Aa.... | 2 | 4 | 4 | - | 4 | 3 | 18 |
| Fév. 12 | .................. | Bb.... | | 4 | 4 | - | 4 | 3 | 18 |
| Fév. 13 | .................. | titre | | 4 | 4 | - | | | |

In order to measure the rhythm of the work and to identify the men who did it, one can compare the above information with that available from another account book, the *Banque des ouvriers*, which shows who printed each sheet. It then becomes clear that on December 7, the press team of Patin and Pousillon began work on sheet A. Having received the standard allotment of paper (four reams and four quires of *papier blanc)*, they produced 4,098 perfected sheets and spoiled only two sheets (their *papier imprimé* came to four reams, three quires, and twenty-three sheets.) On the next day, Vogl and Aberli started printing sheet B. They spoiled eighteen sheets, but they worked faster, because in that week they also ran off the second *forme* of sheet C. The spoilage reached a peak on January 31, when Angol and Gayet completed sheet X, having spoiled twenty-nine sheets while putting in the heaviest week of work among all the printers who labored on that volume: they produced 10,500 impressions (the first *forme* of sheet T and both *formes* of sheets U and X). The actual production of the volume therefore came to 2,071 copies.[5]

While the accounts for *Papier délivré* record the daily transformation of *papier blanc* into *papier imprimé,* the *Banque des ouvriers* shows production from the perspective of the shop foreman. He recorded payments made every Saturday for the labor performed each week on each sheet in the two halves of the printing shop, the *casse*, where the compositors worked at the type cases, and the *presse*, where the printers operated the presses, working in teams of two. The labor on the first nine sheets appears as follows:[6]

| Composition | | | | Tirage | | | |
| --- | --- | --- | --- | --- | --- | --- | --- |
| [sheet] | [worker] | [date] | [wages] | [sheet] | [worker] | [date] | [wages] |
| A | Hallanzi | Dec. 8 | 5-- | A | Patin & Pousillon | Dec. 8 | 6-- |
| B | Offray | Dec. 8 | 5-- | B | Vogl & Aberli | Dec. 15 | 6-- |
| C | | | | C1 | Angol & Gayet | Dec. 15 | |
| D | Hallanzi | Dec. 8 | 10-- | C2 | Vogl & Aberli | Dec. 15 | 6-- |
| | | | | D | Pousillon | Dec. 22 | 6-- |
| E | Patin | Dec. 8 | 5-- | E1 | Vogl & Aberli | Dec. 22 | |
| F1 forme | Patin | Dec. 8 | 2-10 | E2 | Angol & Gayet | Dec. 22 | 6-- |
| F2 forme | Patin | Dec. 22 | 2-10 | F1 | Duthwiler & Rhodes | Dec. 22 | |
| G | Patin | Dec. 22 | 5-- | F2 | Angol & Gayet | Dec. 22 | 6-- |
| H1 forme | Patin | Dec. 22 | 2-10 | G | Roche & Gayet | Dec. 29 | 6-- |
| H2 forme | Fourez | Dec. 22 | 2-10 | H1 | Roche & Gayet | Jan. 5 | |
| I1 forme | Fourez | Dec. 22 | 2-10 | H2 | Patin & Pousillon | Dec. 29 | 6-- |
| I2 forme | Arnaud | Dec. 29 | 2-10 | I1 | Rhodes & Vogl | Jan. 5 | |
| | | | | I2 | Angol & Gayet | Jan. 5 | 6-- |

Compositors received two livres ten sous (in Neuchâtel livres) for every *forme* that they composed.  So at the *banque* (payday) of Saturday, December 8, the foreman paid Hallanzi fifteen livres for setting all of sheets A, C, and D.  He paid Offray five livres for sheet B.  And he paid Patin seven livres ten sous for sheet E and the first *forme* of sheet F.  At the same time in the other half of the shop, the pressmen had begun printing the *formes* supplied by the *casse*.  They received one livre ten sous (in Neuchâtel livres, the equivalent in the local coinage of fifteen batz) for every thousand impressions. Thus, the foreman paid the team of Patin and Pousillon six livres for printing the 2,000 copies of both *formes* of sheet A.  And in the next week he paid Vogl and Aberli nine livres for printing sheet B and the second *forme* of sheet C; and he paid Angol and Gayet three livres for the first *forme* sheet C.

The pressmen ran off sheets as the *formes* became available, so they worked on several different jobs--books, periodicals, ephemera--during the same week.  Compositors labored upstream in the flow of work.  They worked at their own pace, which varied enormously from day to day and man to man; and unless they were paid a fixed wage *(en conscience)* rather than by piece rates, they tended to work on one job at a time.  In the case of the *Système de la nature*, however, where the foreman could cast off copy with great accuracy by following an earlier edition and the book had to reach the market exceptionally fast, the STN employed five different compositors.[7]  They went through the text at irregular rhythms, sometimes working simultaneously, sometimes sequentially.  And they fed *formes* to the pressmen in a still more erratic pattern, as is illustrated in Figure 1.

FIGURE 1: WORK-FLOW

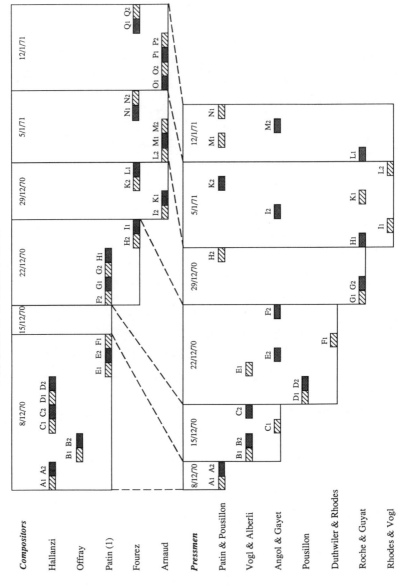

(1) The work force includes two Patins, one at the *casse* and one at the *presse*. Presumably they were relatives.

Thus, for example, *forme* 1 of sheet I was composed by Fourez and printed by Rhodes and Vogl, while *forme* 2 of sheet I was composed by Arnaud and printed by Angol and Gayet.   Then *forme* 1 of sheet K was composed by Arnaud and printed by Roche and Guyat, while *forme* 2 of sheet K was composed by Fourez and printed by Patin and Pousillon.   There was no consistency in the pattern of work, either within the *casse* and the *presse* or between the compositors and the pressmen.

These details may seem esoteric, but they are worth stressing, not only for what they tell us about the nature of work in the preindustrial era but also because of their relevance to textual criticism.  A good deal of Shakespearean scholarship is based on a series of inferences, which run backward from the physical character of the printed work to hypothetical pressmen, hypothetical compositors, and a hypothetical copy text--what Shakespeare must have really written.  Some of those inferences may be correct, but many of them assume stable relations in the pattern of work.  If the compositors and printers who produced the First Folio in Jaggard's shop were as irregular in their behavior as those in the shop of the STN a century and a half later, some readings of Shakespeare could be very wide of the mark.  It may be misleading to think of a perfect reading in the first place, for we may never be able to hypothesize our way back to the original copy.  Perhaps we should settle for a conception of Shakespeare as performance instead of as Ur-text.[8]

It can be safely assumed that the STN's workers did not worry about the implications of their work for Shakespearean scholarship.  They may not have had any interest in the text of d'Holbach.  But by setting that text in type and imbedding it in paper, they did their part in the diffusion of the Enlightenment. That part ended on February 16, 1771, when Patin and Guyat ran off the last sheet and the title page, which had been composed by Arnaud. The foreman then tallied the total costs of labor at the *casse* and the *presse*, and a clerk posted the totals, along with the expense for paper, to another account book, *Brouillard A.*

At this point the accounts begin to reveal more about economic history than the history of labor.  In fact, they make it possible to construct a model of the *Système de la nature* as an economic speculation, and the model can be used to reveal the conditions that determined the financial strategy of Enlightenment publishing.  The figures come from *Brouillard A* and concern only the first of the two volumes in the STN's edition:

Costs
| | | |
|---|---|---|
| Paper ......... | | 498 or 64% |
| Composition ... | 130 | |
| Presswork ..... | 156 | 286 or 36% |
| | | 784 Neuchâtel livres, 1,065 livres tournois |

Projected Income

| | |
|---|---|
| 500 copies at 1 l. 6 s. to Boubers ... | 650 livres tournois |
| 1500 copies at 2 l. ................. | 3,000 |
| | 3,650 l. |
| minus costs ....... | 1,065 |

Projected Profit (excluding overhead)          2,585 l. (+ 243%)

On an outlay of 1,065 livres, the publisher could make 2,585 livres in gross profit, a margin of 243 percent (or of 225 percent if one allows for overhead: see Appendix I--provided he could sell the entire edition, deliver it to his customers, and get them to pay for it. The projected profit for the two volumes was about 5,000 livres, the equivalent of approximately ten years of labor for a skilled workman like one of the STN's compositors. That was what made the illegal book trade so attractive: enormous profits in the face of a certain amount of risk.

How much risk? It is difficult to calculate the danger of marketing a prohibited book from a relatively safe haven such as Neuchâtel, a Prussian principality in Switzerland separated from France by the Jura Mountains. But the STN cut its potential losses to a minimum. It had sold a quarter of the edition in advance: Boubers's advance order for 650 livres, which covered 61 percent of the production costs. As it had set the wholesale price at the modest level of 2 livres (for Volume I), the STN had to sell only 204 more copies to break even. It could turn a profit if most of the edition were confiscated--and it did not need to worry much about the police in any case, because it sold a large proportion of its editions to wholesale dealers scattered around France's borders. They handled the smuggling. Like the STN itself, they often hired "insurers" *(assureurs)*, who contracted to get the books to customers inside the kingdom for a fixed commission (often about 16 percent of the value of the goods plus normal transport costs) and who paid in full for anything they lost to the authorities.

Boubers, too, stood to strike it rich. He advanced no capital; he expected to receive his books before anyone else; and he paid for them, with a year's worth of credit, at 65 percent of the wholesale price. True, he had to organize the smuggling. But he had been working with teams of colporteurs for years, helped by his brother Denis, who operated out of Ostend and Dunkirk, and by Nicolas Gerlache, a dealer with a secret entrepôt in Metz. If Boubers retailed his books at 5 livres, (that is, 10 livres for the two-volume set, a reasonable price in view of the fact that he had sold an edition for 10 livres earlier in 1770, before the demand had crested), he would have to sell only 130 copies, little more than a quarter of his lot, to pay off his debt to the STN. The other 370 copies would bring in 1,855 livres on an investment of 650 livres--a profit rate of 285 percent, as spectacular in its way as the profit of the STN, considering that Boubers functioned only as a middleman, without putting down any capital of his own.

The books actually passed through a whole string of middlemen, their price increasing at every point. It is impossible to follow their sale through all the capillaries of the trade, but there is enough information scattered through the archives for one to reconstruct the general pattern of their diffusion and to give examples of transactions at each stage in the diffusion process:

| Seller | Buyer | Price (Vol. I) |
|--------|-------|----------------|
| STN | Boubers, wholesaler in Brussels | 1 livre 6 sous |
| Boubers | Manoury, wholesaler-retailer | 5 livres |
| Manoury | Segault, peddler in Normandy | 6 livres |
| Segault | Individual clients in Normandy | 7 livres 10 sous and 9 livres. |

These sales, mentioned in letters of various dealers, all took place in the early 1770s, but they did not necessarily involve the STN's edition of the *Système de la nature*; so they give only an approximate picture of the way prices escalated as books were relayed through the underground trade. They make it clear, however, that the cost of a prohibited book could increase fivefold between the publisher and the reader. A systematic study would probably turn up tenfold increases, because prices varied enormously, especially in the remotest branches of the retail trade.

When the books finally came within the range of individual consumers, their price created a boundary to the social character of their diffusion. Skilled workmen, who made 30 or even 60 sous a day, simply could not afford to pay four or five livres for one volume of the *Système,* even if they could read it. But the book fell within the purchasing power of many people in the upper ranks of society. And if the above model corresponds to the realities of the marketplace, the publishers could count on enough purchases to make a killing. What actually happened?

*Brouillard A* includes entries for all the financial transactions of the STN from April 27, 1771, when it finished the printing, to February 3, 1773, when the register ends and a fifteen-month gap in the documentation begins. By studying the accounts, one can trace the sales of the *Système de la nature* day by day until February 1773. At that point, only 329 copies remained in stock. So the diffusion of 1,671 copies, 81 percent of the entire edition, can be mapped as in Figure 2.

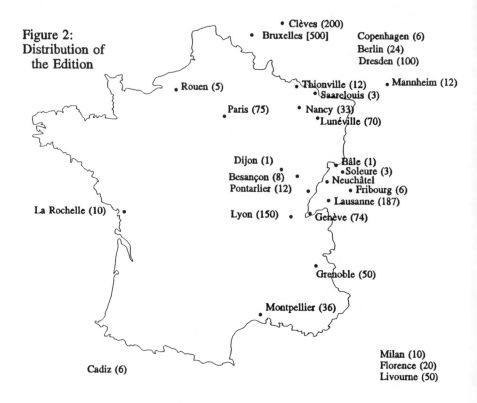

Figure 2:
Distribution of
the Edition

• Clèves (200)
• Bruxelles [500]
Copenhagen (6)
Berlin (24)
Dresden (100)

. Rouen (5)

•Thionville (12)    • Mannheim (12)
•\Saarelouis (3)

.Paris (75)    • Nancy (33)
•Lunéville (70)

Dijon (1)    Bâle (1)
•Soleure (3)
Besançon (8)  •    . Neuchâtel
Pontarlier (12)    • Fribourg (6)
• Lausanne (187)

La Rochelle (10)

Lyon (150)  .    Genève (74)

Grenoble (50)

Montpellier (36)

Milan (10)
Florence (20)
Livourne (50)

Cadiz (6)

Aside from the 500 copies ordered by Boubers, the sales were concentrated in
four areas, which could be considered submarkets within the book trade of
Europe as a whole--that is, of Enlightenment Europe, where nearly everyone
among the educated elite read French:

France: 40%
The Periphery of France (Cleves, Saarlouis, Mannheim,
        Basel, Soleure, Fribourg, Lausanne, Geneva): 42%
The Mediterranean (Milan, Leghorn, Florence, Cádiz): 7%
The North (Copenhagen, Berlin, Dresden): 11%

This sales pattern was fairly typical of the STN's editions and
probably of those of other Swiss houses as well; but it does not reveal the
ultimate destination of the books, because most of the customers were
booksellers, often wholesale booksellers, and they sometimes supplied other

dealers in other towns. It seems likely, for example, that many of the 100 *Systèmes* ordered by Walther in Dresden ended up on bookshelves in Warsaw and Saint Petersburg, and that many of the 66 that went to Grasset in Lausanne were smuggled into France. Pirate publishers usually marketed books in this manner: they would sell half or more of an edition to allied houses, who then portioned their share out to retailers within their own distribution networks. Since so many of the dealers who bought the *Système de la nature* did business in this way, operating from enclaves in Switzerland and the Rhineland, it is safe to conclude that a large majority of the copies eventually filtered into France.

How were the books marketed? The *Système* had caused such a scandal that it could not be advertised and did not need publicity in any case. But the STN had to let potential customers know that it could supply a new edition. As in the case of other dangerous works, it sent messages through the trade grapevine, relying primarily on its commercial correspondence and to a lesser extent on word of mouth. It also took care to adjust its sales pitch to its audience, even when writing to professionals. With Gosse et Pinet, a rather conservative and well-established bookseller in The Hague, it used circumlocution:

> We don't know whether you include in your trade certain
> daring works, which alas have unfortunately all too much
> vogue. We will soon receive a large number of copies of the
> *Système de la nature*. If it suits you to take some of them,
> you will oblige us by telling us so at your convenience.
> Your reply will influence the number that we order.[9]

With Daudet de Jossan, a literary adventurer who peddled forbidden books under the cloak in Paris, it adopted a franker tone: "An edition is being made somewhere of the *Système de la nature*, a tasty morsel for your Parisian stomachs."[10] And in sending a circular to 20 other dealers, all of them trustworthy veterans of the trade, it sounded brisk and businesslike: "As this work has made a great splash, I do not doubt but that this speculation will turn to your advantage."[11]

Everywhere throughout the correspondence one can feel the pulsation of the profit motive. Once the publishers and booksellers woke up to the fact that an enormous demand for illegal literature lay hidden beneath the official literary market, they fell over themselves in the scramble to satisfy it. As the STN explained in a typical letter to a bookseller and smuggler in Pontarlier, "You can strike it rich with this item if you take precautions."[12] Almost never in their letters do the booksellers express the slightest qualms about spreading literature that attacked the official values of the Old Regime. They wanted to make money, "the moving force of everything," as one of the STN directors put it.[13]   So they remained relatively neutral in their role as cultural intermediaries.   In fact, the STN pirated Voltaire's attack on the *Système de la nature*, a short essay entitled "Dieu. Réponse au *Système de la nature*," and included it in its edition of the *Système* in order to gain an edge on the competing editions.   Then, in an effort to make the most of its coup, it pirated two full-length refutations of the *Système*: *Observations sur le livre intitulé "Système de la nature"* by G. F. Salvemini da Castiglione and *Réflexions philosophiques sur le "Système de la nature"* by G. J. von Holland.  Whatever they thought of the Enlightenment when they turned over philosophical questions in their own minds, the bookmen of the Old Regime were eager to sell it in their shops--and to sell the works of its opponents, if the opportunity arose.

Many of them, however, occupied important positions within their local communities.   The STN's own directors included not only Frédéric-Samuel Ostervald, the previously cited banneret of the civil militia and a member of Neuchâtel's governing Conseil de Ville, but also Jean-Elie Bertrand, Ostervald's son-in-law, who was a minister and member of the Vénérable Classe des Pasteurs--not the perfect place from which to publish an atheistic treatise.  Ostervald had cleared the edition with the local censor on the grounds that it would be marketed entirely outside the principality.  But the Vénérable Classe got wind of it, suspended Bertrand, and forced Ostervald to resign from the position of banneret.   Although both men eventually reestablished themselves, the scandal damaged their prestige within the municipal elite.[14]

They continued, nonetheless, to sell their *Systèmes*.   The market seemed insatiable, despite the appearance of a dozen editions within two or three years.   But having marketed their product, the publishers faced a final problem, one that was known in the trade as *le recouvrement* (bill collecting). For it was one thing to sell a book, another to collect payment, and the STN had enormous difficulty in squeezing cash from several of its customers, beginning with Boubers.

Boubers piled speculation on speculation so audaciously that his entire business sometimes threatened to come crashing down.  When critical bills of exchange became due, he cashed in on the demand for hot-selling, high-risk books.  If the crisis passed or the demand had peaked, he pulled out of risky enterprises.  So when the STN failed to get his 500 *Systèmes* to him on time (it shipped Volume II in May instead of February 1771, as promised), he declared the sale null and void: "As to that other work in two volumes, you promised it for February.  It's too late for me to sell it now.  In the case of voguish books like that, you have to sell them while they're hot or give up on them completely."[15]  Boubers would go through with the deal only if the STN agreed to accept, in lieu of cash, an equivalent number of works from his own stock--including a book he had not yet printed and would not name. The STN protested: "We would never have undertaken the reprinting of that book if we hadn't received the order that you made with us in person."[16] But Boubers would not budge:

> If I said it once, I'll say it again: that kind of item can only be sold when it is fresh. Now no one wants it any more. You made me lose a sure profit, because I counted on your promise. Your edition has been offered to me from other sources at a very low price. I don't care what you do now. . . . You have no cause to complain. I am offering to trade my best stuff against something that is going to sit unsold in my warehouse for a long time.[17]

Having failed to make the deadline and to get a written contract, the STN did not have much of a case. But it knew from its own sales that the demand for the *Système* was holding up, so it asked Boubers to return his copies. This, too, he refused, no doubt because he had already sold many of them and was trying to force the STN to accept better terms. Appeals to intermediaries and protectors got nowhere. Boubers would not release the books, and he would not pay for them, except in kind, with books from his own stock, which the STN did not want. Recriminations filled the mail between Brussels and Neuchâtel for years. While the STN denounced Boubers as "an equivocator and a cheat,"[18] he stood his ground and taunted, "It's all the same to me whether you are upright citizens or not."[19]

In the end, Boubers returned 180 copies (they had never got beyond Lorraine, because Boubers's agent in Metz, whom he had also failed to pay, had refused to forward them) and paid 920 livres for the other 320. By this time, he had trained his sights on larger game: nothing less than the manuscripts of Rousseau. Rousseau's death in 1778 touched off a fierce struggle to corner the market for his works among the Enlightenment publishers. Boubers lost in the bidding for the unpublished manuscripts; became embroiled in a quarrel with Rousseau's widow, Thérèse Levasseur, who was in the pay of a rival publisher; attempted nonetheless to go ahead with an edition of his own; and in the midst of the printing disappeared, unable to meet his payments. According to another Brussels bookseller, "He went bankrupt for the biggest sum that you can imagine in the book trade--more than 300,000 livres." Just before a detachment of police had closed in on his shop, Boubers fled with the plates for an illustrated edition of Raynal's *Histoire philosophique et politique de l'etablissement et du commerce des Européens dans les deux Indes* and never was heard from again.[20]

The STN's other customers generally paid their bills on time, but some of them had troubles, too. Marginal dealers faced the same problem as Boubers, though on a smaller scale: when they felt themselves slipping toward bankruptcy, they speculated on the most dangerous books, which brought in the largest profits. And when they could not pay their bills, they threw themselves on the mercy of their creditors or took to the road, abandoning everything.

The problems of dealing with such booksellers stand out clearly in the letters of two men who confessed themselves incapable of paying for their *Systèmes de la nature.* In Clèves, J. G. Baerstecher complained that the publisher of the first edition, Marc-Michel Rey of Amsterdam, had undercut his market by issuing a cheap second edition. Besides, the book was hard going for readers in the Rhineland: "You know as well as I do that the substance of it does not go down well everywhere; the style is too elevated."[21] And finally, to clinch his argument, Baerstecher declared himself insolvent:

> I am too weak to resist violence; and in case you try to overpower me, I will lay down my arms without attempting to defend myself. Will you be any happier and richer from my ruin? I doubt it very much. Or do you want to share your money with the lawyers? So much the worse--for both of us.
>
> . . . . . . . . . .
>
> You know that by violence you can draw blood, but can you make any money out of it?"[22]

Nicolas Gerlache in Metz had even better reasons for not paying:

> I am in a terribly critical situation just now. My mother is on her deathbed, and my wife is about to have a baby, and I'm afraid that my mother's death will upset my wife so badly that something will go wrong with the birth.
>
> . . . . . . . . .
>
> If an unwise creditor tries to bring me to court, I will burn everything I own in order to keep the law from seizing it.[23]

There was as much melodrama in the book trade as in the books of eighteenth-century Europe. The publishers' mail abounded in stories that end with deathbed scenes, furniture auctioned off, wives abandoned, and children reduced to beggary. Many stories were true. In an age of unlimited liability, booksellers often went under, dragging their families with them and leaving great gaps in the accounts of their suppliers.

The final balance in the STN's account for the *Système de la nature* is difficult to estimate, because the documentation gives out after 1773. It seems likely that the book brought in a profit, perhaps something close to 50 percent of costs in two or three years, but nothing like the 243 percent envisaged in the model of costs and profits given above. Economic models are one thing, human behavior another. The potential profit in a speculation like the *Système de la nature* could not be realized in a world composed of characters like Boubers, Baerstecher, and Gerlache. In that world, the difficulty of *recouvrement* offset the profitability of best-sellers, and there was as much risk to be faced from the men who operated the system as from the authorities who tried to repress it. Had it been different, had it been easy to double one's capital in a few months by publishing atheistic tracts, a great many more would have played the game.

But many did play. Some won, some lost, and each in his own way contributed to the circulation of ideas: that was how the Enlightenment reached readers.

## APPENDIX I: OVERHEAD

Although the account books of the STN mention occasional payments for candles, ink, ink ball pelts, rent, presses, and fonts of type, they do not present them in a manner that lends itself to an accurate calculation of overhead costs. The modern concept of overhead probably did not exist among eighteenth-century printers. But the printers knew very well that their work involved a significant load of incidental expenses. In French-speaking areas, they referred to those expenses as *étoffes*. Thus the entry on *étoffes* in the printer's manual by A.-F. Momoro:

> *Etoffes* are non-durable goods necessary for printing. The term *étoffes* includes tympan blankets, tympans, wool, the wood of the printer's balls, the leather of the balls, gray paper for the underlays, oil for the balls, and olive oil. Without those items, one cannot print at all; and they get worn out every day; they must be constantly renewed. Of course they cost money, but they are a prime necessity. With good *étoffes*, one can do good work; but without *étoffes*, or rather with supplies of poor quality, one cannot produce anything worthwhile.
>
> A printer who wants to see his presses turn out handsome work never spares the *étoffes;* he does not even allow the pressmen to work with *étoffes* that are slightly worn.[24]

Because the expenditure on *étoffes* varied throughout the year and from year to year, printers adopted a rule of thumb in order to incorporate it into their calculations of the cost of a *feuille d'édition*: they set it at half the combined cost of composition and presswork. For example, in 1780 the directors of the STN asked a confidant, the Parisian printer Jacques-François Pyre, to provide them with information on printing costs in Paris. He replied as follows:

> As to the cost of printing commissioned by booksellers in Paris, one usually reckons it in the following manner: first one determines the cost of printing [*sic*: a slip for composition] and presswork, and then one takes half of that sum for the *étoffes*--that is, for wear and tear of the type, the press, and so on--and a third for the profit. For example, in the case of a sheet of ordinary pica without notes, composition normally comes to 8 livres tournois and

presswork to 2 livres 10 sous for a thousand impressions,
which makes 5 livres with the reiterations [the printing of the
second *forme*]:

| | |
|---|---|
| Composition | 8 l. |
| Tirage | <u>5</u> |
| Total | 13 |
| Moitié | 6 l. 10 s.  *pour les étoffes* |
| Tiers | <u>4 l.  5 s.</u> |
| | 23 l. 15 s. |

This example is valid for all kinds of type, no matter what
the difficulty of the work. However, if the composition costs
are too great, owing to complications in the typesetting, one
usually reduces the third that the printer takes for his profit--
that is, one bargains with him.  Such is the best and the
surest way to calculate the costs of a job here [in Paris].[25]

Pyre's calculations are confirmed by those of Eméric David, the
printer of Aix-en-Provence, who filled a notebook with typographical
observations during a journey through France and Switzerland in 1787.  David
set the costs of a *feuille d'édition* printed on *papier ordinaire* at a pressrun of
750 (one and a half reams) as follows:[26]

| | |
|---|---|
| Composition | 8 l. |
| Tirage | 5 |
| 1 *rame* 1/2 *de papier à* 12 l. | 18 |
| *Caractère, étendage*, etc. | <u>6</u> |
| | 37 l. |

That is, David set the incidental costs (6 livres) at roughly half the combined
cost of the composition and presswork (13 livres), precisely as Pyre did, except
he rounded off instead of including sous in his calculation.  Pyre, too, did
some rounding: his calculation of profit (4 livres 5 sous) is not exactly a third
of the cost of composition and presswork (13 livres).  One can find a few
variations on these figures among the thousands of letters in the STN archives
(for example, a letter of the STN to the Société typographique de Berne of
April 4, 1774, where the various *faux frais* are set at only a quarter of the
labor costs), but these proportions seem to have prevailed throughout the
printing trade in France.
     The French practice coincided fairly closely with that of contemporary
London printers, who favored the traditional "third" in setting costs--that is,
they added composition and presswork, halved the sum, and used that half to

cover overhead and profits, which therefore came to a third of their total bill (assuming they did not pay for the paper.)[27] But the "third" mentioned by Pyre represents a different calculation: one-third of the composition and presswork, which the printer added to his bill in order to cover his profit *after* taking half of the labor costs to cover overhead.

If this way of reckoning costs were applied to the STN's printing of the *Système de la nature*, Vol. I, its overhead, at least in the eighteenth-century sense of *étoffes*, would come to 143 Neuchâtel livres or 191 livres tournois. That was a modest sum considering the scale of the enterprise, which the STN conducted both as a printer and as a publisher. If one subtracts 191 l. in *étoffes* from the projected profit of 2,585 livres, 2,394 livres remain--that is, a profit of 225 percent on an investment of 1,065 livres. Overhead was too small an ingredient of manufacturing costs to have much relevance to the general model of the *Système de la nature* as a speculation.

## APPENDIX II: PAPER

The Account for Paper

Papier de Monnier bâtard mi-fin, petit format

1770
Nov 15  Reçu 12 balles de 16 rames......  192 R
Mars 1  Reçu  6 balles..................   90 R

| | | | | | DELIVRE | | | | | |
|---|---|---|---|---|---|---|---|---|---|---|
| | | | Numéro des presses | Papier blanc | | | | Papier imprimé | | |
| | | | | R | M | F | | R | M | F |
| Dec | 7 | pour Ouvrage F. | A | 3 | 4 | 4 | - | | 4 | 3 | 23 |
| | 8 | " | B | 3 | 4 | 4 | - | | 4 | 3 | 7 |
| | 13 | " | C | 3 | 4 | 4 | - | | 4 | 3 | 8 |
| | 15 | " | D | | 4 | 4 | - | | 4 | 3 | 18 |
| | 17 | " | E | | 4 | 4 | - | | 4 | 3 | 8 |
| | 21 | " | F | 2 | 4 | 4 | - | | 4 | 3 | 5 |
| | 24 | " | G | | 4 | 4 | - | | 4 | 3 | 13 |
| | 27 | " | H | | 4 | 4 | - | | 4 | 3 | 18 |
| | 31 | " | I | 2 | 4 | 4 | - | | 4 | 3 | 20 |
| 1771 Jan | 2 | " | K | 4 | 4 | 4 | - | | 4 | 3 | 15 |
| | 4 | " | L | 2 | 4 | 4 | - | | 4 | 3 | 16 |
| | 7 | " | M | 2 | 4 | 4 | - | | 4 | 3 | 21 |
| | 8 | " | N | | 4 | 4 | - | | 4 | 3 | 15 |
| | 14 | " | O | | 4 | 4 | - | | 4 | 3 | 10 |
| | 18 | " | P | | 4 | 4 | - | | 4 | 3 | 11 |
| | 21 | " | Q | | 4 | 4 | - | | | | |
| | 22 | " | R | | 4 | 4 | - | | | | |
| | 25 | " | S | | 4 | 4 | - | | 4 | 3 | 17 |
| | 26 | " | T | | 4 | 4 | - | | 4 | 3 | 7 |
| | 30 | " | U | | 4 | 4 | - | | 4 | 3 | 8 |
| | 31 | " | X | | 4 | 4 | - | | 4 | 2 | 21 |
| Fév. | 4 | " | Y | | 4 | 4 | - | | 4 | 3 | 21 |
| | 5 | " | Z | | 4 | 4 | - | | 4 | 3 | 17 |
| | 7 | " | Aa | 2 | 4 | 4 | - | | 4 | 3 | 18 |
| | 12 | " | Bb | | 4 | 4 | - | | | | |
| | 13 | " | titre | | 4 | 4 | - | | | | |

The production costs of books in early modern Europe differed fundamentally from those of today. At a time when every sheet of paper was made individually from pulped rags by highly skilled craftsmen, paper usually cost as much as the labor of the compositors and the pressmen combined. In large editions, it could represent three-quarters of the printer's expenses. So printers kept careful accounts of their paper. The STN's *Registre de papier délivré* provides a record of how its pressmen transformed each sheet of Monnier's *bâtard mi-fin, petit format* from *papier blanc* to *papier imprimé*, while printing the *Système de la nature*.

The three columns on the right in Figure 3--under R, M, and F for *rames, mains* and *feuilles*--show the actual output of perfected sheets and so, by extension, the rate of spoilage. Thus the pressmen who printed sheet A at press number 3 produced 2,098 perfected sheets (4 reams, 3 quires, 23 sheets), spoiling only 2 of the 2,100 sheets (4 reams, 4 quires) given to them. By consulting the *Banque des ouvriers* (Appendix III), one can determine who those pressmen were: Patin and Pousillon. It thus becomes clear that, as one might expect, the greatest spoilage (29 sheets of signature X) occurred in the week of the greatest production: the week of February 2, 1771, when the team of Angol and Gayet printed the first *forme* of sheet T and both *formes* of sheets U and X, an output of 10,500 impressions. The spoilage of sheet X meant that the actual size of the printing came to 2,071 copies rather than the round figure of 2,000, which served as the ostensible production goal.

The gap between the actual and the ostensible pressruns is worth noting, because the extra copies could make a crucial difference to the profit margin. In fact, the surplus sheets printed from the *chaperon*--the extra quires allotted to cover spoilage, usually at the rate of one quire for every ream of the pressrun, or 4 quires in the case of the *Système de la nature* --were not always used as *défets,* to complete deficient copies or to serve as scrap paper and packaging *(maculature).* By printing a few extra sheets (in this case, for example, sheets F and X) publishers could produce scrap editions. A lively trade in *scrap* books grew up in response to the demand for best-sellers like the *Encyclopédie,* and specialists like Batilliot of Paris made large sums by buying up the leftover sheets that cluttered printers' warehouses everywhere in France and the surrounding territory.[28] Many of those scrap editions now sit proudly in rare book rooms, where they can provide endless puzzles for bibliographical investigation.

# APPENDIX III: LABOR

| | Composition | [date] | [gages] | | Tirage | [date] | [gages] |
|---|---|---|---|---|---|---|---|
| A | Hallanzi | Decembre 8 | 5-- | A | Patin & Pousillon | 6 | 6-- |
| B | Offray | 8 | 5-- | B | Vogl & Aberli | 15 | 6-- |
| C | Hallanzi | 8 | 10-- | C 1 | Angol & Gayet | 15 | 6-- |
| | | | | C 2 | Vogl & Aberli | 15 | 6-- |
| D | | | | D | Pousillon | 22 | 6-- |
| E | Patin | 8 | 5-- | E 1 | Vogl & Aberli | 22 | 6-- |
| | | | | E 2 | Angol & Gayet | 22 | 6-- |
| F 1 | Patin | 8 | 2-10- | F 1 | Duthwiler & Rhodes | 22 | 6-- |
| F 2 | Patin | 22 | 2-10- | F 2 | Angol & Gayet | 22 | 6-- |
| G | Patin | 22 | 5-- | G | Roche & Guyat | 29 | 6-- |
| H 1 | Patin | 22 | 2-10- | H 1 | Roche & Guyat | Janv. 5 | 6-- |
| H 2 | Fourex | 22 | 2-10- | H 2 | Patin & Pousillon | 29 | 6-- |
| I 1 | Fourez | 22 | 2-10- | I 1 | Rhodes & Vogl | 5 | 6-- |
| I 2 | Arnaud | 29 | 2-10- | I 2 | Angol & Gayet | 5 | 6-- |
| K 1 | Arnaud | 29 | 5-- | K 1 | Roche & Guyat | 5 | 6-- |
| K 2 | Fourez | 29 | 5-- | K 2 | Patin & Pousillon | 5 | 6-- |
| L 1 | Fourez | 29 | 2-10- | L 1 | Roche & Guyat | 12 | 6-- |
| L 2 | Arnoud | 1771 Janv. 5 | 2-10- | L 2 | Rhodes & Guyat | 5 | 6-- |
| M | Arnoud | 5 | 5-- | M 1 | Patin & Pousillon | 12 | 6-- |
| | | | | M 2 | Angol & Gayet | 12 | 6-- |
| N | Fourez | 5 | 5-- | N 1 | Patin & Pousillon | 12 | 6-- |
| | | | | N 2 | Angol & Gayet | 19 | 6-- |

Ouvrage de Boubers à Bruxelles

APPENDIX III: LABOR (Continued)

| | | | | | | | |
|---|---|---|---|---|---|---|---|
| O | | | | O 1 | Guyat & Roche | 19 | 6-- |
| | | | | 2 | " | | 6-- |
| P | Arnaud | 12 | 10-- | P 1 | Vogl & Rhodes | 19 | 6-- |
| | | | | 2 | Angol & Gayet | 19 | |
| Q | Fourez | 12 | 5-- | Q 1 | Rhodes & Vimer | 26 | 6-- |
| | | | | 2 | Angol & Gayet | 26 | |
| R | Arnaud | 12 | 5-- | R 1 | Angol & Gayet | 26 | 6-- |
| | | | | 2 | Rhodes & Vimer | 26 | |
| S | | | | S 1 | Angol & Gayet | 26 | 6-- |
| | | | | 2 | Rhodes & Vimer | 26 | |
| T | Arnaud & Patin | 26 | 15-- | T 1 | Angol & Gayet | Fev. 2 | 6-- |
| | | | | 2 | Rhodes & Vimer | 26 | |
| U | | | | U | | | |
| X 1 | Arnaud & Patin | Fév. 26 | 2-10- | X | Angol & Gayet | 2 | 12-- |
| 2 | Patin | 2 | 2-10- | | | | |
| Y | Arnaud | 2 | 5-- | Y 1 | Angol | Fev. 9 | 6-- |
| | | | | 2 | Veibel & Vogl | 2 | |
| Z 1 | Arnaud | 2 | 2-10- | Z | Angol | 9 | 6-- |
| 2 | Patin | 2 | 2-10- | | | | |
| Aa | Arnaud | 2 | 5-- | Aa 1 | Rhodes & Vimer | 16 | 6-- |
| | | | | 2 | Angol & Gayet | 16 | |
| Bb | Arnaud | 9 | 5-- | Bb 1 | Angol & Gayet | 16 | 6-- |
| | | | | 2 | Patin & Guyat | 16 | |
| Titre | Arnaud | 9 | 5-- | Titre | Patin & Guyat | 16 | 6-- |
| | Composition | £ 130 | | | | £ 156 | |
| | Tirage ci-contre | 156 | | | | | |
| | | £ 286 | | | | | |
| | Rapporté au Bd. F.o. | 83 | | | | | |

Figure 4, a page (folio 71) from the *Banque des ouvriers* kept by the STN's shop foreman, provides an inside view of work in the printing shop and of the history of work itself. Every Saturday, or *journée de banque*, the foreman recorded the amount of work done on each job by each worker during the preceding week and the amount that each worker received in pay from the cash box. The structure of the document is revealing in itself, because the foreman organized his accounts in a way that corresponded to the organization of labor on the shop floor. He divided the page vertically into two halves, which represent the basic division of the work force into *la casse* (compositors) on the left and *la presse* (pressmen) on the right. The columns of letters on the left side of each half stand for sheets, the basic unit of production; so one can follow the labor on each sheet and on the volume as a whole, week by week, as it progressed through the *casse* and the *presse*.

When the volume was completed, the foreman tallied the sums paid for presswork on the right, 156 livres, and added them to the sum of the composition on the left, 130 livres. The total, 286 livres, was posted to the account book known as the *Brouillard*: hence the note at the end, *"Rapporté au Bd., fo. 83."* That sum can be found in the *Brouillard* itself, on folio 83, exactly as indicated, in an entry that debits the general account of the *Système: "Ouvrage de Boubers doit aux suivants . . . à Caisse 286 l. pour composition et tirage du tome 1, apert Banque des Ouvriers fo. 71."* The STN's accountant, following the standard techniques of double-entry bookkeeping, had debited the account for the *Système* 286 livres and had credited the same amount to the account for the cash box (*Caisse*) from which the workers had been paid. Each account in turn was posted to a general *registre*, the *Grand Livre*, where the directors of the STN could check the state of each of the dozens of accounts that collectively constituted their business.

Taken as a whole, therefore, folio 71 of the *Banque des ouvriers* represented a general unit of work--the total labor costs for producing Volume I of the *Système de la nature*, or in the printer's jargon, an *ouvrage*, as indicated by the title at the top of the page, *Ouvrage de Boubers*. The foreman organized his accounting according to *ouvrages,* or jobs, each of which corresponded to one of the STN's accounts. So the labor on the *Système* could be conjugated through the STN's books by means of "posting," or transmitting sums through increasingly abstract levels of reckoning: from the *Banque des ouvriers* to the *Brouillard* and the *Grand Livre*. At the same time, the *Ouvrage de Boubers* could be broken down into smaller units, each of which had a value expressed in *livres tournois:* the overall work at the *casse* and the *presse* and then, within each of them, the labor on individual sheets or on the two *formes* used to produce each sheet.

The pieces fit together perfectly in a highly integrated structure, but the structure existed only in the rational world of accountancy, where the accountant himself had an account and disappeared in the abstractions of his own creation. The men who actually manufactured the *Système de la nature* belonged to another world, the world of the printing shop, which was constantly erupting in jokes, brawls, and breaks for rounds of drinks in the tavern. Despite the disparity between the irregular behavior of the workers and the mathematical patterns of the account books, one can nonetheless catch something of the rhythm of labor in the printing shop. Closer analysis of the *Banque des ouvriers* and the account for *Papier délivré* makes it possible for one to measure the flow of work on the *Système* with considerable precision (see Figure 1).

It should be remembered, however, that the above documents only concern labor performed on the *Système de la nature*. Pressmen worked on many other jobs each week, because they printed *formes* as they became available from the compositors; and the compositors themselves frequently shifted from job to job. Also, the account for *Papier délivré* has some gaps: it does not give the output of perfected sheet in four cases, and it gives the number of the press at which the work was performed in only nine cases. So these documents do not provide enough information for one to measure the weekly output and income of every worker, even though they make it possible for one to reconstruct the pattern of labor that went into the *Système*.

Whatever his exactitude in keeping accounts, the foreman does not seem to have managed the labor very efficiently. As Figure 1 shows, the compositors kept getting far ahead of the printers, and the shop's general output varied erratically from week to week, both at the *casse* and at the *presse*. In the first week, which ended on December 8, 1770, three compositors completed 11 *formes*, while one press team printed only 2 *formes*. In the second week, the compositors did no work at all on the *Système*, while two other teams of pressmen ran off only four *formes*. By January 12, 1770, the *casse* was seven formes ahead of the *presse*. So the foreman had to shift a heavy proportion of the *presse* to the *Système* in late January and early February in order to complete the volume by February 16, which was far behind the deadline set by Boubers.[29]

Output looks equally erratic when studied at the level of individual workers. By casting off copy from the printed text supplied by Boubers, the foreman could have different chunks of the text set simultaneously by different compositors. Hence the output in the week of December 8, when Hallanzi (working with *paquetiers?*) set 6 *formes*, Offray set 2, and Patin set 3. In the end, the text passed through the hands of five compositors, each of whom worked at his own pace. It seems likely, moreover, that they occasionally collaborated in combinations that can only be guessed at. In the week of January 26, the foreman credited Arnaud and Patin together with composing 7 *formes:* presumably they worked with one or two *paquetiers*, or compositors, who set only pages, which freed Arnaud and Patin to concentrate on the more skilled work of imposition and complex corrections. So the typesetting did not follow any distinct pattern. Different men, and combinations of men, worked at different rhythms on different segments of the text.

The presswork was just as irregular. Output for the *presse* as a whole varied from two *formes* (4,000 impressions) to seven *formes* (14,000 impressions) per week. The pressmen printed formes as they became available from the *casse,* so the printing was scattered throughout the presses, and individual compositors did not feed work to individual printers in a consistent manner. In fact, the teams of pressmen often split and re-formed, presumably as a result of absenteeism and turnover in the work force. Thus Pousillon worked with Patin in the week of December 8, then worked by himself at half press in the week of December 22, and took up with Patin again in the week of December 29; and Rhodes worked with Duthwiler in the week of December 22 and with Vogl in the week of January 1, 1771.

The press numbers *(numéros des presses)* and the dates of the distribution of *"Papier blanc"* given in the account for *"Papier délivré"* make it possible to follow the labor of the pressmen still more closely. One might expect the printers to remain at a given press and to run off whatever *forme* arrived at that press from the compositors working upstream to them. But the printers of the STN apparently shifted from press to press as well as from job to job. Assuming the press numbers indicate who worked at what press, it seems that sheets A, B, and C were printed at press 3 by three different teams. Patin and Pousillon began to print sheet A on December 7, 1770, and finished by payday, December 8. Vogl and Aberli began to print sheet B on December 8 and finished it well before the next payday, December 15. At that point apparently the foreman shifted them to another job at another press. Soon afterward Angol and Gayet became free, and the foreman put them to work on press 3 printing the first *forme* of sheet C, which they, too, finished a few days before December 15. So the foreman shifted them to another job. Then, as Vogl and Aberli in turn became free, he put them back on press 3, where they printed the second *forme* of C in time to collect for it on the same payday. Presumably the labor on make-ready made it easier to maintain the printing of a given job at the same press and to shift press teams to other presses as *formes* from other jobs became available.

Admittedly, this interpretation involves some speculation. But the way the accounting was kept for *Papier délivré* suggests that the four reams, four quires were allotted to given presses on given days; and the *Banque des ouvriers* indicates that printers moved around those presses in response to the pressure of the available work. The pattern can be seen more clearly during the weeks between December 27, 1770, and January 12, 1771, when the *Système* was being printed at press 2 and press 4. The following table shows which printers worked at those presses from the dates when the paper was distributed and what formes they printed.

| Distribution of Paper | Number of Press | Printers | Formes | Work Completed by Pay-day on |
|---|---|---|---|---|
| Dec. 31 | 2 | Rhodes & Vogl | I1 | Jan. 5 |
| Dec. 31 | 2 | Angol & Gayet | I2 | Jan. 5 |
| Jan. 2 | 4 | Roche & Guyat | K1 | Jan. 5 |
| Jan. 2 | 4 | Patin & Pousillon | K2 | Jan. 5 |
| Jan. 4 | 2 | Roche & Guyat | L1 | Jan. 12 |
| Jan. 4 | 2 | Rhodes & Vogl | L2 | Jan. 5 |
| Jan. 7 | 2 | Patin & Pousillon | M1 | Jan. 12 |
| Jan. 7 | 2 | Angol & Gayet | M2 | Jan. 12 |

It seems clear from this table that the workers shifted frequently from press to press. For example, Rhodes and Vogl finished *forme* I1 at press 2 a day or two after December 31 and then went to another job at another press. Angol and Gayet succeeded them at press 2, where they printed I1. And then Rhodes and Vogl returned to press 2 and printed *forme* L2 in time to collect for it and for I2 on payday, January 5. But why did the foreman not keep them at press 2 throughout that week? Presumably a *forme* of another job became available; he did not want to delay work on it; and no other pressmen were free to print it--that is, the compositors produced more than the pressmen could handle. The two halves of the shop seem to have been out of balance, and the foreman directed the flow of work as best he could by shifting around printers.

Whatever its rationale, the pattern, or lack of pattern, suggests that work did not flow smoothly through the shop. It went by fits and starts, in currents and eddies, according to rhythms set by the workers themselves and despite the foreman's efforts to channel it in directions of his own choosing. Other shops may have operated differently. But work itself was different 200 years ago from what it is today--that seems to be the most general implication of these highly specific data.

## NOTES

1. This paper was originally given as a lecture at the University of Michigan in 1976. Later versions were presented at the Enlightenment Congress in Budapest in 1987 and the Library of Congress Symposium on Publishing and Readership in Revolutionary France and America in 1989.

2. The best bibliographical survey of all the Holbachean works is still Jeroom Vercruysse, *Bibliographie descriptive des écrits du baron d'Holbach* (Paris: Lettres Modernes, 1971). The information on Rey's second edition comes from a letter to the Société typographique de Neuchâtel by J. G. Baerstecher, a bookdealer in Clèves, dated November 30, 1771: "After having published the first edition, M. Rey of Amsterdam immediately put out a second one and set its price so low that it is impossible for me to sell yours in competition with it" (Papers of the Société Typographique de Neuchâtel [referred to henceforth as STN], Bibliothèque publique et universitaire, Neuchâtel, Switzerland). These archives are the main source for this study. The letters are classified by the names of the STN's correspondents.

3. Samuel Fauche to STN, Nov. 24, 1770.

4. Boubers's dossier in the STN papers contains 35 letters, which are full of information about the speculation; but they are so tendentious that they have to be read with a good deal of skepticism--and also in conjunction with the STN's own letters as well as those of its other correspondents, notably Charles Triponetty, a merchant who specialized in the lace trade and who kept an eye on Boubers for the STN, and Gosselin *père et fils*, merchants in Lille, who also represented the STN's interests.

5. Output varied enormously in printing shops during the era of the common press. Whether one studies the same team of printers over several weeks or several teams during the same week, the production could double or halve. Donald F. McKenzie found that weekly averages of impressions per day at the Cambridge University Press in 1700 fluctuated between 3,450 and 1,566: McKenzie, *The Cambridge University Press 1696-1712* (Cambridge: Cambridge University Press, 1966), vol. 1, chaps. 3 and 4. The above figures on the output of printers do not represent their entire labor for a given week, because they usually worked on other jobs beside the *Système de la nature*. In 1770-71, the STN's foreman organized his accounts by the job rather than by the total amount of work done in the shop for a week. The latter system was adopted by Barthélemy Spineux, the foreman who directed the shop in the late 1770s and 1780s, when weekly output per worker can be measured more accurately. See Jacques Rychner, "Running a Printing House in Eighteenth-Century Switzerland: The Workshop of the Société Typographique de Neuchâtel," *The Library*, 6th series, vol,. 1, no. 1 (1979), pp. 1-24; and Robert Darnton, *The Business of Enlightenment: A Publishing History of the Encyclopédie, 1775-1800* (Cambridge, Mass.: Harvard University Press, 1979), chap. 5.

6. I have transcribed the manuscript without emandation and have enclosed my own additions in square brackets. The two Patins who appear among the workers seem to have been a father and a son who tramped around the printing shops together.

7. In the unusually productive week of Jan. 26, 1771, the foreman recorded payments to "Arnaud et Patin" for the composition of sheets S, T, U, and *forme* 1 of sheet X. This entry could indicate that the foreman paid Arnaud and Patin the allotted sum per *forme* and that they then distributed the money among other workers, presumably *paquetiers*, who set the type for pages under their direction, leaving them to do the more complicated task of imposition.

8. For a general discussion of these issues, see Donald F. McKenzie, "Printers of the Mind: Some Notes on Bibliographical Theories and Printing-House Practices," *Studies in Bibliography* 22 (1969), pp. 1-75.

9. STN to Gosse et Pinet, Nov. 5, 1770.

10. STN to Daudet de Jossan, Oct. 30, 1770.

11. Circular letter addressed to twenty booksellers in the STN's *Copie de lettres,* March 14, 1771.

12. STN to Faivre, Sept. 10, 1771.

13. Abram Bosset de Luze to STN from Paris, April 10, 1780. In a similar letter of March 31, 1780, written to the home office during this business trip to Paris, Bosset insisted: "But, I must emphasize once again, our problem is not to find wonderful, magnificent works to print. The key to everything, the goal that we must keep in mind at all times, is before printing any work to make sure that we can get some cash for it." For a further discussion of the values and the profit motives among eighteenth-century booksellers, see Robert Darnton, "The World of the Underground Booksellers in the Old Regime," in *Vom Ancien Regime zur Französischen Revolution. Forschungen und Perspektiven,* ed. Ernst Hinrichs, Eberhard Schmitt, and Rudolf Vierhaus (Göttingen: Vanderhoeck und Ruprecht, 1978), pp. 439-478.

14. Ostervald to Lentulus, the governor of the principality of Neuchâtel and Valangin, July 4, 1771. On the local context of this affair, see Charly Guyot, "Imprimeurs et pasteurs neuchatelois: l'affaire du *Système de la nature* (1771)," *Musée neuchâtelois* 33 (1946), pp. 74-81 and 108-116.

15. Boubers to STN, April 7, 1771.

16. STN to Boubers, Oct. 27, 1771.

17. Boubers to STN, Oct. 4, 1771.

18. STN to Charles Triponetty, a merchant in Brussels who tried to arrange a settlement, Jan. 6, 1772.

19. Boubers to STN, May 17, 1776.

20. Delahaye to STN, Jan. 2, 1783. For an account of Boubers's imbroglios from a Belgian point of view, see Jeroom Vercruysse, "L'édition neuchâteloise du *Système de la nature* et la librairie bruxelloise," in *Aspects du livre neuchâtelois,* ed. Jacques Rychner and Michel Schlup (Neuchâtel: Bibliothèque publique de l'université de Neuchâtel, 1986), pp. 77-88.

21. Baerstecher to STN, Nov. 30, 1771.

22. Baerstecher to STN, Dec. 23 and Dec. 15, 1772.

23. Gerlache to STN, July 6, 1772, and April 17, 1773.

24. Antoine-François Momoro, *Traité élémentaire de l'imprimerie, ou le manuel de l'imprimeur* (Paris: Veuve Taillard et Fils, 1793), pp. 167-168.

25. Pyre to STN, April 15, 1780.

26. "Mon Voyage de 1787," Bibliothèque de l'Arsenal, ms. 5947, fo. 50 verso.

27. See William M. Sale, *Samuel Richardson: Master Printer* (Ithaca, N.Y.: Cornell University Press, 1950), p. 24. Richardson set his profit at half the combined costs of composition, presswork, and proof reading. Sale makes no mention of any calculation for overhead, so it would seem that the English equivalent of "étoffes" came out of the provision for profit. Hence the disparity between the profit margin in London (half the labor costs) and in Paris (one third of the labor costs on top of the half taken to cover "étoffes.") However, the French sources do not refer to proofreading as a factor in the printer's price per sheet, while Richardson allowed for it in his calculations: he paid a workman 2 d. to the shilling on the price paid to the compositor.

The shop foreman usually read proof at the STN, and so the cost of that function was absorbed in his salary, which was fixed at the beginning of the year.

28. See Robert Darnton, "A Bibliographical Imbroglio: Hidden Editions of the *Encyclopédie*," in *Cinq siècles d'imprimerie genevoise*, vol. 2, ed. Jean-Daniel Candaux and Bernard Lescaze (Geneva: Societé d'histoire et d'archéologie, 1981), vol. 2, pp. 71-101.

29. Of course the irregularities in the labor on the *Système* could have been compensated by work on other jobs underway at the same time. So what appears to be irrational at the level of the *"ouvrage"* could be efficient at the level of the shop: that was the point of the system of concurrent production, which seems to have been adopted in most early modern printing shops. But the STN needed to print the *Système* quickly in order to meet the deadline set by Boubers. Furthermore, its correspondence shows that it was dissatisfied with the work of its foremen until later in the 1770s, when the talented *prote* from Liége, Barthélemy Spineux, took over the direction of the shop. Spineux changed the system of accounting in the *Banque des ouvriers* so that entries were arranged by all the work done throughout the shop in a given week, rather than all the work done on a given job over several weeks--an indication that he sought to balance output at the shop level. On Spineux and the general character of printing at the STN, see the superb studies by Jacques Rychner: "Fonctions et tribulations d'un prote au XVIIIe siècle: Jacques-Barthélemy Spineux," in *Aspects du livre neuchâtelois*, ed. Jacques Rychner and Michel Schlup (Neuchâtel: Bibliothèque publique de l'université de Neuchâtel, 1986), pp. 187-269; and Rychner's "Running a Printing House in Eighteenth-Century Switzerland: The Workshop of the Société Typographique de Neuchâtel," *The Library*, 6th series, 1 (1979), pp. 1-24.

# A SILENT REVOLUTION: BENJAMIN FRANKLIN AND PRINT CULTURE

*Larzer Ziff*

Benjamin Franklin was a printer and beyond others in his day, even of fellow printers, he comprehended the change in consciousness that print was effecting. Printing, to be sure, had been established centuries before Franklin took up the trade, but in his America print was spreading from centers of learning and population into the countryside of towns and hamlets with a rapidity unmatched in Europe. The printing press followed the flow of settlement as an institution of the common life. Franklin realized that print's capacity to produce a multitude of identical copies worked toward the depersonalizing of discourse. As print culture expanded, he perceived, the authority texts had once derived from the person of their authors--an authority inherited from oral culture, wherein speaker and spoken were inseparable--would be transferred to the reader who absorbed the replicated text at a physical and temporal distance from its producer.

Franklin grasped the difference between the usual practice of writing a piece for a circumscribed audience, such as a sermon or treatise on the law, and then printing it, and writing for print itself. The former, retaining assumptions of the speaker's authority and the audience's specificity, carried into print the habits of the oral tradition and writing's association with an elite or learned class. The latter seized upon print's capacity to disembody the author and reach a large, indeterminate audience as a condition that made possible a new range of written matter and dictated a new manner of writing it.

Jonathan Edwards, eighteenth-century America's greatest philosopher, as well as American Puritanism's greatest theologian, was Franklin's contemporary. During his lifetime he printed a large amount of what he wrote and preached. But even in print the speaker was a minister who derived his authority from his learning combined with his piety and addressed an audience in a printed relationship that sought to recapture the immanence of preacher and congregation. When Edwards writes about the exalted moments of religious revival, he describes the condition that printed discourse, in his view, cannot even hope to approximate:

> Our public assemblies were then beautiful; the congregation
> was alive in God's service, everyone earnestly intent on the
> public worship, every hearer eager to drink in the words of
> the minister as they came from his mouth; the assembly in
> general were, from time to time, in tears while the Word
> was preached: some weeping with sorrow and distress, others
> with joy and love, others with pity and concern for the souls
> of their neighbors.[1]

The condition of the physical proximity of speaker and audience is intense and the corporeality of response is emphasized. Neither can be expected when the sermon is published and then experienced by a reader apart from both speaker and other listeners.

A good proportion of Edwards's writings, to be sure, were philosophical discourses prepared for print and so addressed to the reason rather than the sensibility of the reader. But while recognizing this, Edwards also recognized that print was thus a second best, because for him the essential fact of human existence, the possession of grace, was not a matter of reason or judgment. In opposition to reason he called this possession a "divine taste" and explained it by analogizing it to natural taste. As he argues in his *Religious Affections*, while judgment proceeds abstracted from corporeality, taste, its superior, springs directly from physical presence. A majestic reasoner, Edwards nonetheless appeals to the judgment as an inadequate substitute for a preferred address to physical presence. He thus exemplifies the way in which print's difference from speech was viewed by many as a decline in power.

In contrast, Franklin seized upon print's capacity to obliterate presence, seeing it as a means to diffuse information, thought, and sentiment free from the limitations of place and moment. He sought to develop print's potential to create communities of readers from across the boundaries of community previously defined by class, religious belief, or occupation, and he twitted the two groups, clergymen and lawyers, who dominated written discourse but failed to grasp the intrinsic nature of print.

Taking the sermon, the preeminent oral performance of his day, as his target, Franklin lampooned its format once it is viewed in cold print, and said of the preachers:

> Let them have the Liberty of repeating the same Sentence in
> other Words; let them put an Adjective to every Substantive,
> and double every Substantive with a Synonmia, for this is
> more agreeable than hawking, spitting, taking Snuff, or other
> Means of concealing Hesitation. Let them multiply

> Definitions, Comparisons, Similitudes, and Examples.
> Permit them to make a Detail of Causes and Effects,
> enumerate all the Consequences, and express one Half by
> Metaphor and Circumlocution. Nay, allow the Preacher to
> tell us whatever a Thing is negatively, before he begins to
> tell what it is affirmatively; and suffer him to divide and
> subdivide as far as *Two and fiftiethly*.[2]

When, however, a discourse is to be printed, "bound down upon Paper," as Franklin put it, then, he insisted, the brief, the perspicuous, and the direct was called for because the discourse must stand without the aid of the speaker's presence.

Similarly, Franklin lampooned the verbosity of legal writings in a day when print made them available to common readers: "You must abridge the Performance to understand them; and when you find how little there is in a Writing of vast Bulk, you will be as much supriz'd as a Stranger at the opening of a Pumpkin."[3] He then went on slyly to suggest that legal wordiness was a contrivance of scriveners who were threatened by the increasing availability of print.

Franklin's first published writings were designed for the *New-England Courant*, the newspaper his brother founded in Boston in 1721, and throughout his career he shaped his writing for an assumed audience of intelligent, busy people who had the capacity to understand even technical subjects if they were presented in a clear and simple--even homely--style within the relatively brief compass of the usual journal article. Each of his pieces proceeds from the pen of a persona; none presumes to be written by an individual whose reputation having gone before him establishes the authority of what is said. Each piece must take its independent chance, deriving its effect from what it can work on the reader. Franklin's acknowledged masters, the great English essayists of the early century such as Addison and Swift, had guided his style, but in one respect, at least, he went beyond them. Influenced by American conditions, he accepted the indeteriminate nature of his readership--neither learned nor ignorant, interested in gossip yet hungry for facts, alert to personal profit while sympathetic to schemes of social benevolence--and called forth the audience that from his day to this exists substantially yet elusively under the title of the common reader.

The American world of print that Franklin's mastery shaped is put into relief by the notes of a young scholar who had been formed by it. Studying in Göttingen in 1819, George Bancroft marveled at what he called the "democracy" of German literary culture. America had not prepared him for a land in which a class of men could earn their living by learning and publishing regardless of their birth. In his homeland democratic opportunity extended to economic and social mobility but did not encourage learning as a trade; in Germany, he noted, "Much knowledge is collected that one may have a chance of selling himself at a higher price." There was also, however, a price to be paid. Whereas in America similar knowledge was purveyed to the public by Franklinesque writers whose articles and books were outgrowths of occupations and concerns broader if more shallow than those of professional scholars, in Germany, "the learned write for the learned." As a result, while the writings that issued from American presses were received as matters of public consequence, in Germany, "the literary class has little or no influence on the people."[4]

When Franklin, educated by print outside college walls, proposed a university that unlike all then existing in America would be founded free of sectarian interest and devoted to preparing a range of young men for the social and economic conditions of their country rather than to either finishing the wealthy or furnishing the clergy, he was compelled to acknowledge the hold oratory had on the popular mind. "*History* will show the wonderful effects of *Oratory*," he admitted, "in governing, turning, and leading great Bodies of Mankind." But that was in another day. So after the students are "struck with Admiration" at what oratory once had wrought and the beauties of the ancient speeches are pointed out to them, the instructor should move on: "Modern Political Oratory, being Chiefly performed by the Pen and Press, its Advantages over the Ancient in some Respects are to be shown, as that its Effects are more extensive, more lasting, &c."[5] The phrase "in some Respects" is typical Franklin demurral; the best persona for a proposer is one of modesty and openness to persuasion. In point of fact, his discourse indicates no advantages that speech has over pen and press.

The way print culture spread in America was greeted with dismay by many and with misunderstanding by even more. The dismay was felt by those on both the conservative and liberal sides of the political division and for contrasting reasons. On one hand, there was the remarkable Joseph Dennie, a staunch Tory even in a time of nationalistic fervor. From his days in the cradle in Lexington, where he was born in 1768, through his Harvard education to his career as a literary journalist, Dennie appears to have had one overwhelming ambition in the pursuit of which he never waivered: to be a great man of letters on the model of such English giants as Samuel Johnson. In Boston in 1791 he founded *The Tablet*, an ambitious literary journal that proved too ambitious. Relocating in Walpole, New Hampshire, the very location an indication of the dispersal of printing, he became editor of the *Farmer's Weekly Museum*; and drawing around him a circle of politically minded wits with literary ambitions, he improved that journal into one that had a readership in all of the states while also placing it fully in the Federalist camp. In 1799 Dennie moved to Philadelphia, where after other journalistic efforts he founded *The Port Folio* in 1801, a magazine that for fifteen years went unrivalled as the best literary journal in the country.

Dennie's view of literary excellence was fixed firmly on the English tradition, and his Federalism was an expedient substitute for his true allegiance, which was to a class society of monarch, aristocrats, club wits, and elegant satirists disdainful of the mob. Writing to his parents in the year before he founded *The Port Folio*, Dennie with characteristic acerbity said:

> Had not the *Revolution* happened; had I continued a subject to the King, had I been fortunately born in *England* or resided in the City of London for the last 7 years, my fame would have been enhanced; and as to fortune I feel a moral certainty that I should have acquired by my writings 3 or 4 thousand pounds. But in this *Republic*, this region covered with the Jewish and canting and cheating descendants of those men, who during the reign of a Stuart, *fled way* from the claims of the Creditor, from the tithes of the Church, from the allegiance to their Sovereign and from their duty to their God, what can men of liberality and letters expect but such policy treatment as I have experienced?

He went on to state what was already manifest: "foul is the day in our Calendar, and bitterly are those *patriotic* and Indian traitors to be cursed who instigated the *wretched* populace to declare the 4th of July, 1776, a day of Independence."[6]

None of Franklin's contemporaries was so equally qualified to grasp the implications of the spreading print culture as was Dennie. His mother was a Green, a member of one of the first families in the history of American printing,[7] and he sensed the modifications print required of existing genres. The most popular of his own writings, the lively moralistic essays that first appeared in the *Farmer's Weekly Museum* and were then published and republished in book form, were titled *The Lay Preacher*. Modelled on the sermon, they were written rather than preached by a persona who was a genteel, almost dandyish, wit rather than a pious preceptor. They exemplify Dennie's acute ability to conserve the outline of a traditional oral form while abbreviating its length and substituting opinions on manners, morals, and politics for the doctrinal issues customarily drawn from biblical texts by the ministry.

Viewed from the safe distance of some two centuries, Dennie's outrageous prejudices expressed with an insistent smirk of superiority are rather engaging. Especially attractive is an unabashed modernizing of the Bible that translates texts weighted with moral and theological glosses into lessons in contemporary manners and politics. Franklin did the same but did so with rather too heavy an allegorical intent. Dennie was defter if more supercilious.

But Dennie was indeed in the wrong place at the wrong time. He was unable to separate the keen journalistic sense he acquired from his familiarity with the press from an ideal of literature as the property of the sophisticated few that would be degraded in direct proportion to the number of persons for whom it was shaped. He spoke often of the "natural malignity of our rascal populace."[8] As a consequence, he regarded Franklin as the central villain of the American drama in which circumstances had so cruelly placed him. Politically, he said, Franklin was "the first to lay his head in the lap of French harlotry," and economically Franklin encouraged "a low and scoundrel appetite for small sums" that "degraded our national character." As for his writing, Franklin "was the founder of that Grubstreet sect, who have professedly attempted to degrade literature to the level of vulgar capacities, and debase the polished and current language of books by the vile alloy of provincial idioms, and colloquial barbarism, the shame of grammar and akin to any language, rather than English."[9]

Ironically, the shrewdest counter to Dennie's anglophiliac view was provided not by the American "Jacobins" he despised but by a Briton. Writing in the *Edinburgh Review* in 1806, Francis Lord Jeffrey said that Franklin's

> style was formed entirely by his own judgement and occasional reading, and most of his moral pieces were written while he was a tradesman, addressing himself to the tradesmen of his native city. We cannot expect, therefore, either that he should write with extraordinary elegance or grace; or that he should treat of the accomplishments, follies, and occupations of polite life. He had not great occasion, as a moralist, to expose the guilt and the folly of gaming or seduction; or to point a poignant and playful ridicule against the lighter immoralities of fashionable life.[10]

Jeffrey's concluding observation acutely directs us to the most vulnerable aspect of the work of Dennie and other American belles-lettrists of his day devoted to an ideal of English elegance. The style they admired was formed in expression of the concerns of a particular segment of a specifically English society. American society differed, and to pursue the same style in application to it was to address concerns that existed in America only as literary conventions. The "lighter immoralities of fashionable life" were, in America, a shadow cast by a transatlantic substance.

The lesson of Dennie's shortcomings was taken by the young Washington Irving, who shared his basic distaste for republicanism and imitated Oliver Oldschool, the editorial persona of *The Port Folio*, in his papers of Jonathan Oldstyle (1802), as well as in the persona of Launcelot Langstaff of *Salmagundi* (1807), the latter, indeed, based even more particularly on Irving's direct personal impression of Dennie. But Irving soon recognized the lack of fit between such literature and the substance of American society, and opting for the former, took himself to England to observe a more congenial subject matter.

If some at one end of the political spectrum were dismayed by the literature promoted by American print culture because it degraded literature in a pretense of elevating an inevitably vulgar populace, some at the other end were dismayed because it degraded an intelligent populace with writing beneath its capacity. Charles Jared Ingersoll of Philadelphia wrote poetry (he published a poem in *The Port Folio*), drama, and social treatises. But Jeffersonian Republican that he was, he regarded his literary activities as a natural adjunct of his career as a lawyer, politician, and sometimes congressman rather than as a profession that deserved support in its own right. For Dennie, a work of literature was an event in the history of literature, a history that enjoyed an essential independence from political history. For Ingersoll, a work of literature grew from the condition of the society in whose history it participated, and in a republic would, ideally, be the expression of the concerns of those who wrote from their experience in a variety of occupations rather than because they were professional writers. His dismay at the effects of the spread of print culture was therefore addressed to its failure to meet the needs and capacities of a republican readership:

> I consider rational liberty, useful learning, and solid science, more endangered from what is called the freedom of the press, than from all the hosts of ignorance and tyranny. The discovery of printing has been incalculably beneficial to the mass of mankind, but like all other benefits this is susceptible of corruption and abuse. The magazines, reviews, and newspapers that are spreading over the face of Europe and North America, threaten to deface and obliterate every vestige of the good sense and information to be derived from well chosen reading and unprejudiced inquiry. In the United States particularly, where the people in general are so well informed, there is less occasion than in any other country, for these little lights; and more occasion and a better atmosphere, than in any other, for the greater luminaries of science and instruction.[11]

For Ingersoll, the press had failed to keep step with the rise of general intelligence consequent upon a democratic revolution; the extramural university of print so vital in a free country had degenerated into a school of scandal. Dennie might well smile and point out that such levelling was inevitable in a nation ruled by public opinion; true literature by definition was restricted to the few. Ingersoll's and Dennie's agreement about the deplorable state of what was printed and their difference as to the cure defined the cultural conflict of modern democratic society. In asserting the standard of the best literature of the past, the traditionalist also endorses the necessary conservation of the social values that nurtured such a literature, while the believer in social progress stands ready, accordingly, to change literary standards, as was Ingersoll when he said: "Poetry, music, sculpture, and painting may yet linger in their Italian haunts. But philosophy, the sciences, and the useful arts, must establish their empire in the modern republic of letters, where the mind is free from power or fear."[12]

Unlike Dennie and Ingersoll, John Adams's contemplation of the effects of print was a consequence of his fascination with Franklin's phenomenal fame, which he viewed with a mixture of bafflement, outrage, and envy, yet also with a degree of shrewd penetration. He could not quite put the pieces together. He sensed that that fame was something new in the world of letters because although it resulted from Franklin's writings, still, unlike the reputation of other men of letters, say of John Locke, it was not confined to readers: "His name was familiar to government and people, to kings, courtiers, nobility, clergy and philosophers, as well as plebeians, to such a degree that there was scarcely a peasant or a citizen, a *valet de chambre*, coachman or footman, a lady's chambermaid or a scullion in a kitchen, who was not familiar with it, and who did not consider him as a friend to human kind."[13] But as he puzzled over why this was so, Adams was too readily attracted to an answer that hinted at conspiracy:

> He had been educated a printer, and had practiced his art in Boston, Philadelphia, and London for many years, where he not only learned the full power of the press to exalt and spread a man's fame, but acquired the intimacy and the correspondence of many of that profession, with all their editors and many of their correspondents. This whole tribe became enamored and proud of Mr. Franklin as a member of their body, and were consequently always ready and eager to publish any panegyric upon him that they could procure. Throughout his whole life he courted and was courted by the printers, editors, and correspondents of reviews, magazines, journals, and pamphleteers, and those little busy meddling scribblers that are always buzzing about the press in America, England, France, and Holland.[14]

To be sure, Franklin, as we now say, enjoyed a good press, but the reasons for his reputation extended beyond the puffing he thus received. Adams had hold of a better answer when he noted: "His rigorous taciturnity was very favorable to his singular felicity. He conversed only with individuals, and freely only with confidential friends. In company he was totally silent."[15] But blinded by the way his own reputation had suffered from the press, Adams left the point unanalyzed and fixed on the more obvious circumstance of Franklin's standing in the fraternity of printers.

Franklin's celebrated silence seems, indeed, to be at the root of the matter. Even in deliberative assemblies he spoke infrequently and then only briefly--never more than "ten minutes at a time, nor to any but the main point,"[16] Jefferson recalled. He acted from a conviction so deeply held that it was an essential trait of character rather than an idea, a conviction that speech was fittest for private moments and print for public. Since the deliberations in which he participated as a representative were to eventuate in public documents, he aimed at the shaping of those documents rather than the display of his personal views and reserved his force for the closed-door conferences and committees concerned with drafting.

Michael Warner acutely identifies the ideological context of Franklin's outlook: "Social authority, like truth, holds validity not in persons but despite them; it is located not in the virtuous citizen nor in God nor in the king but in the light of day, in the scopic vision of publicity itself. Thus print--not speech--is the ideal and idealized guardian of civic liberty, as print discourse exposes corruption in its lurking holes but does so without occupying a lurking hole of its own."[17] And he amplifies his perception thus: "Developed in practices of literacy that included the production and consumption of newspapers, broadsides, pamphlets, legal documents, and books, the republican ideology of print arranged the values of generality over those of the personal. In this cognitive vocabulary the social diffusion of printed artifacts took on the investment of the disinterested virtue of the public orientation, as opposed to the corrupting interests and passions of particular and local persons."[18]

Presenting his general self replicated in print time and again, Franklin exemplifies the ideology that disembodied him. The personal self was not to be written and was not even to be spoken in public. Indeed, so guarded was personality that for Franklin to write, was, in effect, to publish even if print were not the goal, and he regarded all writing as public property.

Thus in justifying his release to a jounal of the confidential letters Governor Hutchinson and Lieutenant Governor Oliver of Massachusetts had dispatched to their correspondents in the British government, Franklin cooly stated, "It is in vain to say, this would be betraying private Correspondence, since if the Truth only was written, no Man need be ashamed or afraid of its being known; and if Falsehoods have been maliciously covered under the Cloak of Confidence, 'tis perfectly just the incendiary Writers should be exposed and punished."[19] There may well be more than a touch of sophistry in this argument that nothing should be written, even in confidence, unless it can bear public exposure; that, in effect, there is no such thing as private correspondence.    The contention reminds us that Franklin was the first American printer of *Pamela* (1740), by Samuel Richardson, another printer by trade, the work that set the style for the age's popular, epistolary novels, revelations of private albeit fictional letters, and also gives us second thoughts about the way Franklin may have viewed his duties when he occupied the office of postmaster.  For Franklin, to write was to publish.

Carried to a logical extreme, such a contention means that, in effect, there is no such thing as intellectual property.  Once a person commits ideas to writing, they become the legitimate possession of all who can read. Franklin's  scientific career proceeded from this premise as he exchanged theories of electricity with his correspondence or declined to patent his stove because it was designed for all who could read about its merits, and he even, notoriously, applied it to plagiarism in defense of a minister who without acknowledgment preached sermons he had not written.   "I stuck by him" Franklin said, "as I rather approv'd his giving us good Sermons compos'd by others, than bad ones of his own Manufacture."[20]  For him ideas were general property, and their consequences rather than their origin were what counted.

The argument that maintains the publicity of writing implies the legitimacy of secrecy in all matters kept from writing.  Conduct that is not on public display and speech that is not overheard have no obligation to be consistent with what comes under public view.  The taciturnity of the personal is, for Franklin, the logical complement of the publicity of the general.

"Oratory in this age?" Adams exclaimed in disgust at its decline. "Secrecy! Cunning! Silence! *voilà les grandes sciences des temps modernes.* Washington! Franklin! Eternal silence!  impenetrable secrecy! deep cunning! These are the talents and virtues which are triumphant in these days."[21]  And he thought he knew the reason:

> Silence is most commonly design and intrigue.  In Franklin it was very remarkable because he was naturally a great talker.  I have conversed with him frequently in his garrulous humors, and his grandson, Billy, has told me that he never knew a greater talker than his grandfather.   But at other times he was as silent as midnight, and often upon occasions and in relation to subjects on which it was his duty to speak. Arthur Lee told me he had known him to sit whole evenings in London, without uttering a word, in company, when the conversation had turned upon subjects on which he was supposed to be well informed.
>
> Whether the age of oratory will ever return I know not.  At present it seems to be of little use, for every man in our public assemblies will vote with his party, and his nose is counted before his seat.[22]

While the rise of parties, polarized especially by opposed reactions to the French Revolution, diminished the consequences of oratory in the public assemblies, it augmented the importance of print because of the press's role in influencing voters to elect members of one or more party. Thomas Green Fessenden, the feisty poet of federalist doggerel, scolded his party for "not taking pains to circulate anti-jacobin newspapers and other periodicals, as antidotes to the poison of the Aurora, the Democratic Press, the Chronicle &c. It is folly to say that exertions of that kind will have no effect. Our adversaries ought to have taught us better. Their maxim is command the press and we command the union."[23] Fessenden, however, underestimated the avidity with which his party seized the lesson. Federalist journals were every bit as demagogic in their rhetoric as were the journals of the "jacobin" opposition which they attacked.

The establishment of the United States and the spread of print went hand in hand. The replacement of the individual with its corporeal connotations by the general with its truth claims, which was generated by the spread of print culture, was linked to the growth of personal as opposed to real property in the economy and the shift from immanence to representation in the political process. Even the stoutest patriotic opponents of the argument that the American colonists were virtually represented by Parliament quickly came to see that the notion of literal representation--of the body of representatives being a replication of the body of the people--was a greater fiction than that of virtual representation. Women and the propertyless, for example, were not replicated in the republic's assemblies. Replicated representation, however, was the lifeblood of the press which kept that ideology alive by claiming to be the voice of the people even as it promoted the notion that the people were one.

Benjamin Franklin's extension of the craft of the printer into trade and politics was not only emblematic of the American success story he consciously offered it as being; it also exemplified the way in which literary culture grew out of the dynamics of commercial and political representation. There were in his day and there would continue to be those who sought to keep literature free from such dependency. But they beat against the current. The silent yet voluble, secret yet published Benjamin Franklin stands as an illustration of the revolution in perception accomplished by printing, a revolution without which political revolution would not have occurred, and yet a revolution whose claims for generality were intimately connected with the concealment of the individual.

## NOTES

1. Jonathan Edwards, "A Faithful Narrative," *The Great Awakening*, ed. C. C. Goen (New Haven, Conn.: Yale University Press, 1972), p. 151.

2. Benjamin Franklin, "On Literary Style," *The Papers*, ed. Leonard W. Labaree et. al. (New Haven, Conn.: Yale University Press, 1959), vol. 1, p. 330.

3. Benjamin Franklin, "On Amplification," *The Papers*, ed. Labaree et. al. (New Haven, Conn.: Yale University Press, 1960), vol. 2, p. 146.

4. Orie William Long, *Literary Pioneers* (Cambridge, Mass.: Harvard University Press, 1935), p. 122.

5. Benjamin Franklin, "Proposals Relating to the Education of Youth in Pensilvania," *Writings*, ed. J. A. Leo Lemay (New York: Library of America, 1987), p. 336.

6. Harold Milton Ellis, *Joseph Dennie and His Circle* (Austin: University of Texas Press, 1915), p. 116.

7. In "The First Hundred Years of Printing in British North America: Printers and Collectors," *Proceedings of the American Antiquarian Society*, Vol. 99, Part 1, 1989, William S. Reese finds that of the American born and trained printers "thirteen of the nineteen were connected to the ubiquitous Green family, descended from the Cambridge printer Samuel Green, Sr. [who established his press in 1649], and related by blood, marriage, or apprenticeship" (p. 344).

8. Joseph Dennie, *The Lay Preacher*, ed. Harold Milton Ellis (New York: Scholars' Facsimiles & Reprints, 1943), p. 124.

9. *The Port Folio* (Feb. 14, 1801), in *Benjamin Franklin's Autobiography*, ed. J. A. Leo Lemay and P. M. Zall (New York: W. W. Norton, 1986), pp. 252-53.

10. Ibid., p. 254.

11. Charles Jared Ingersoll, *Inchiquin, the Jesuit Letters* (New York: I. Riley, 1810), p. 126.

12. Charles Jared Ingersoll, *A Discourse Concerning the Influence of America on the Mind* (Philadelphia: A. Small, 1823), p. 11.

13. *Benjamin Franklin's Autobiography*, ed. Lemay and Zall, p. 245.

14. Ibid., p. 246.

15. Ibid.

16. Thomas Jefferson, *The Life and Selected Writings*, ed. Adrienne Koch and William Peden (New York: Modern Library, 1944), p. 61.

17. Michael Warner, "Franklin and the Letters of the Republic," *Representations* 16 (Fall 1986), p. 116.

18. Michael Warner, "Textuality and Legitimacy in the Printed Constitution," *Proceedings of the American Antiquarian Society*, Vol. 97, Part 1 (1987), p. 74.

19. Benjamin Franklin, "On the Hutchinson Letters," *Writings*, ed. Lemay, p. 687.

20. Benjamin Franklin, *Autobiography*, ed. Lemay and Zall, p. 1400.

21. *The Spur of Fame, Dialogues of John Adams and Benjamin Rush, 1805-1813*, ed. John A. Schatz and Douglas Adair (San Marino, Calif.: Huntington Library, 1966), p. 59.

22. Ibid., p. 64.

23. Thomas Green Fessenden, *Pills, Poetical, Political and Philosophical* (Philadelphia: Printed for the Author, 1809), p. vi.

# PUBLISHING AND THE LAW

# THE DILEMMAS OF REPUBLICAN PUBLISHING, 1793-1799

*Carla Hesse*

In 1789 French revolutionaries led by the journalist Jacques-Pierre Brissot de Warville revolted against the publishing world of the Old Regime. They declared their intention to liberate the minds of citizens from royal *inquisitors* and to free the presses, as Brissot put it, in order to "spread enlightenment in every direction."[1]  Between 1789 and 1793 they translated this cultural program into legislative action and systematically dismantled the entire legal and institutional infrastructure that had organized French publishing under the absolutist monarchy.  In order to liberate thought and "spread enlightenment," the French Revolution inaugurated an era of freedom of commerce in the world of ideas.

      The declaration of "freedom of the press" on August 26, 1789 put a definitive end to prepublication censorship.  In 179O, the Royal Administration of the Book Trade was closed down as well. It was this administration which registered and enforced royal literary *privilèges* on books, the predecessors to copyrights that granted an exclusive claim upon a publication to an author or publisher.  The army of bureaucrats and inspectors who policed the book trade in order to prevent the circulation of subversive literature and pirate editions of *privileged* works was suppressed as well.  In 1791, the National Assembly definitively abolished the exclusive monopoly of the Publishers' and Printers' Guild on the trades of publishing, printing, and bookselling, thus opening these trades to all.  Finally, proclaiming nothing less than a "declaration of the rights of genius," in 1793, the National Convention for the first time legally recognized the property rights of living authors and abolished all former royal literary *privilèges*, or any private claims upon the works of authors who had been dead for more than ten years.  As a consequence, the entire literary inheritance of France, which had been monopolized by the Royal Book Guilds of France through these exclusive privileges granted by the crown, was released from private hands into the public domain.  Anyone was now free to publish Racine and Molière, as well as Voltaire and Rousseau. Thus by 1791 the entire legal and institutional framework that had restricted and regulated the circulation of printed matter had been destroyed.  The old corporate publishing regime was gone.

Between 1789 and 1792 chaos reigned in the Parisian publishing world.  There were no laws regulating literary property.  Literary piracy ran rampant, and the old Parisian book publishers were driven to bankruptcy. Finally, in 1793, the government decided to take action to restore order to the commercial publishing world.  A new legal depository was established at the Bibliothèque Nationale by the law of July 19, 1793 to protect the property claims of authors and their publishers.  But registration of a work at the *dépôt* was to be completely voluntary, for the author's own protection alone, rather than for the purposes of government surveillance as had been the case with the royal administration of the book trade.  In fact, the new law did not establish any national administration to regulate, inspect, or police the book trade. Publishers and authors would have to police the book trade themselves, and pursue claims against literary pirates retroactively in the courts.

What were the consequences of this massive deregulation of the printing and publishing world?  What happened to book publishing in particular during the French Revolution?  The purpose of this chapter is to examine the consequences of the revolutionary effort to institute a free market in ideas as a means of realizing the cultural ideal of an enlightened nation, and as well to explore the fate of the most treasured cultural invention of the early modern period, the printed book, in face of these efforts.

## THE IRONIES OF LIBERTY, 1793-1794

The new law of 1793 was intended to restore book publishing to a sound legal footing after the abolition of royal literary privileges by recognizing books as a form of property created by the author and protected by the law until ten years after the author's death.  But it was set into place as the Revolution entered its darkest moment.  Although the law guaranteed authors property rights and gave publishers clear legal protection against literary pirates, it was to be near impossible for them to make use of, let alone benefit from, this new legal situation.

The revolutionary wars against the major powers of Europe, along with the civil war in the Vendée, wreaked havoc on the economic and commercial life of the nation.  By July of 1793, the new official paper money, the *assignat*, had lost approximately 75 percent of its face value.[2]  The government then responded to soaring inflation with the *maximum*, a set of price limits, first on bread alone, but extended to all goods and services, including printing, publishing, and bookselling, on September 29, 1793.[3] Further, because of the wars, the government prohibited exports of any kind to hostile nations.  As a consequence, the extensive French book trade in

Austria, Belgium, England, and Spain ground to a halt. Trade with neutral countries, most notably Switzerland, was disrupted as well.[4] Domestic commerce was equally chaotic as a result of federalist revolts in the south and civil war in the west.

Here is how Jean-Baptiste Lefebvre de Villebrune, the director of the Bibliothèque Nationale, described the newly liberated publishing world in the spring of 1794:

> There is total stagnation. . . Something must be done . . . as much for the general good of the fatherland, as to avert the total ruin of the publishers of Paris, who have already, as is well known, suffered enough from present circumstances.[5]

Villebrune outlined the central causes of the crisis in the publishing world in the following manner:

> First: Fewer customers; [In former times,] many useless people fastidiously formed libraries that they were unable to read. Incapable of being republicans, they have fled the country.

> Second: Those who educate themselves and read in order to educate themselves, absorbed by the defense of the fatherland or by the posts that they occupy, are not reading or are reading much less.

> Third: The interruption of commerce with hostile countries has closed this branch of export.

> Fourth: The obstacles imposed on commerce with neutral countries.[6]

The war had devastated the book trade by depriving dealers of aristocratic and foreign markets, and by turning the attention of virtuous citizens to more pressing tasks than self-edification.

Statistics confirm the grim picture of commercial book publishing painted by contemporary witnesses. Despite the law on literary property of July 1793, which had promised to restore order and prosperity to the publishing world, book publishing was at a near standstill. The legal deposit, founded to administer the new laws on literary property, registered only 73 works in the first four months of operation, in comparison with the nearly 2,000 titles registered by the royal authorities four years earlier in 1789![7] And many of these works were not even new titles, but rather editions dating back to 1791. Robert Estival, the most noted bibliographer of the period, considered the entries at the legal depository for 1793 so statistically insignificant that he chose not to include them in his tabulation of legal deposits for the revolutionary period.[8] In the entire year II (September 21, 1793 to September 21, 1794), the *dépôt* recorded receipt of barely 300 titles. Moreover, very few of these works were actually book length. They were mostly plays, music, and political or educational pamphlets. This picture is confirmed by other statistical evidence as well. Martin, Milne, and Frautschi show in their massive *Bibliographie du genre romanesque français*, that the publication of novels dropped dramatically in 1789 from several hundred new novels a year to only *16* in 1794.[9]

The disruption of the commercial book trade by the war and the wartime economy was not the only source of unemployment in the Parisian printing and publishing community. Political repression, of both producers and consumers of the printed word, played a crucial role as well. The laws of December 4, 1792, and, especially, March 9, 1793, turned political journalism into a potentially lethal profession: any call for the dissolution of the present government became punishable by death.[10] The "law of suspects," which supplied the legal basis for the Terror on September 17, 1793, still further smoothed the path from the printing press to the guillotine by ordering the arrest of anyone whose "conduct, talk, or writings" raised suspicion of counterrevolutionary sympathies.[11]

Not surprisingly, between 1792 and 1793 the number of journals published in Paris dropped by one-half, from 216 to 113.[12] In the year II (1793-94) the number of periodicals circulating in Paris hit its low-water mark for the revolutionary period: 106. But the pursuit of unpatriotic printed matter was not limited to political journals. No genre was above suspicion. Surveillance extended from posters and pamphlets to book-length publications such as novels and scientific works.[13] Even the character of a bookdealer's clientele could come under scrutiny.[14]

The war and the Terror thus conspired with scissor-like inevitability to cut down the desperate along with the militant and courageous. And it was not just the new young printers of political journals and *nouveautés* like the Hébertist, François-Jean Momoro, who found their careers aborted by the Terror. Formerly wealthy and respected old members of the Paris Printers' and Publishers' Guild such as Phillipe-Denis Pierres, Jacques François Froullé, and Gaspar-Joseph Cuchet, who, having suffered the abolition of their *privilèges* and witnessed the collapse of their businesses, now too found themselves driven into the production of illicit ephemera in order to survive.[15] Cuchet, like Pierres and Froullé, was one of the wealthiest members of the Printers' and Publishers' Guild in 1789.[16] He specialized in publishing scholarly and scientific works.[17] By July of 1794, however, Cuchet presented the following account of his career since the beginning of the Revolution:

> [A] zealous partisan of the Revolution, I embraced it with the
> enthusiasm of a free man.  An elector in 1789, I was one of
> the first to take up arms.  The morning of July 14, I was in
> town, and in the afternoon I marched among the brave
> French Guards to take the Bastille. . . . On October 5 I
> marched with the Parisian army . . . to Versailles.  I have
> proof of all of these facts.

> After these great events, I was overcome by the darkest
> misfortunes; I went bankrupt.  Heartbroken, pursued by
> creditors, menaced by captivity . . . I lost my spirit, I lost
> my reason, and weakened by torment, I clung to any branch
> that could save me from the storm. . . .

> Citizens, I am not guilty of treason, I succumbed to the
> excesses of woe.  I printed three or four works on the
> monarchy.[18]

Whatever his actual political beliefs, Cuchet was driven by the collapse of the book trade from publishing scientific books into the shady world of political ephemera, only to stand trial before the Revolutionary Tribunal.

Faced with similar circumstances, others simply chose not to publish. The Paris agent Le Breton reported to the Minister of the Interior on March 3, 1794:

> Printers are complaining that, independent of the modest
> wages they are paid, they can no longer find any work
> because of the number of printing shops that have been
> suppressed.  And they are saying that if everyone's minds
> were left free to pursue their thoughts, they would no longer
> find themselves in need [of work]. . . . , there wouldn't be
> enough of them in the city to meet demand.[19]

The stifling of public discussion and dissent, as well as the more general fear of arousing suspicion merely by printing and publishing, left the commercial presses idle.

To make matters worse for the commercial book publishing world, the political repression of the year II (1793-94) was accompanied by an intensive effort to ensure governmental and national unity by centralizing and expanding government literary patronage, as well as official publishing and printing. Less than a year after the abolition of the royal academies and literary societies, in 1793 the Committee of Public Safety initiated an effort to establish a corps of official writers who could be depended upon to produce schoolbooks, political pamphlets, and newspapers, as well as literary and scientific works in all genres, imbued with unquestionable republican principles.[20] Further, while systematically repressing lucrative political publications that had to some extent compensated commercial publishers for their losses in book sales, the government now too committed significant funds, and its own presses, to both the publication of officially sanctioned and unofficially subsidized books, journals, and ephemeral literature.[21] Commercial publishers thus now had to compete with the government to attract politically acceptable authors and publishing ventures.

Finally, the imperative to achieve national unity in the face of war led to an effort to centralize the publication of laws. On November 18, 1793, the National Convention heard a report from the Committee of Public Safety proposing that the government centralize the promulgation of laws by publishing a single exclusive *Bulletin des Lois*, printed and distributed solely by a national printing shop.[22] This measure, wrote the reporter Billaud de Varenne

> is simple, because it will do away with all outside subcontracting to intermediaries, no longer leaving any separation between the legislator and the people. . . . This luminous idea was put before . . . the Constituent Assembly. . . . Be wise enough to marshall it now, and put it to your use to consolidate the Republic.[23]

The Convention put this plan into law a month later, in December of 1793.[24] The "intermediaries" between government and people, that is, the commercial and departmental publishers and printers, were removed from the process of printing and publishing government documents and laws.

A new national "Legal Printing Shop" (the *Imprimerie des Lois*) was constructed in the maison Beaujon in the faubourg St. Honoré in the winter and spring of 1794.[25] The presses for this huge shop were supplied, in part, through the confiscation of the presses of suppressed printers.[26] Thus when Anisson-Duperron, the director of the former Royal Printing Shop, perished in the Terror in the spring of 1794, his presses were moved to the maison Beaujon.[27] The presses of suppressed printers such as Momoro, Hebert, Gattey, Froullé, and Nicolas (all convicted as counterrevolutionary conspirators) met with the same fate. The government thus wielded repression and centralization hand-in-hand in its effort to deploy the printing press to create a unified national political culture.

The expansion of government publishing did not benefit the Paris publishers and printers. In fact, it further deprived them of resources and opportunities. Throughout the fall and spring of the year II (1793-94), Paris printers sent desperate appeals to the government for work.[28] Bust had

followed boom.    Deprived of its most lucrative commercial domestic and
international markets in elite literary culture, the largest government contracts,
such as schoolbooks and laws, and its printing houses suppressed and
confiscated for the nation's service, by 1794 the newly liberated publishing
world of Paris had ground to a virtual halt.    Thus they protested to the
National Convention: "If there is to be only one printing shop in Paris, what
meaning will 'freedom of the press' have?"[29]


## GOVERNMENT INITIATIVES

The nation's new cultural administration, the Committee of Public
Instruction, was soon made painfully aware of the initial results of its
deregulationist policies.    By declaring the freedom of the press, they had
liberated man's reason from the inquisitorial institutions of the Old Regime,
and through the new laws on literary property they had consecrated his genius
and its fruits.    They had abolished private claims upon the great classical and
Enlightenment texts and made them the inheritance of all.    And they had freed
access to the means of spreading thoughts--that is, the professions of printing,
publishing and bookselling--at least in principle, to all.    But it was patently
clear that enlightenment was not "spreading in every direction" as a
consequence of these measures, at least not through the medium of the
commercially printed book.

By the spring of 1794 the Committee was ready to hear the  appeals
from the director of the Bibliothèque Nationale, Villebrune, urging immediate
government intervention in order to revive the book trade.[30]    First and
foremost, Villebrune argued that books should be exempted from the wartime
laws against foreign export.    With the exception of rare books and military
maps, Villebrune suggested, there could be no reason to prohibit the export of
printed matter, even to hostile nations.    The economic benefits were obvious.
An ardent Jacobin, however, Villebrune, was not a man of narrow commercial
concerns.    He appealed to the cultural vision of the Committee of Public
Instruction as well:

> It is important to the French nation that its revolutionary
> principles are propagated beyond its frontiers, because then,
> the diverse peoples who surround us, impregnated with
> liberty, will resist all the more the perfidious plots of their
> tyrants.[31]

By reopening the export market to commercial publishing, commercial
publishing could thus be transformed into an agent of cultural expansionism
and global revolution.

There was no guarantee, however, that the commercial publishing houses, if revived, would rise as a vanguard of republican literary culture. In fact, the streets of Paris offered ample evidence to the contrary. For example, the undercover agent Mercier, reported to the minister of the interior that "[Parisian] dealers in new releases are selling lots of books better suited to corrupt morals than to shape minds. Without morals there can be no true republicans."[32] Was it in the interest of the nation to bail out commercial publishing and leave it free to propagate whatever texts it would? Villebrune anticipated this question and offered the following diagnosis of the situation:

> Let us for a moment consider the publisher as an ordinary manufacturer. His work augments or diminishes in proportion to the demands that he receives, and he devotes his industry to the genres for which the demand is greatest. . . . But at the same time as the fantasies of the moment determine the genres that he produces, he, by the works with which he inundates his fatherland, influences, in turn, his fellow citizens, by implanting in an even greater number of minds the dreams and futilities which a few opinionmakers have made the torrent of the moment. This is the relationship between the morality of the publisher and public morals. When the caprice of fashion turns him toward a genre of study that is destructive of reason, or toward immoral reading matter, the publisher spreads this venom into all classes of society. . . . [This is how] the immorality of the court under the Old Regime was spread into the furthest reaches of the country.[33]

This cycle of cultural reproduction was thus extremely difficult to break, because publishing did not simply mirror demand, it created it.

As Villebrune astutely observed, the problem was how to intervene in such a manner so as to break the cycle of reproduction without undermining or compromising the newly instituted rights of freedom of commerce, of expression, and of the press. The solution, he admitted, was not simple:

> Where minds are not already shaped, it is to be feared that the tastes of consumers imbued with prerevolutionary ideas will not be in harmony with the spirit of the nation. In this situation, the mercantile interests of the publisher do not coincide with the national interest, and it becomes necessary for the government to intervene in the publishing world....

> But in what way? The prohibition of works contrary to
> republican principles is indispensable in a revolutionary
> government. But there are other works, as dull as they are
> useless to the development of the mind: they cannot be
> prohibited merely for that. Works of this genre form the
> large majority of what is printed, they are the most sought
> after. . . . Among these works are compilations, excerpts,
> [and] almost all novels. . . . The publisher is not guilty for
> engaging in this kind of business . . . because these works
> have no other vice than their uselessness.[34]

If this decadent literary culture of the Old Regime could not be
censored, then how were the reading habits of the nation to be reformed?
Villebrune thought he had an answer:

> [T]he fatherland should offer the publisher a compensation
> that will balance in his eyes the benefits that he sacrifices for
> the greater good. . . . What should this advantage be?
>
> First: Civic recompense to the publisher who in the course
> of the year has published the greatest number of useful
> books.
>
> Second: The Convention having decreed that a national
> library will be formed in the administrative seat of every
> district, to honorific recompense could be added the
> acquisition of copies of works judged to be useful. . . . By
> this organization of encouragements, the book trade will
> preserve all the liberty it needs to keep itself alive, and the
> government, by a constant, but not onerous, policy, could
> redirect people's minds from their former emptiness toward
> more useful objectives.[35]

The Old Regime had attempted to shape minds through a system of *privilèges*
and censorship. Under the Republic these mechanisms were to be replaced by
"recompenses" and "encouragements." The principles of freedom of
commerce, expression, and the press, could thus be upheld.

Villebrune's report marked an important shift in both the underlying
principles and the practical organization of the revolutionary government's
policies in relation to book publishing. His proposal betrayed a recognition
that a "free market in ideas" was not an adequate means to ensure the
enlightenment of the nation, that the minds of citizens, if freed from
prescriptive constraints, might not naturally, nor easily, incline toward reason,

enlightenment, or self-improvement, let alone the public good. Indeed, the very technology upon which the government had placed so much faith as an agent of cultural change, the printing press, had proved that, if left to its own devices, it could equally act as a force for obstructing progress by reproducing and multiplying demand for an aristocratic reading diet of books for idle pleasure. These sober insights of the year II (1793-94) were to lead to a significant redefinition and expansion of the government's patronage of book publishing. Until 1794, publishers had benefited only indirectly from government patronage of writers or commissions for pedagogical works.[36] Henceforth the government would "encourage" publishers directly. They would patronize *editions*, as well as authors, of books useful to citizens and the nation.

The records of the Commission of Public Instruction reveal that the publishing world was soon to receive millions of livres of "encouragements." In the wake of the fall of Robespierre, the Commission of Public Instruction formed a special Office of Encouragement and Recompense for the Arts and Sciences. Between 1794 and 1796 this office poured over two and a half million livres in encouragements and over 16 million livres in government loans into patronage of useful books.[37]

Government patronage, accompanied by peace and the reopening of international markets after 1795, resulted in an extraordinary revival of French book publishing during the period of the Directory (1795-1799).[38] The years 1796 to 1798 witnessed the emergence of a whole new generation of publishing houses. Robert Estival's computation of the total number of book titles registered at the legal depository confirms the picture disclosed by my calculations of publishing establishments. He shows that the number of titles registered declined steadily from 1789 to 1795 and then turned upward again from 240 in 1796 to 815 in 1799.[39] A significant number of the new book publishing houses, like Bernard, Marchand, Huzard, or Duprat, specialized in scientific and educational publishing. They, among others, can be directly linked to the government's subsidized revival of scientific publishing during the period of the Directory (1795-1799).[40]

Peace not only reopened markets for French publishers, it also brought a renewal of civilian life, and an increase in the leisure time of citizens. Greater leisure led to a marked rise in the demand for, and consequently the production of, novels and fiction, as well as scientific works. Thus, Martin, Milne, and Frautschi, show that after a dramatic drop in the production of novels from 1789 to 1794, the trend reversed in 1795, with steady and increasing rises in the number of novels published between 1795 and 1799.[41]

## CONCLUSION

The book publishing renaissance of the Directory period was to be short-lived. Again, bankruptcy statistics offer striking testimony of renewed difficulties for book publishers from 1800 well into the imperial period.[42] Fiscal crisis and a partial government bankruptcy in 1797 brought drastic cutbacks in cultural subsidies.[43] The budgets of the Committee of Public Instruction show that by 1799 government patronage of commercial publishing had dried up almost completely.[44] But why was commercial book publishing essentially unable to survive without government assistance? The government began to make its own inquiries into the problem between 1803 and 1810. And fortunately, the responses of numerous publishers have survived.

More important than the short-term vicissitudes of the war and the Terror, or even the ills of state patronage, publishers testified unanimously that the underlying and persistent problem for commercial publishing was the law on literary property of 1793. It was both legally and institutionally inadequate as a basis for commercial book publishing. The Paris publisher Lamy is typical in his views:

> In 1793 the law which came to regulate us destroyed the
> foundations of literary property. It resulted in the undoing
> of the premier publishing houses and in universal disorder.
> Immorality supplanted the good faith of yore.[45]

There was a united call for greater regulation of the publishing world than the law supplied. Two issues lay at the heart of publisher's complaints: *contrefaçon* and *concurrence*, pirating and unregulated competition.

The law of 1793, they explained, was totally ineffectual in protecting against pirating. The head of the Paris Office of Arts and Manufactures assessed the law as follows:

> The lacunae in the law are numerous, and their nature is
> such that it is impossible for either the administration or the
> courts to apply the law in a uniform or regular manner.

In order to pursue someone for having produced a pirate edition, he explained:

> It is necessary to present endless memoranda, to send along
> with the formal accusation, a copy of the pirated edition
> [and] a copy of the original, with proof of its deposit at the
> Bibliothèque Nationale. . . . That is not all. One is obliged
> to wait until the court has made its determination [before

taking a further action]. This results in innumerable delays,
and as a consequence the unscrupulous pirate, now informed
of the proceedings which have been proposed against him,
has ample time to rid himself of the pirated works.[46]

Equally, if not more devastating than pirate editions, was the problem of
unregulated competition of different editions of works in the public domain.
Thus the publisher Briand observed:

"Modern publishing" designates all the books that are
ceaselessly reprinted, in which no one has property rights,
and which anyone can make use of in consequence of the law
of 1793. This branch of publishing [is] the most extensive
and the most certain . . . because it encompasses the best
books.

Everyone prints the same books without being able or
without desiring to coordinate their editions; they print them
in competition with one another, and end up remaindering
them. But the public does not even benefit, because the
editions are truncated, inexact and poorly executed.[47]

Similar testimony could be multiplied at length. Publishers were driving each
other under by undermining one another's markets. And even if they had
wanted to try to cooperate, they lacked the institutional means to do so. The
stipulations of the law of 1793 organizing the national legal depository at the
Bibliothèque Nationale had made deposit voluntary, rather than obligatory. As
a consequence, for the entire republican period there was no exact national
record of editions in print for publishers to consult before deciding whether or
not to embark on an edition.

There were no winners in these publishing wars. Even in cases where
publishers initially set out to cooperate with one another. This is vividly
illustrated by the publishing history of a work now celebrated as one of the
great typographic monuments of the revolutionary period: the 1798 Houel
edition of the *Oeuvres complètes de Condillac, . . . augmentées de la langue
des calculs.*[48]    Six printers and publishers of Paris formed a business
association to produce the edition.[49]    The association began with every
advantage. They enjoyed a government subsidy in the form of a guaranteed
purchase of 150 copies by the minister of the interior. They had agreed by
written contract that upon dividing up the edition, they would maintain
minimum wholesale and retail prices that none of them would undersell.
Everything went smoothly until one of the associates, Guillaume, was ruined

by a pirate and forced into bankruptcy. In order to bail himself out, he made a fast move. Thus one of the associates reported:

> Citizen Hué, dealer in Rouen came to buy some Condillacs this morning. He offered me an impossible price. It seems that Guillaume is selling the work off to colporteurs at a vile price. I ask you to do me the favor of locking up the warehouse.

Guillaume, cut down first by a literary pirate, then dragged his associates under with him through a desperate, but unprofitable price war. Three more of the associates were soon driven to bankruptcy as well. Thus even with government assistance, the elegant posthumous edition of Condillac's *Language of Calculation*, a monument to Enlightenment science and republican typography, ended up in the remainder bin of the revolutionary literary market.

In sum, the law of 1793 had rendered book publishing commercially inviable. The limiting of private copyright claims to ten years after the author's death reduced the commercial value of a copyright to a single edition. Pirating was rampant because there was no effective mechanism to prevent it after the suppression of the National Administration of the Book Trade. But most important was the problem of competing editions of works in the public domain, because such editions made up the majority of book commerce. The lack of a national administration, and of a compulsory system of registration of works in print, meant that there was no effective mechanism for regulating competition, even by the publishing community itself. The fundamental dilemma of commercial publishing under the Republic was that commerce in the printed word had been rendered "too free" to be capable of fulfilling Brissot's revolutionary dream of "spreading light in every direction"--at least through the medium of the printed book. Books require government protection in order to exist. Faced with this insight, by the year II the Revolution's cultural elites were compelled to abandon their laissez-faire idealism of 1789 and to rethink how the ideal of a free *and* enlightened Republic could best be achieved.

## NOTES

1. Cited by Eugène Hatin, *Histoire politique et littéraire de la presse en France*, vol. 5 (Paris: Poulet-Malassis, 1860), pp. 22-23. All translations are my own unless otherwise noted.

2. Alfred Cobban, *A History of Modern France*, vol. 1 (Middlesex: Penguin, 1963), p. 226.

3. François Furet and Denis Richet, *La Révolution française*, (Paris: Marabout, 1973), p. 518.

4. Archives Nationales, AA 56 (1525), letter from Batillot, publisher in Paris, to the Committee of Public Safety, 12 floréal, an II (May 1, 1794). See also Lefebvre de Villebrune, "Considérations sur le commerce de la librairie française," 29 ventôse, [an II] (March 19, 1794), in M. J. Guillaume, ed., *Procès-verbaux du Comité d'Instruction Publique de la Convention Nationale*, vol. 3 (Paris: Imprimerie Nationale, 1897), pp. 612, 613, and 617.

5. Bibliothèque Nationale, Nouv. acq. fr., 2836, feuille 27, report from Villebrune to the Committee of Public Safety on the state of the book trade, 12 ventôse, an II (March 2, 1794).

6. Lefebvre de Villebrune, "Considérations sur le commerce de la librairie française," in *Procès-verbaux*, Guillaume, ed., vol. 3, p. 613.

7. Bibliothèque Nationale, Archives modernes, CXXIX: "Dépôt légal des livres imprimés, registre 1, 1793-an VII [September 1799]."

8. Robert Estival, *La Statistique bibliographique de la France sous la monarchie au XVIIIe siècle* (Paris: Mouton, 1965), p. 415.

9. Angus Martin, Vivienne G. Milne, and Richard Frautschi, *Bibliographie du genre romanesque français* (Paris: France Expansion and London: Mansell, 1977), pp. xxxvi-xxxix.

10. Claude Béllanger, ed., *Histoire générale de la presse française*, vol. 1 (Paris: PUF, 1969), p. 504.

11. For the application of this law against journalists, see ibid., p. 508.

12. Ibid., pp. 436 and 504.

13. For an example of censoring posters, see Chemin fils, printer, 26 messidor, an II (July 14, 1794), Archives Nationales, F7 4645, doss. 2. For pamphlets, see Archives Nationales, Froullé, printer, and Levigneur, bookseller, 8 ventôse, an II (February 26, 1794), W 332 no. 566; and Archives Nationales, AF*II 294, fols. 107-108; Pierres, printer, and Barbra, bookseller, 25 nivôse an II (January 14, 1794), Archives Nationales, BB 3, 81A, fols. 361-364; and Charlier and Senneville (Rioux-Maillon), booksellers, germinal-thermidor, an II: Archives Nationales, F7 4774, 93, doss. 3; Archives Nationales, F7 4775, 17, doss. 4; Archives Nationales, F7 4637, doss. 4; and Archives Nationales, AF*II, fol. 145. For an example of novels and scientific publications, see Cuchet, publisher, 8 thermidor, an II, Archives Nationales, W 53, doss. 3401; and Archives Nationales, F7 4658, doss. 4.

14. For suspect clientele, see Desenne, bookdealer, September 19, 1793, Archives Nationales, F7 3688, 3, doss. 2.

15. See Archives Nationales, BB3 81A, fols. 361-364, Pierres, printer, 25 nivôse, an II (January 14, 1794). For Froullé, see Archives Nationales, F17 1005A, doss. 743bis, letter from Froullé to the Committee of Public Instruction, July 27, 1793; and Archives Nationales, W 332, no. 566, 8 ventôse, an II (February 26, 1794). Finally, for Cuchet, see Archives

Nationales, F7 4658, doss. 4, 24 messidor, an II (July 12, 1794); and Archives Nationales, W 53, 3401, 8 thermidor, an II (July 26, 1794).

16. They all appeared in the top quarter of the *capitation* tax roll for the Guild in 1789. See Bibliothèque Nationale, mss. fr. 21861, "registre de la communauté des imprimeurs et libraires de Paris," 1789.

17. See Archives Nationales, F7 4658, doss. 4, 24 messidor, an II (July 12, 1794). This dossier gives a list of some of Cuchet's stock. See also Archives Nationales, AD VIII 7, "Consultation pour le citoyen A. J. Dugour, propriétaire du *Cours d'Agriculture* par Rozier." Dugour bought Cuchet's business, including this work, in 1796.

18. Archives Nationales, F7 4658, doss. 4, Cuchet, printer-publishers, 24 messidor, an II (July 12, 1794).

19. Pierre Caron, *Paris pendant la terreur, rapports des agents secrets du ministre de l'intérieur*, vol. 5 (Paris: Klincksieck, 1958), p. 50, "Rapport de Le Breton, 13 ventôse an II" (March 13, 1794).

20. The National Convention suppressed all official societies and academies by their decrees of August 8 and 12, 1793. For the plans of the Committee of Public Safety, see Archives Nationales, F17 1008B, doss. 1487, letter from the Committee of Public Safety to the Committee of Public Instruction requesting a list of patriotic writers, 17 frimaire, an II (December 7, 1793). See Archives Nationales, F17 1258, doss. 2, for the decree ordering printing and distribution of the *Receuil des actions héroiques et civiques des républicains français*, 13 nivôse, an II (January 2, 1794); and Archives Nationales, F17 1258, doss. 8, Committee of Public Safety calls for patriotic poems, hymns, and plays, 27 floréal, an II (April 16, 1794).

21. For officially and unofficially subsidized journals, see Albert Mathiez, "Mélanges: la presse subventionnée en l'an II," *Annales révolutionnaires* 10 (1918), pp. 112-113; and Béllanger, ed., *Histoire générale de la presse française*, vol. 1, p. 510.

22. Report by Billaud de Varenne to the National Convention, 28 brumaire, an II (November 18, 1793), cited in F. A. Duprat, *Histoire de l'imprimerie impériale de France* (Paris: Imprimerie Impériale, 1861), pp. 144-146.

23. Duprat, *Histoire de l'imprimerie impériale de France*, p. 146.

24. Ibid., p. 147.

25. Ibid., p. 154.

26. Ibid., p. 152. One hundred new presses were ordered from the shop at the Imprimerie du Louvre, but there is only an actual record for the delivery of 30 new presses.

27. Ibid., p. 165.

28. See Archives Nationales, F17 1008c, doss. 1559, letter from Beauvais, Paris printer, to the Committee of Public Instruction, requesting to be requisitioned in their service as a consequence of the decree, n.d. [an II];

Archives Nationales, F17 1009Abis, doss. 1992, letter from Lavoye, printer, to the Committee of Public Instruction, 25 pluviôse, an II (February 13, 1794); and Archives Nationales, F17 1009B, doss. 2071, letter from Deltufo, printer, to the Committee of Public Instruction, 9 prairial, an II (May 28, 1794). Finally, the Committee of Public Instruction registered receipt of an appeal from "printers without occupation," 5 prairial, an II (May 24, 1794); see Guillaume, ed., *Procès-verbaux*, vol. 4, p. 471.

29. Archives Nationales, AA 56 (1525), Petition to the National Convention from the printers of Paris, n.d. [22 pluviôse an III (February 10, 1795)].

30. Bibliothèque Nationale, Nouv. acq. fr. 2836, feuilles 27-29, report from Villebrune to the Committee of Public Safety concerning the state of the book trade, 12 ventôse, an II (March 2, 1794), forwarded to the Committee of Public Instruction on 24 ventôse, an II (March 14, 1794); and Archives Nationales, F17 1009C, doss. 2216, report from Villebrune to the Committee of Public Instruction, entitled "Considérations sur le commerce de la librairie française," n.d., received by the Committee on 29 ventôse, an II (March 19, 1794). This second report has been edited in Guillaume, ed., *Procès-verbaux*, vol. 3: pp. 612-618.

31. Ibid., p. 614.

32. Pierre Caron, *Paris pendant la terreur, rapports des agents du ministre de l'intérieur*, vol. 3 (Paris: Picard et fils, 1910), p. 211; "Rapport de Mercier," 17 nivôse, an III (January 6, 1795).

33. Lefebvre de Villebrune, "Considérations sur le commerce de la librairie française," [March 19, 1794], in Guillaume, ed., *Procès-verbaux*, vol. 3, p. 614.

34. Ibid., p. 615.

35. Ibid., pp. 615-616.

36. For revolutionary patronage of authors from 1789 through 1794, see the decrees of the National Assembly of February 6, 1790, August 3 and 14, 1790, October 16, 1790, March 24, 1791, and September 9, 1791. For commissions of school textbooks, see Guillaume, ed., *Procès-verbaux*, vol. 1, pp. 36, 57, 84-85, 92-101, 493, and 495; vol. 2, pp. lxii, 127, 216, and 306; and vol. 3, pp. xi, 364, 371-372; and Archives Nationales, F17, 1258, doss. 2, 9 pluviôse, an II (January 28, 1794).

37. The budgets are still extant in the archives of the Bibliothèque Nationale, Nouv. acq. fr. 9193, feuille 49, "Collection Ginguené: Compte sommarie des dépenses de la Commission de l'Instruction Publique, an II-IV." For authorizations of expenditures, see, for example, Archives Nationales, F17 1258, doss. 2, 17 vendémiaire, an III (October 8, 1794) (allocation by the National Convention of 300,000 livres in "encouragements" for arts and sciences).

38. For the exact calculations, see Carla Hesse, "Res Publicata: The Printed Word in Paris, 1789-1810," Ph.D. diss., Princeton University, 1986, p. 237. The number of new publishing houses founded in Paris during the republican period were: 1793, 13; 1794, 16; 1795, 22; 1796, 31; 1797, 51; and 1798, 51.

39. Estival, *La Statistique bibliographique de la France sous la monarchie au XVIIIe siècle*, p. 415.

40. This expansion of scientific publishing is further confirmed by the statistics and evidence compiled by the historian of science, Jean Dhombres. See Jean Dhombres, "Books: Reshaping Science," in *Revolution in Print: The Press in France, 1775-1800*, ed. Robert Darnton and Daniel Roche (Berkeley: University of California Press, 1989), pp. 179-180.

41. Angus Martin, Vivienne G. Milne, and Richard Frautschi, *Bibliographie du genre romanesque français*, pp. xxxvi-xxxix. New titles for 1794 were 16; for 1795, 41; for 1796, 54; for 1797, 73; 1798, 96; and for 1799, 174.

42. See Carla Hesse, "Economic Upheavals in Publishing," in *Revolution in Print*, ed. Darnton and Roche, p. 86. The number of bankruptcies registered by Paris publishers, and now found in the Archives de Paris, jumped from 0 in 1800-1801, to 3 in 1802, 11 in 1803, and 7 in 1804.

43. Martyn Lyons, *France under the Directory* (Cambridge: Cambridge University Press, 1975), pp. 180-184.

44. Bibliothèque Nationale, Nouv. acq. fr. 9193, feuilles 6, 23, and 141-177, Papiers Ginguenés (an IV-VII, 1796-1800).

45. Archives Nationales, F 18, carton 11A, plaque 1, Lamy, publisher in Paris, May 8, 1810.

46. Archives Nationales, F 18, carton 10A, plaque 1, doss. XVIII, "Rapport au gouvernment: exposition des principes qui doit dirigé la rédaction du projet d'une loi relative à la propriété des auteurs ...," Costaz, chef du bureau des arts et manufactures, Paris, 28 nivôse, an XI (January 18, 1803).

47. Archives Nationales, F 18, carton 11A, plaque 1, report from Briand, Paris publisher, April 2, 1810.

48. The complete history of this edition is documented in the correspondence and business records of the publisher Maginel and the printer Loret, both of Paris. See Archives Nationales, AQ 24, carton 6, private papers of the publisher Maginel, dossier: C. Loret, Paris printer, an 7 [1798-99]. An extensive discussion of the contribution of this edition to scientific publishing and the history of science can be found in Jean Dhombres, "Books: Reshaping Science," in *Revolution in Print*, ed. Darnton and Roche, pp. 177-202.

49. Gratiot, Gide, Loret, Guillaume, Houel, and Prudhomme.

# GOVERNMENT, LAW, PUBLIC OPINION, AND THE PRINTED WORD IN EIGHTEENTH-CENTURY AMERICA

*James Gilreath*

All books and pamphlets printed in America before 1800 that are in the Library of Congress are chronologically arranged in a special room in the Rare Book and Special Collections Division. A glance down the shelves in this room reveals the dramatic and exponential rise year after year in the number of printed items produced in colonial America. Bibliographies record that fewer than 100 titles were printed in the colonies in 1700. In 1740, not more than 200 works were issued; but by 1800, the number shot up beyond 2,500, an increase of more than twelvefold in 60 years. Of course, there were more Americans in 1800 than in 1740; but the existence of a larger audience is only a partial reason for the jump. The estimated population of 2.3 million in 1740 certainly could have supported more than 200 pieces of native American printing. And it is equally certain that the fifteen printers at work in America in 1740 would have had little trouble producing more than 200 imprints. Finally, the rapid growth of the press during this period far outstripped the increase in population, which merely doubled during the last six decades of the century.

The burgeoning output of the press at the end of the century was at least partially due to a new force at work in society that had become linked to the printed word and had grown more powerful than ever: public opinion. At the beginning of the century, public opinion had a limited role in governing society and was seldom broadcast in print. Word of mouth ignited Bacon's Rebellion in Virginia in the seventeenth century in contrast to the phalanx of pamphlets, broadsides, and newspapers that drove the American Revolution forward a century later. The new American government's recognition that its legitimacy and authority were ultimately rooted in the approval of the people strengthened public opinion as an active agent in society. Americans' inbred distrust for all forms of government led them to believe that even their newly created public institutions could be only imperfect vehicles for the expression of the public mind; and so, they looked to printed publications as additional legitimate tools for discussing and manipulating public affairs.    At the beginning of the eighteenth century, many printers were financially dependent on government and often published information that came from and was disseminated through official channels.    But at the end of the eighteenth century, printers could become prosperous and successful without relying on government patronage, freeing them to print whatever they wanted. Paradoxically, the government, at the insistence of its citizens, passed laws protecting opposition views, thereby making debate outside government forums often as important as discourse within them.

The career of printer James Franklin, older brother of the renowned Benjamin, demonstrates in an anecdotal way the situation of the early eighteenth-century printer vis-à-vis the government.    After an apprenticeship as a printer in London, James Franklin returned to his native Boston in 1717 to set up shop as one of the colonies' few pressmen.    Over the next ten years, Franklin frequently ran afoul of the Massachusetts civil and ecclesiastical leaders for publishing criticisms of them.    Though it was not customary for American printers at this time to take such challenging stances, Franklin had been exposed during his apprenticeship to the English press and printers, who were not only more involved in public affairs than their colonial counterparts but were also more partisan in their views.    In Massachusetts, printers were alert to the fact that government could intervene in their business at any given moment, as had happened in the suppression of the newspaper *Publik Occurrences* and other similar cases.

Franklin's problems stemmed partially from his association with members of the Hell Fire Club, a loosely organized group that was willing to criticize Massachusetts public figures.[1]   With club members' help, Franklin started a newspaper, the *New England Courant*, only the fourth such undertaking in the colonies, and modeled it on Addison and Steele's *The Spectator*.   The distinguishing feature of both publications was an introductory essay written in a witty style that freely commented on current events or personalities.    One essay in the *New England Courant* so enraged officials by satirizing the government's inability to control the pirates who were plundering shipping along the New England coast that Franklin was jailed.[2]   The General Court directed him never again to publish anything without prior approval, but he managed to circumvent this restriction by issuing the *Courant* under younger brother Benjamin's name.    Both legal and social pressure mounted on James Franklin to conform to the role expected of printers in Massachusetts.    Cotton Mather charged the newspaper with being "full freighted with nonsense, unmannerliness, raillery, profaneness, immorality, arrogance, calumnies, lies, contradictions, and what not, all tending to quarrels and division."[3]   In the end, Franklin decided to leave Boston.

Though the license Franklin took in expressing his views in the *New England Courant* may seen innocent today at a distance of more than 250 years, it clearly taxed the patience of early eighteenth-century Massachusetts authorities. The nature of the threat posed by Franklin's newspaper is better understood by comparing the *Courant* with its two rivals, *The Boston News-Letter* and the *Boston Gazette*. The first of these adorned its masthead with the phrase "Published by Authority," clearly implying a special relationship to Boston officials. The editorial policy of Franklin's second journalistic rival, the *Boston Gazette*, was succinctly summarized by its editor, Joseph Campbell, when he declared that his newspaper did not offer any "opinions, ideas, or arguments." Both *The Boston News-Letter* and the *Boston Gazette* printed only speeches by British officials in Massachusetts, addresses by the king or members of Parliament, announcements of government appointments, and some foreign news.

Citizens of the period had few channels of public communication in which common issues could be analyzed or debated that were not to some extent under the watchful eyes of the crown or the pulpit. The *Courant* forged a new path. Mass communication, as it existed at this time, went in one direction. Ordinances, acts and laws, and proclamations were issued by the public printer to inform the people about their new responsibilities rather than to encourage open debate. On the other hand, petitions to the royal governors or the assembly were presented in private and were not circulated for public review. During the early eighteenth century, public information when printed was meant to be authoritative and accurate--free from private prejudice and personal opinion. When the editors of the *Boston Gazette* stated that their newspaper was "Published by Authority," they did not mean that it was an organ of the government but rather that it had access to unimpeachable, official information. The Massachusetts leaders feared that the highly personal *Courant* essays might fragment the public mind by luring into the controversy citizens who were not directly involved with the incidents. It was better to resolve any problem in private and later notify the people what had been done in their behalf. Elected assemblymen in the colonies viewed themselves not as representing the public will but as able to divine what was in the best interest of the people.

Public opinion, in the sense of an active independent entity that was potentially free from governmental influence and could compete with other forces in society--such as we know it today--did not exist in early eighteenth-century America, at least not in printed communication. Contesting parties inadvertently put their arguments in print before the public, and then the disputants always saw the public as passive, unprejudiced, and having no interest of its own in the matter. A case in point was the disagreement between Pennsylvania Governor William Keith and James Logan, a member of the Pennsylvania Council and a confidant of the Penn family, about the proper division of power in the colony among the proprietor, the governor, and the assembly.

In *A Letter from Sir William Keith*,[4] Keith tried to refute charges James Logan had leveled against him in *The Antidote*.[5] Keith at the outset expressed his indignation that Logan had aired his complaints in a "Printed Paper." Conceding the fact that the matter was now public, Keith concluded that he could at least have the impartial reading public as his witness during the debate, implicitly regarding literate citizens as having no stake or opinion in this struggle for political leadership in the colony. Keith wrote that he was "referring these my thoughts, nevertheless, unto more indifferent persons, than either you and I can supposed to be."[6] Later in the piece, Keith returned to this theme:

> But of all that has drop't from your Pen on these occasions, I think Your Letter to John Salkeld, which direct him to Publish, is the most extraordinary Piece: For if those Private Instructions from the Widow Penn to Me, were (as You there acknowledge) such as would not bear the Light, without reflecting on Those who had Contrived them; Who, before an unprejudiced Judge, do You think will have the most Blame? You that Hatched the Mischief, or I that in my own Just and Necessary Defence, Communicated them to the Assembly, as Private Instructions, fit only to be perused by Those whose Interest was nearly Concerned in them?[7]

In this passage, Keith laid bare the dual issues of an innocent public incapable of making knowledgeable judgments about private governmental matters and the ability of the printed word to encourage just such uninformed individuals to form an opinion. And opinion was almost always subjective, dangerous, and based on insufficient evidence.[8] The printed word was supposed to form a consensus in society that leaders could employ for governing. The primary power of the printed word originated in its official authoritative nature rather than in its ability to air a variety of personal views or in its potential as an agent of change.

That the public channels of printed communication were meant to be clear of controversy is also suggested by the fact that the printers rather than the writers of opinions objectionable to the government were usually singled out for punishment, for it was only the printer who could make statements public. To be sure, the printers were the custodians of their publications and hence ultimately responsible for the contents. However, that truth itself was no defense in libel trials at this time reveals another dimension to early American censorship cases. Even if a printer published a verifiable and just criticism of the government or one of its officials, he still chanced a retaliatory action. What was crucially at stake was governmental authority rather than truth, justice, or freedom of information. The fact that the criticism was public was a more serious offense than the criticism itself, for it was the public nature of the criticism that was the real threat to government power. To hearken back to the Franklin example, officials in Massachusetts were aware of the people's concern about pirates. Several pamphlets had reported their acts, though without criticizing the government.[9] Surely a few of the many who had lost boats, friends, employees, and even loved ones in several very bloody incidents must have voiced the opinion that Massachusetts needed to do more. But it was only when Franklin printed these concerns that the criticism became worthy of censure and the cause for action.

There was more to Franklin's decision to leave Massachusetts and his choice of Newport, however, than his sporadic problems with the law in Boston. If he was on the one hand critical of government, he was on the other hand dependent on it for success. Because of the controversial articles in his paper, Franklin knew that he would never receive any of the lucrative government printing contracts. The possibility of securing a government printing contract in Rhode Island must have been a powerful lure for Franklin; and, in fact, he did print the colony's first compilation of laws a few years after arriving. Though the imprints recorded in Charles Evans's *American Bibliography* for the pre-1801 in America period are incomplete, the numbers suggest the financial importance of government printing to printers during these early years. For 1735, Evans listed 178 books, pamphlets, and broadsides as being printed in all the English colonies in America. Twenty of those, or more than one in ten, were government imprints. The ratio was undoubtedly higher; because Evans's bibliography is less reliable for government imprints than for other types of works; and it also did not include any stationery forms needed by government. To further dramatize the disproportionate amount of government printing, many of the official publications were several hundred pages long, whereas non-governmental work was typically only a few dozen pages.[10] Working for the colonial government was relatively secure and yearly stipends were sometimes paid to law book printers, an obvious attraction at a time when hard currency was often scarce. Such was the condition of the pre-Revolutionary printer: directed to be a publisher of information rather than opinion and often financially beholden to those who had a vested interest in monitoring his viewpoint.

America differed, however, from a country like France with an elaborate official censorship system. There were relatively few colonial laws restricting American printers' actions; nevertheless, there existed an implicit code of conduct based on English legal precedent. For instance, the English Bible patent reserved for a few London printers the privilege to print this very popular and profitable book. None of the colonies formally adopted a Bible patent; but no American dared print a Bible, a book so popular it would have guaranteed a printer a munificent income.[11] Likewise, the Statute of Anne and the earlier Stationer Company printing patents controlled the right to print the works of popular English authors such as Laurence Sterne.  Again, though no American colonial law to my knowledge formally acknowledged the extension of these legal restrictions to America, nevertheless, no celebrated British writer's works were reprinted in the colonies, despite the great demand for their books that were imported at considerable expense from London by American booksellers.

Because no centralized licensed censoring structure existed in the colonies, American printers found themselves in legal trouble for violating the rather vague principle of legislative or parliamentary privilege rather than any particular local statute.  Such an unstructured situation helps explain how the printers could so tenaciously cling to the belief that they operated in a free press tradition although, as Leonard Levy demonstrated in *The Emergence of a Free Press*, the small number of pressmen in America provoked an inordinate amount of punitive legal attention.[12]  As was done in the Zenger case,[13] embattled printers could blame their trouble on personal animosity or on the poor judgment of some local official rather than on the law.  Infractions were arbitrarily punished.[14]  To return once again to Franklin, at other times he criticized the government more sharply than he did about the pirate problem; yet he was not arrested for these infringements.  Before leaving for Newport, Franklin wrote and published *The Life and Death of Old Father Janus*, in which he assumes the identity of Janus, a satiric poem that did not rail against institutions but against individuals.  Franklin concluded the poem by emphasizing that corrupt individuals have poisoned the system:

> Like Nonsense Fraught, shall Jinglers swarm the Town
> Like Rats & Mice, when once the Light's Withdrawn:
> The Golden days of Ignorance return,
> And Wit, like Janus, meet with grievous Scorn.[15]

It was this fragile, albeit rhetorically fervent, tradition of an American free press that enabled printers to leap so enthusiastically after 1765 into the fray over the Stamp Act, the Intolerable Acts, and finally the separation from Great Britain itself.  In a rare display of unanimity, today's historians and eighteenth-century observers share a belief in the crucial nature of the role of the press in articulating America's need for separation from Great Britain and finally in convincing the colonies to sever their relationship with the mother country.  As Samuel Miller noted in 1803, the newspapers were "immense moral and political engines" that drove the countries apart.  And in *Prelude to Independence*, Arthur Schlesinger compiled a wealth of evidence to flesh out Miller's generalization by showing how Revolutionary sentiment infused the world of print in newspapers, broadsides, pamphlets, and even almanacs.[16]  What boosted the printers' confidence to launch this attack on British authority, unprecedented in American history, was their belief that they had the support of a large segment of the colonial population. Just as print had been used earlier to control or to instruct the governed, now words were beginning to be used in ways that were openly independent of official views. These new public views were empowered as active agents in society not by the government but directly by the citizens themselves.

The lasting and significant decisions debated in the publications American printers produced gave the printed word an ideological caste that it had not had before in America. To some extent, the printer embodied the publications' ideology in the public's eyes, because the simplicity of the publishing operations at this time encouraged the belief that the products of his press were an expression of the printer's own opinions. Printers sometimes were seen as threats to the warring parties, and there are numerous instances of violence or threats directed against pressmen by both loyalist or patriot and Federalist or Republican factions. For instance, as soon as British troops landed in Massachusetts, patriots thought it necessary to move the printer Isaiah Thomas and his pro-Revolutionary press from Boston to Worcester on the night of April 16, 1775. A reader opening an American pamphlet printed after 1765 delved into a much wider and more public world than he would have previously encountered when much of American reading was devotional, private, and focused on the community's expectations of the individual. By mid-century, individuals and groups were expressing in print what they expected of the community and its institutions.

In 1763, the Stamp Act, which required the colonists to pay a tax to Great Britain on all printed paper, was an especially important force in coalescing a unified American opinion. Before its enactment, newspapers in each colony emphasized home colony news and events in Great Britain, seldom recognizing any common interests among the colonies. In fact, England encouraged this division by declaring that the colonies had no legal relationship to each other except through the mother country. But as printers and merchants in each colony objected to what they considered the illegal tax of 1765, they also began to recognize and feel strengthened by the identical reactions to events by their counterparts in other colonies. After the tax was enacted, many newsletters suspended normal operations in protest and instead issued special supplements. For instance, the *Pennsylvania Gazette* stopped publication in November of 1765 and its publishers issued *Remarkable Occurrences*, a four-page special report dedicated to the Stamp Act controversy, printed on unstamped paper. What was particularly interesting about this publication was that it was almost entirely devoted to emphasizing the point that opposition to the tax occurred in all the colonies. Here, as seldom before in the colonies, a united, common, and vocal American front faced the world. The authors of *Remarkable Occurrences* made explicit their vision of an American voice by writing that the Stamp Tax was an affront to "the Spirit of the People, not only of this City and Colony, but of neighboring

Colonies." In *Symbols of American Community, 1735-1775*, Richard Merritt analyzed references in colonial newspapers to home colonies and to the continent (meaning all colonies) and concluded that an explosion of continental references occurred between 1761 and 1765, a rise that continued consistently during the period he studied.[17]  The forging of a distinctly American voice occurred at a time when public opinion in the colonies operated outside the sanction of official government approval.  A united American opinion was born in opposition.

Public opinion in the pamphlets and newspapers of the Stamp Act era transcended individual colonies' boundaries and continued to do so throughout the polemical debates of the entire Revolutionary period, still playing a key role in society even after the end of hostilities.  Soon after the Treaty of Paris in 1789, national documents such as the Constitution and the Bill of Rights needed to be printed, dispersed as widely as possible among the citizens, discussed, and either approved or rejected.  These national documents appeared in the most common and democratic kinds of formats, such as almanacs, making them part of the country's folk culture, accessible to the widest possible audience.  This popularization of the nation's most important documents and their unrestricted distribution contrasts with the official pronouncements of the earlier colonial period that were distributed through a limited network that was approved by the government itself.  But most importantly, because the Constitution and other documents needed popular review, the people became accustomed to having their opinions sought on important national issues.  These documents were presented not as binding declarations issued from an authoritarian source but rather as matters for citizens' consideration.

Revolutionary-period leaders viewed printers as allies during the desperate struggle with Great Britain, influencing the new nation's officials to provide handsomely for books and printers in the United States Constitution, the Bill of Rights, the Postal Act of 1794, the tariffs of 1792 and 1796, and the Copyright Act of 1790.  Many Americans feared that an entrenched authority could control the press in order to isolate the people from one another and thereby dampen debate on public policy.  Consequently, they provided in the Bill of Rights that the government could make no law abridging the freedom of the press--a sweeping statement from planners who were not only very careful about enumerating the specific powers each institution could exercise but who also were committed to balancing forces within government itself.  This provision was, in Levy's words, "almost without precedent."  The 1792 and 1796 tariffs increased the tax on imported goods, including books, to 5 and then 10 percent, respectively, making books produced in England more expensive and thereby less attractive,[18] thus benefiting  American printers.  The Postal Act of 1794 allowed printers to use the public mails to distribute their books at advantageous rates, a significant economic boost.  The national

Copyright Act of 1790 and Article I, Section 8 of the Constitution were intended not to help the few poets and novelists who were struggling in the larger urban areas but rather to encourage the informative and technical books that would educate the populace and thereby ensure the success of the American republican experiment.[19]    The copyright law represented Americans' growing confidence in the power of the public dimension of the printed word, which promised to improve not only the spiritual nature of the individual soul but also the physical and political condition of the secular nation.  The Copyright Act was an expression of the Enlightenment's view of knowledge as being cumulative if free from restraint and as being able to improve reality rather than simply describing some ideal or theoretical state. In effect, written communication shared in the young government's efforts to encourage with legislation what one writer called "public utilities" meant to serve the common good, in much the same way as roads, ferries, and bridges, were public improvements.[20]  The common man who wrote and read was linked with virtuous citizens in other colonies, gaining a new standing in the community.  In fact, during the debate about the form of the Constitution it was preferable to be seen as an anonymous member of the general public who was expressing his views in print rather than as one of the elite who might be suspected of trying to usurp the public's right to make up its own mind. Essays in *The Federalist*, for example, were signed "Publius," which is close to the Latin verb *publico*, which means to tell the people, and to the Latin adjective *publicus*, which means pertaining to the community of people.  Many ordinary citizens wrote letters to newspapers to express their opinions, and the printers eagerly printed them.   These letter writers directly addressed the people, sometimes through the person of the printer, and took pride in being common citizens.  For instance, an individual using only the name Alonzo wrote to the North Carolina *State Gazette* in support of the proposed Constitution and described himself as "uncommitted with party or faction, and not expecting or desiring to be one of the leaders of the people, but to be one of the governed."[21]   The very title of Thomas Paine's enormously popular *Common Sense* indicated the author's intentional appeal to the ordinary citizen.

These appeals to public opinion about the political structure soon widened to other matters, including social issues, as people brought various grievances to the attention of their fellow citizens.  It became commonplace in the young Republic for authors to address the public directly in order to redress some perceived private inequity (often inflicted by the government), indicating not only a close relationship between writers and the reading public but also a respect for the power of public opinion.  This mode of address was a far cry from the solicitous presentations to royalty or patrons in many pre-Revolutionary books and broadsides.   Examples of this new tradition of addressing the general public were the *Address to the Inhabitants of Alexandria, and Other Seaports from a Proprietor of the Lands on the Scioto*

(1790), John Nicholson's *Address to the People of Pennsylvania; Containing a Narrative of the Proceedings Against John Nicholson* (1790), and *An Address to the Numerous and Respectable Inhabitants of the Great and Extensive District of Maine [from] a Number of Your Representatives* (1791). In these and other cases, the printed word was the medium through which the public was transformed from the passive witness that Keith perceived in 1725 to an active force that could influence the fate of ordinary citizens by harnessing the power of the community.

The role of the printers in society was elevated by association with the products of their press. Shortly after 1800, a printer wrote that newspapers "exact a controlling influence on public opinion, and decide almost all questions of a public nature."[22] Though his point of view is exaggerated, his argument has some basis in fact. Comparing printers' reactions to the British Stamp Act of 1765 and the Massachusetts-imposed Stamp Act of 1785 further underscores the progression of the printers' sense of their enlarged role in society because of the transformation of the public word in print. Much of the protest of the pressmen against the 1765 act was couched in constitutional or economic terms. But the 1785 Massachusetts act brought objections that the state legislature's threat against the press was a blow to an institution that had become absolutely indispensable for good government itself. The *Massachusetts Spy* rejoiced over the repeal of the 1785 act with these words: "Heaven grant that the FREEDOM of the PRESS, on which depends the FREEDOM of the PEOPLE, may, in the United States, be ever guarded with a watchful eye, and defended from Shackles, of every form and shape."[23] The parallel capitalization of "FREEDOM of the PRESS" and "FREEDOM of the PEOPLE" was clearly the printer's deliberate attempt to emphasize the mutual dependence of the people and the press.

But the power of the printing press flew into the face of an unresolved question in American society that was endlessly debated during the formulation of the Constitution. Many thought that the press served as a more direct conduit for the people's opinion than did government itself. Such a sentiment was to some degree behind Jefferson's often-quoted opinion: "If it were left to me to decide whether we should have a government without newspapers, or newspapers without a government, I should not hesitate a moment to prefer the latter." The basic issue was how directly the will of the people should be brought to bear on events. Some writers, like Thomas Paine, hoped that the people's representatives would be neutral media for the people's minds. Writing in support of frequent elections, Paine argued: "the elected [should] never form to themselves an interest separate from the electors, prudence will point out the propriety of having elections often: because the elected might by that means return and mix again with the general body of the electors in a few months, their fidelity to the Public will be secured by the prudent reflexion of not making a rod for themselves."[24]  Others were not so certain.  For instance, James Madison in *Federalist* no. 10 put forth the view that a government's job was "to refine and enlarge the public views, by passing them through the medium of a chosen body of citizens, whose wisdom may best discern the true interest of the country."

During the post-Revolutionary period, elected Federalist officials viewed with dismay the attacks on their administration from a press that was beginning to see itself as almost an equal partner with the government in determining the nation's future. An important theme in Federalist rhetoric leading to the Sedition Act of 1798, in part a tool to suppress opposition printers and consequently public opinion, was that the public, encouraged by the press, was too fickle to be given a direct hand in government affairs. Gouveneur Morris wrote at the time: "Those who court the People have a very capricious Mistress, a Mistress which may be gained by sacrifices, but she cannot be so held for she is insatiable."[25] That the Constitution originally proposed that the Senate be elected by the state legislatures rather than directly by the people and that a senator's term of office be a lengthy six years, insulating him from sudden and transitory shifts in voters' opinions, demonstrated a widespread fear of the public's rapidly swinging moods.

Yet, it was precisely because many Americans feared that government might turn a deaf ear to the public that citizens looked to newspapers and pamphlets as very desirable forums for their debates, which should always be free from legal interference. Correspondents exchanged letters printed in newspapers over a period of months as they debated issues point by point. Throughout the winter and spring of 1772, for instance, Bob Short wrote letters about the Massachusetts charter that were published in the loyalist *Boston Newsletter*. Tom Long (both names are clearly pseudonyms) responded to Short's missives with his own series of letters in the patriot *Massachusetts Spy*.[26] Bernard Bailyn saw in the pamphlet literature of the time what he described as "chain-reacting personal polemics: strings of individual exchanges--arguments, replies, rebuttals, and counter-rebuttals--in which may be found heated personifications of the larger conflict. A bold statement on a sensitive issue was often sufficient to start such a series, which characteristically proceeded with increasing shrillness until it ended in bitter personal vituperation."[27] No less a contemporary observer than Isaiah Thomas, founder of the influential *Massachusetts Spy* and author of *The History of Printing in America*, believed that the proliferation of newspapers and presses at the end of the eighteenth and beginning of the nineteenth century was caused by the necessity of airing the numerous vituperative political exchanges. Pressmen were not just printers but were loyalist or patriot printers and, later, Federalist or Republican printers.

Three of the most powerful forces in American society at the end of the eighteenth century were: government and the law, public opinion, and a free press (not limited to the newspaper press). But even in the act of conceiving their government, the people and their leaders distrusted the very thing they created. The first attempt at establishing a government, the Articles of Confederation, made that government as weak as possible. Thomas Paine expressed a widely held sentiment when he called "government even in its best state . . . but a necessary evil: in its worst state an intolerable one" and remarked that it was "like dress . . . a badge of lost innocence."[28] Many Americans were careful to distance themselves from government, making it out to be something that could not quite encompass the entire spirit of the people. In *A Letter from George Nicholas of Kentucky to His Friend in Virginia*, Nicholas wrote, "the genius of . . . the opinions of the people of the United States, cannot be overruled by those who administer the government."[29] Ironically, one of the democratically designed governments that sought to measure its success by its ability to represent the people directly was nonetheless judged at the outset as something of a failure and as an entity sometimes separate from, and possibly antagonistic to, its citizenry. Such distrust allowed the press to compete, in effect, with elected representatives to express the public mind. Not only did the world of print become a place where citizens could debate issues, but it also assumed the mantle of watchdog or ombudsman for the people's interest. Unlike the beginning of the eighteenth century, when government and the press enjoyed a synergistic relationship, the end of the century saw the power of print often coming from opposition to established authority.

The political sequence of events set in motion by Great Britain around the middle of the century stimulated a reaction in the colonies that inevitably reached beyond the narrow geographical limits that necessarily restrict any oral culture. During this time, printed works were the only form of communication that could break down these geographical restraints, giving segments of the world of print an urgency and importance that it did not previously have. Later, the uneasiness with which Americans viewed their own national government, the creation of regional and even national forms of public opinion, and the high economic and social expectations that the new order envisioned for the broadest sweep of citizens continued the transformation that the conflict with Great Britain began. Instead of being authoritative and uniform, the printed word became more subjective and fragmented. Once viewed as static and the conveyor of ancient tradition, the printed word was now often expected to produce change, sometimes outside legal and governmental channels. Instead of the subject of private meditation, print invited contentious debate, even requiring it if the Republic was to succeed. The printed word had not achieved its full potential in American society, nor had all Americans shared in its riches. But America had established an agenda for literate culture at the end of the eighteenth century, and legislators passed legislation which they hoped would ensure that this agenda would be integral in furthering the lofty goals of their democratic experiment.

## NOTES

1.Jeffrey A. Smith, "James Franklin," in *American Newspaper Journalists, 1690-1872*, ed. Perry J. Ashley, *Dictionary of Literary Biography*, vol. 3 (Detroit: Gale Research, 1985). Perry Miller, Introduction to *The New England Courant: A Selection of Certain Issues Containing Writings of Benjamin Franklin* (Boston: American Academy of Arts and Sciences, 1956). Benjamin Franklin, *The Autobiography of Benjamin Franklin*, ed. J. A. Leo Lemay and P. M. Zall (Knoxville: University of Tennessee Press, 1981), pp. 18-30.

2. See the June 11, 1722, issue of the *New England Courant*.

3. John T. Winterich, *Early American Books and Printing* (Boston and New York: Houghton Mifflin Company, 1935), p. 40.

4. William Keith, *A Letter from Sir William Keith, Bart., Governour of Pennsylvania to Mr. James Logan, secretary to the Proprietorship of the Said Provence, on Occasion of Mr. Logan's Having Sent to Sir William a Copy of His Printed Paper, Called The Antidote* (Philadelphia: Andrew Bradford, 1725).

5. James Logan, *The Antidote. In Some Remarks on a Paper of David Lloyd's Called a Vindication of the Legislative Power. Submitted to the Representatives of all the Freedom of Pennsylvania* (Philadelphia: Andrew Bradford, 1725).

6. Keith, *Letter*, p. 7.

7. Ibid., p. 15.

8. See Daniel Boorstin's chapter "How Opinion Went Public" in his *Democracy and Its Discontents* (New York: Random House, 1974). In "Public Spirit to Public Opinion" in his *Beyond Liberty and Property: The Process of Self-recognition in Eighteenth-Century Political Thought* (Montreal: McGill-Queen's University Press, 1983), J. A. W. Gunn traces the history of the nature of the public life of the community in England as moving from individuals being interested in the commonwealth to the concept of public opinion itself being the foundation of government.

9. See, for example, John Barnard's *Ashton's Memorial; An History of the Strange Adventures, and Signal Deliverances, of Mr. Philip Ashton* (Boston: Samuel Gerrish, 1725).

10. George Selement, "Puritan Publications," *William and Mary Quarterly*, 3d ser., 37 (1980), pp. 219-241.

11. Isaiah Thomas discusses his fellow printers' fears about printing a Bible in the colonies on pages 107 and 108 of his *History of Printing in America* (Albany: Joel Munsell, 1874).

12. The most convenient and persuasive compilation of such cases is in chap. 2, "The American Colonial Experience," in Leonard W. Levy's *Emergence of a Free Press* (New York: Oxford University Press, 1985).

13. Ibid., p. 28. Also see Leonard W. Levy's *Freedom of Press from Zenger to Jefferson* (Indianapolis: Bobbs Merill, 1966).

14. Examples of arbitrary enforcement are given in Jeffrey Smith's "A Reappraisal of Legislative Privilege and American Colonial Journalism" in *Journalism Quarterly* 61 (Spring 1984), pp. 97-103.

15. James Franklin, *The Life and Death of Old Father Janus, The Vile Author of the Late Wicked Courant* (Boston: James Franklin, 1726), p. 7.

16. Arthur Schlesinger, *Prelude to Independence, the Newspaper War on Great Britain* (New York: Knopf, 1958).

17. Richard L. Merritt, *Symbols of American Community, 1735-1775* (New Haven, Conn.: Yale University Press, 1966). See also Richard L. Merritt's "The Colonists Discover America: Attention Patterns in the Colonial Press, 1735-1775," *William and Mary Quarterly*, 3d ser., 21 (April 1964), pp. 270-287.

18. Rollo Silver, "The Book Trade and the Protective Tariff: 1800-1804," *Papers of the Bibliographical Society of America* 46 (1952), pp. 33-44.

19. See "American Literature, Public Policy, and the Copyright Laws before 1800" on pages xv through xxv in Elizabeth Carter Wills and James Gilreath's *Federal Copyright Records, 1790-1800* (Washington, D.C.,: Library of Congress, 1987).

20. Lawrence N. Friedman, *A History of American Law* (New York: Simon and Schuster, 1973), p. 65.

21. Louise Irby Trenholme, *The Ratification of the Federal Constitution in North Carolina* (New York: AMS Press, 1967), p. 123. A similar story is told in Linda Grant De Pauw's *The Eleventh Pillar: New York State and the Federal Constitution* (Ithaca, N.Y.: Cornell University Press, 1966).

22. Stephen Botein, "Printers and the American Revolution," in *The Press and the American Revolution*, ed., Bernard Bailyn and John B. Hench (Worcester: American Antiquarian Society, 1980), p. 49.

23. John Hench, "Massachusetts Printers and the Commonwealth Advertising Tax of 1785," *Proceedings of the American Antiquarian Society* 87 (1977), pp. 199-211.

24. Thomas Paine, *Common Sense: Addressed to the Inhabitants of America* (Philadelphia: R. Bell, 1776), p. 5.

25. James Morton Smith, *Freedom's Fetters: The Alien and Sedition Laws and American Civil Liberties* (Ithaca, N.Y.: Cornell University Press, 1956).

26. Thomas Marton, "The Long and the Short of It: A Newspaper Exchange on the Massachusetts Charter, 1772," *William and Mary Quarterly*, 3d ser., 43 (January 1986), pp. 99-110.

27. Bernard Bailyn, *The Ideological Origins of the American Revolution* (Calcutta: Scientific Book Agency, 1969), pp. 4-5.

28. Paine, *Common Sense*, p. 2.

29. George Nicholas, *A Letter from George Nicholas of Kentucky to His Friend in Virginia* (Philadelphia: James Carey, 1799).

# A TALE OF TWO COPYRIGHTS: LITERARY PROPERTY IN REVOLUTIONARY FRANCE AND AMERICA[**]

*Jane C. Ginsburg*


## INTRODUCTION

The French and U.S. copyright systems are well-known as opposites. French copyright law, it is said, enshrines the author, while U.S. copyright law gives first place to the public domain. As the U.S. Congress has observed, "Not primarily for the benefit of the author, but primarily for the benefit of the public [is copyright] given. . . . [Copyright] is not based upon any natural right that the author has in his writings, . . . but upon the ground that the welfare of the public will be served."[1] By contrast, France's leading modern exponent of copyright theory, the late Henri Desbois, proclaimed that "[t]he author is protected as an author, in his status as a creator, because a bond unites him to the object of his creation. In the French tradition, Parliament has repudiated the utilitarian concept of protecting works of authorship in order to stimulate literary and artistic activity."[2]

Traditional depictions of French and Anglo-American copyright further portray the regimes' substantive differences not only as extensive, but as at the origins of each law's enactment. Thus, many contend that France has always rejected instrumentalist theories in favor of copyright as the natural right of creators. For example, in his treatise, Professor Claude Colombet labels one of the "fundamental ideas" of the revolutionary copyright laws the principle that "an exclusive right is conferred on authors because their property is the most justified because it flows from their intellectual creation."[3]

This kind of characterization is typical of modern descriptions (both French and Anglo) of late-eighteenth-century French copyright.[4] The facts, however, suggest a contrary conclusion. The speeches in the French revolutionary assemblies, the text of the laws, and the court decisions

---

construing the laws, all indicate at the least a strong instrumentalist undercurrent to the French decrees of 1791 and 1793.[5] By the same token, while it is true that the law of U.S. letters predominantly reflects "utilitarian" policies, it was not impervious to natural rights influence.

I propose to examine the rhetoric and policies of, and the practice under, the first French and U.S. copyright laws. I believe this examination will demonstrate that the principles and goals underlying the revolutionary French copyright regime were far closer to their U.S. counterparts than most comparative law treatments (or most domestic French law discussions) generally acknowledge. If the two systems are now often seen in opposition, this result may stem from late-nineteenth- and early-twentieth-century developments in French courts and in legal writings more than from any great philosophical gulf at the laws' inception.

## COPYRIGHT BEFORE 1791 (MODELS AVAILABLE TO REVOLUTIONARY LEGISLATORS)

First, a brief glance at the ancien régime. Under the edicts of 1777-78, the French crown afforded printing privileges to both authors and publishers. The author's privilege was perpetual, but once ceded to the publisher, or if initially acquired by the publisher, it lasted only during the life of the author.[6] By the end of the ancien régime, much rhetoric proclaiming the sanctity and self-evidence of exclusive literary property rights had infiltrated the copyright debate. Most of this rhetoric was propounded by publishers invoking authors' rights for the publishers' benefit, and some of it by government advocates invoking authors' rights to curb publishers' assertions.[7]

The system of printing privileges was conditioned upon compliance with formalities: deposit of copies in national libraries, inclusion of the text of the privilege in each printed copy, and registration of copies with the publishers' guild.[8] Remedies afforded by the privilege included injunctions and damages, seizure, confiscation and destruction of infringing copies.[9] In addition to the right to publish the work, the Crown also regulated rights of public performance of dramatic works by vesting in the Comédie Française the exclusive right to perform such works.[10]

On the Anglo-American side, England was the first nation to substitute a statutory rule of copyright law for a regime of royal favor. The first copyright statute, known as the Statute of Anne, was enacted in 1710. Its title and preamble enunciate the policy which became the essential rationale for both English and American copyright laws: copyright is an incentive to authors to create so that the public may have access and be enriched by their works. The Statute of Anne is titled "An Act for the Encouragement of Learning by vesting the Copies of Printed Books in the Authors or Purchasers of such Copies." Its preamble states that the act is to discourage piracy and is "for the Encouragement of Learned Men to Compose and Write useful Books." The statute sought to accomplish these goals by conferring a reproduction right on authors for fourteen years, renewable for another fourteen, if the author was still living. However, because "Persons may through Ignorance offend against this Act," the statute imposed the formalities of registration and deposit of copies as prerequisites to protection. Remedies included destruction of infringing copies and damages.[11]

The United States Constitution, drafted in 1787, and available in France in Philip Mazzei's French translation by at least 1790, authorizes a national copyright regime. In terms reminiscent of the Statute of Anne's incentive/access policy, and suggesting the Framers' intent to employ copyright as a means of furthering public education, the Constitution declares "Congress shall have Power . . . to promote the Progress of Science and useful Arts, by securing for limited Times to Authors and Inventors the exclusive Right to their respective Writings and Discoveries."[12] The first U.S. copyright statute, from 1790, is titled "An Act for the encouragement of learning, by securing the copies of maps, charts and books, to the authors and proprietors of such copies, during the times therein mentioned."[13] As did the English law, the U.S. statute granted protection in these works to the author or his assigns for fourteen years, renewable for another fourteen, if the author was still living. Moreover, the U.S. legislation displayed a public domain bias reminiscent of the Statute of Anne: the Act's formalities included deposit and registration and obliged the author to place a notice of the copyright registration in newspapers published in the United States for a period of four weeks.[14] Remedies included forfeiture of infringing copies and damages.[15]

Despite U.S. copyright's predominantly instrumentalist origins, natural rights rationales for copyright were not absent from the American scene. Before the enactment of the Constitution, states were entirely responsible for the regulation of literary property. The Continental Congress, under the Articles of Confederation, encouraged the thirteen states to pass copyright laws.[16] While some of the ensuing state statutes were modeled after the Statute of Anne, many others mingled public benefit rationales with natural rights rhetoric. For example, the preamble to the Massachusetts Act of 1783 first announced a public benefit rationale drawn from the English precedent, but then stated: "As the principal encouragement such persons can have to make great and beneficial exertions of this nature, must exist in the legal security of the fruits of their study and industry to themselves; and as such security is one of the natural rights of all men, there being no property more peculiarly a man's own than that which is procured by the labor of his mind."[17]

For what kinds of works was U.S. copyright sought or litigated in the eighteenth century? Petitions to Congress before enactment of the first U.S. copyright statute seek exclusive privileges for works overwhelmingly instructional in character. For example, petitioners in 1789 included the authors of *The American Geography, or a View of the present Situation of the United States of America, embellished and illustrated with two original maps*, and of *A new and complete System of Arithmetic*.[18] A recent comprehensive study of copyright deposit records covering the first ten years of the federal copyright system discloses a preponderance of useful, instructional texts in deposits made pursuant to the first federal copyright statute.[19] For example, of 80 copyright deposits recorded from 1790 through 1792 in Pennsylvania and Massachusetts (the states where most works were published), 34 were of grammars, geographies, or similar instructional texts, and another 26 comprised informational works such as histories and almanacs.

One scholar of publishing history attributes the dominance of textbooks in copyright registers in part to national pride: "In the post-Revolutionary textbook boom, the demand for primers, geographies and arithmetics, in both German and English was high, as American books patriotically replaced the British texts that had been used before."[20] The titles of several of the instructional works deposited for copyright convey their personally and patriotically uplifting aims. For example, Jedidiah Morse titled another work, registered for federal copyright in Massachusetts on July 10, 1790, as follows: *Geography made easy; being an Abridgement of the American Geography -- to which added a geographical Account of the European settlements in America & of Europe, Asia & Africa; illustrated with eight neat maps and [wood]cuts -- calcuated particularly for the use & improvement of Schools in the United States*; and Noah Webster titled one of his prolific educational endeavors, registered for federal copyright in Massachusetts on October 7, 1790, as follows: *An American Selection of Lessons in Reading and Spelling. Calculated to improve the minds and refine the taste of Youth. And also, to instruct them in the Geography, history and politics of the United States*.[21] Perhaps not surprisingly for a young republic, instructive, civics-oriented works dominate the publishing catalogues. The relative paucity of fiction may well reflect republican values. Thomas Jefferson is attributed as saying that "a great obstacle to good education is the inordinate passion prevalent for novels, and the time lost in that reading which should be instructively employed."[22]

U.S. copyright litigation, albeit sparse, appears also to have been reserved to quarrels over informational and similar works. A leading study has cited no decisions before 1791, and only two lower court decisions between that time and the U.S. Supreme Court's first copyright decision, *Wheaton v. Peters* in 1834.[23] Both lower court cases concerned compliance with federal copyright formalities. Both also concerned works more of utility and of laborious compilation than of imagination; in one, a "federal calculator" and in the other, a *Pharmacopoeia of the United States of America*. *Wheaton v. Peters* involved a claim of copyright in reports of U.S. Supreme Court decisions.[24]

## THE FRENCH ENACTMENTS OF 1791 TO 1793

While traditional comparisons of French to Anglo-American copyright law assert that France rejected instrumentalist theories in favor of copyright as the just and fair prerogative of creators, research in primary sources prompts a different conclusion. The various legislative texts reveal a hesitating and uneven progress toward protection of authors' rights. In neither the 1791 law, conferring a public performance right in dramatic works, nor in the 1793 law, conferring a reproduction right in writings of all kinds, are authors securely at the core of the new literary property regime. Rather, in both texts, broader public concerns divide or even overshadow the legislators' attentions. The 1791 text predominantly is preoccupied with the recognition and enlargement of the public domain. The committee report in favor of the 1793 law emphasizes that protecting authors will not prove detrimental to society.

In the 1791 decree, the author's concerns do not occupy center stage. The report on the 1791 decree arises in a dispute between dramatists and the Comédie Française -- the latter once the beneficiary of the exclusive right to produce theatrical works, the former once effectively indentured to the only approved theater. The decree's main goal was to proclaim the right of all citizens to open their own theaters and produce plays. So states the decree's first article. Authors' rights are an adjunct to this freedom; just as any citizen may be a theatrical producer, so may any living author (or the successors of one dead for up to five years) authorize the production of his work anywhere he wishes them to be produced and only where he (or his successor) wishes them to be produced. Plays by authors dead over five years are declared part of the public domain. The decree thus was designed to break the Comédie Française's monopoly on the works of Corneille, Molière, and Racine.[25] Seen in its overall context, the decree's recognition of authors' rights is principally a means to terminate the exclusivity once enjoyed by the Comédie Française.

The authors' rights, it bears emphasis, are hardly ascendant. The reporter Le Chapelier is often quoted as a great exponent of author-oriented rationales for copyright. Almost invariably, the passage quoted is taken out of context.[26] Le Chapelier did declare that "the most sacred, the most legitimate, the most inattackable, . . . the most personal of all properties, is the work which is the fruit of a writer's thoughts."[27] But he said it with respect to *unpublished* works. Once disseminated, Le Chapelier went on to assert, the work is "give[n] over to the public . . . by the nature of things, everything is finished for the author and the publisher when the public has in this way [through publication] acquired the work."[28] According to Le Chapelier, the main principle is the public domain, to which authors' rights are an exception. He stressed that the new French law put the principle and its exception in the right place: were the exception to replace the principle that "a published work is by its nature a public property," "you will no longer have any basis for your law." Indeed, he criticized the English copyright law for setting up a strongly protected right rather than appreciating the principle of the public domain.

The text of the 1791 law followed Le Chapelier's organization of principles and exceptions: Article 1 pronounced the right of all citizens to erect theaters and to perform plays of all kinds; Article 2 declares that works of authors who have been dead for over five years are public property; not until Article 3 does the 1791 law set forth affirmative authors' rights by conditioning performances of the works of living authors upon their written consent.[29]

A subsequent decree on playwrights' copyright, of August 30, 1792, also reflected Le Chapelier's weak embrace of authors' rights. The January 1791 decree had not satisfied the authors' demands. The public's right to establish theaters appears to have come into conflict with the dramatists' right to authorize public performances; particularly in the provinces, theater owners were producing plays without paying the authors the full sums demanded. Beaumarchais petitioned the Assemblée Nationale for a law that would better assure authors' property interests. The ensuing decree announced in preamble that "the right to publish and the right to public performance, which incontestably belong to the authors of dramatic works, have not been sufficiently distinguished and protected by the law."[30]

However, the actual articles of the 1792 decree made the dramatist's public performance rights appear even more vulnerable than under the 1791 decree. The 1792 decree subjected the dramatist's right to compliance with formalities. It imposed on the author the burden, at the time of the play's publication, to notify the public that the author had retained the public performance right. The notice was to be printed at the head of the text of the play and deposited with a notary (Arts. 4-6). Without fulfillment of these conditions, the dramatist's right would never vest.[31] Moreover, the decree declared that plays may be freely performed at the expiration of ten years following publication (Art. 8). In substituting a ten-year period for the 1791 decree's life plus five, the 1792 measure may have shortened the duration of many playwrights' protection.[32]

By 1793, however, the revolutionary legislators' copyright rhetoric had shifted away from Le Chapelier's public domain principle and toward recognizing a property right in authors' works, even after publication. But this shift did not markedly amend the prior reserved characterization of authors' rights, much less break with it. In the new formulation, authors would still not receive protection primarily for their own sake; rather, recognition of their rights would serve to promote the public welfare. Indeed, jurisdiction over elaboration of a copyright law had been transferred from the Committees on the Constitution and on Agriculture and Commerce, to the Committee on Public Instruction.[33] Enacting a copyright law formed part of a grander scheme of public education.

The report of Joseph Lakanal on the law granting exclusive reproduction rights, another document often quoted selectively, does indeed announce in its first sentence a property right in works of authorship. Lakanal also dubbed the proposed law the "Declaration of the Rights of Genius" thus stressing copyright's kinship to other great Rights of Man. But other aspects of the report reveal ambiguities. For example, Lakanal's pronouncement of an author's property right is guarded. Unlike ancien régime advocates of literary property, Lakanal did not assert that "the author is the master of his work or no one in society is master of his property."[34] Indeed, unlike Le Chapelier, Lakanal does not even affirm "the most sacred," "the most personal of properties." Rather, he proclaims that this right is "[o]f all rights the least subject to criticism; a right whose increase can neither harm republican equality, nor offend liberty."[35] The rhetoric here displays a looking-over-the-shoulder quality inconsistent with a firm conviction of the centrality of authors' personal claims.[36]

Some nineteenth-century commentators buttress this conclusion. For example, in his 1858 study *Etudes sur la propriété littéraire en France et en Angleterre*, Edouard Laboulaye voiced disappointment that Lakanal's report failed to affirm a true property right for authors. He charged that in Lakanal's report "one sees that nothing has changed either in ideas nor in legislation: the word *property*, it is true, has replaced that of *privilege*, but this property is still but a charitable grant from society."[37]

The text of the 1793 decree also undercuts arguments that this law protects authors primarily because they are authors. Although the version of the decree reported by Lakanal on July 21 contained no formalities, the final text incorporated the requirement of deposit as a prerequisite to suit. Conditioning the exercise of copyright upon compliance with state-promulgated and administered rules undercuts the notion of a right inherent in the author.[38] Indeed, several early court decisions under the 1793 law held that deposit of copies, rather than simply meeting a procedural requirement, *gave rise to* the copyright.[39] That is, without deposit, no copyright protection attached to the work. At the least, failure to deposit the work could result in an initially protected work's falling into the public domain.[40] These rulings suggest a judicial view that the act of authorship does not itself afford a basis for recognizing or maintaining protection of authors' rights. Commentators closer than we to the 1793 text contended that it did not afford authors powerful guarantees of exclusive rights. Thus, parodying the Le Chapelier and Lakanal reports, Edouard Laboulaye lamented that under the 1793 law copyright had become "of all property rights, the most humble and the least protected."[41]

If the motivations for enacting the first French and U.S. copyright laws were similar, what of the works they yielded? Comparison of the subject matter the two laws covered suggests that the two nations sought to promote dissemination of different kinds of works. The U.S. Constitution authorized Congress to create a copyright system to "promote the progress" of knowledge. Congress adopted a rather pragmatic view of the kinds of works that achieved that objective: the first U.S. copyright law protected maps, charts, and books-- in that order. The great majority of works for which authors or publishers sought copyright protection under that first statute were highly useful productions.

The first French copyright law conferring a right of reproduction extended not merely to "writings of all kinds" but to "all productions of the *beaux arts*."[42] Putting the two texts side by side, one might conclude that one law promoted Utility, while the other sought Beauty. In fact, reports of French copyright infringement cases through 1814 indicate that, as in the U.S. and England, works of information or instruction were most often the subject matter of copyright litigation.

Moreover, even when the complaint of the French copyright owners concerned works of higher Arts and Letters, the arguments of the advocates would nonetheless sound familiar to an Anglo-American copyright litigant: incentive rationales loom large in the reasoning of the lawyers and the courts.[43] The French copyright law may have protected a broader range of subject matter, but in both French and American cases, the subject matter advanced state interests. If the U.S. framers feared that art might distract hard-working citizens from useful achievements, the French revolutionaries saw art, or at least some kinds of art,[44] in the service of utility.

Art glorified the French Revolution and spread its ideals. A criminal copyright infringement affair from the Year VII of the Republic illustrates the point. The work at issue was a play. Theatrical works were among those creations the Revolution sought to encourage.[45] The pleading stressed the utility of dramatic works in disseminating the Enlightenment and the Revolution. The prosecutor, complaining of inadequate enforcement of dramatists' rights in the provinces, queried: "Shall literary properties be less sacred in the eyes of the republican judge than other properties?" And then declared:

> It is to the wise men, to dramatic authors, to all literary
> authors that we principally owe the uncontested superiority
> of the French language over all the languages of Europe. It
> is they who render all nations tributaries to our arts, to our
> tastes, to our genius, to our glory; it is through them that the

> principles and rules of a wise and generous liberty penetrate
> beyond our borders and sphere of activity.[46]

I turn now to a more systematic review of copyright infringement actions and decisions under the law of 1793 (through 1814). Of the 37 controversies I have been able to gather, the subject matter of 21 concerns informational works; another 15 cases concern works of drama, music, art, poetry, or fiction; and the subject matter of one case is undisclosed. However, the initial subject matter distinction between information and art is not entirely satisfactory: many of the works of drama and poetry at issue purport not merely to entertain but also to educate.[47] Moreover, this subject-matter breakdown does not purport to reflect the overall relationship of published works of utility to published works of entertainment;[48] rather, identification of the kinds of works that spawned litigation serves to indicate the kinds of works that generated sufficient popular demand to encourage piracy.

Regarding to the claims or defenses at issue, of these 37 controversies, 11 decisions concern formal or procedural defects in the copyright or its enforcement. Reference to the many decisions involving formal or procedural defects may elucidate the efficacy of the 1793 law at protecting author's rights. Frequent foundering of authors' claims on these rocks suggests a copyright regime ill adapted to vigorous enforcement of, and therefore perhaps not warmly receptive to, the author's monopoly.

Many decisions as reported forego detailing the courts' rationales; they simply state the subject matter and the result. From the decisions that do more, what approach to copyright emerges? While some decisions invoke or presume a natural rights basis for copyright, others, perhaps the majority, express or rely on more external justifications for protection. In the first group, a controversy from the Year II [1794].[49] The controversy involved sales of unauthorized copies of memoirs which defendant contended it had acquired before passage of the July 1793 copyright law. Challenging the retroactive application of that law, defendant disclaimed liability for prior acts of copying and distribution.

The court ruled for plaintiff, holding that "natural fairness, the first of all laws, sufficiently warned the printers and booksellers that it was not permitted to appropriate the productions of others, and that anytime one harms the property of another, one is essentially obliged to compensate the harm which he has suffered." The court's reasoning presumes that, even in the absence of a law regulating booksellers, the author has a "property" right. Yet, the court identifies no formal source of this property right[50] but apparently perceived it as arising out of the creation of the work. Moreover, the court did not refer to any public benefit derived from protecting authors.

A later decision, from the Year XI, *Buffon c. Behmer,*[51] also recognized copyright protection for pre-1793 works, but this time not exclusively on grounds of general fairness, or an inherent property right. Rather, the Tribunal de Cassation ruled that privileges granted under the 1777-78 edicts, if not expired under their own terms, remained in force.[52] The reasons offered for the persistence of ancien régime printing privileges are of particular interest to this study.

Buffon's widow had charged copyright infringement of *Natural History*, whose 40-year printing privilege granted under the ancien régime had not yet expired. Defendant responded that the August 4, 1789, decree generally abolishing ancien régime privileges had terminated the work's protection and cast it into the public domain, and that the August 20, 1789, decree establishing freedom of the press entitled defendant to publish whatever he wished. Buffon's widow appealed to the Tribunal de Cassation, arguing that the August 4 decree did not apply to an author's rights under the prior edicts, because these rights were not feudal, and therefore were not targeted by the general abolition of privileges. Similarly, she contended, the August 20 decree simply recognized that "each man being the master of his own thoughts may write and publish them as he desires"; the decree in no way authorized the appropriation of the works of others.

In holding that the 1777 decrees remained in force until prospectively superseded by the 1793 law, the court declared:

> the decrees of August 1789, which abolished privileges and distinctions and set the press free, have no relation to the property acquired by an author in his work, which is simply the legitimate compensation for his work, and the price naturally owing for the enlightenment which he spreads throughout society.

The court invoked both personal and external justifications for protection; it grounded the author's rights both in the act of creation and in the public benefits flowing from it. Thus the court first endorsed the notion that authors have property rights in their works as the fruit of their labors, but then invoked the policy (fundamental to Anglo-American copyright) that copyright rewards authors because they contribute to the advancement of public instruction.

Other cases also contain reasoning consistent with the twin Anglo-American copyright goals of encouraging investment in, and the creation of, works of authorship in order to promote public education.[53] One of these, the protracted affair of the *Dictionary* of the Académie Française,[54] merits attention both for the statements of the government official intervening on behalf of the plaintiffs, and for the Tribunal de Cassation's holding. The plaintiffs were publishers who succeeded to rights granted by the revolutionary authorities to a prior publisher to prepare a fifth edition of the *Dictionary*. A new edition had been in preparation when the Académie Française was suppressed by the decree of August 8, 1793. Plaintiffs' edition, incorporating the academicians' notes for new articles, appeared in the Year VI [1798]. Three years later, defendants published a new edition of the *Dictionary*, based on the edition last published by the Académie, and updated with defendants' own new articles.

In the ensuing infringement action, the defendants disputed plaintiffs' copyright interest, arguing that with the abolition of the Académie Française, the *Dictionary* became public property, available to all to republish or revise. Defendants also indicated that if anyone had a property interest in the *Dictionary*, under the terms of the 1793 law granting copyright to "authors"[55] and designating the "true owner" as the person to whom the infringer must pay damages,[56] that person could only be the *Dictionary*'s actual writers, not the state, nor the state's publisher-grantees. Countering this defense, the *commissaire du gouvernement* Merlin evoked a concept of authorship and of copyright which we would now consider far more American than French. Today the French copyright system generally proceeds from the principles that the "author" is the actual physical creator of the work, and that the creator's status as an employee or commissioned party in no way affects authorship or initial title to copyright.[57] (By contrast, U.S. copyright has embraced the doctrine of "works made for hire," designating as "author" and initial owner the employer or, in certain circumstances, the commissioning party.[58]) Construing the 1793 French law to favor plaintiffs' ownership claims in the *Dictionary*, Merlin declared that plaintiffs were the lawful grantees of the State, and the State was the proper copyright owner of the *Dictionary*, he elaborated:

> The word *authors* does not have, under the law, a meaning
> as restrictive as defendants have asserted. The word
> designates not only those who have themselves composed a
> literary work, but also those who have had it written by
> others, and who have had the work done at their expense. .
> . . The rights which belong to the nation belong to it
> because it is the nation which itself instituted and paid the
> Académie Française to compose this dictionary.

The court upheld the plaintiffs' assertion of a copyright interest on the ground that plaintiffs were the "true owner" envisioned by the 1793 text:

> In the letter, as well as the spirit of the law, the true owner
> to compensate for the infringement is the owner of the
> original publication, that is, the publisher, because under the
> tort of infringement only the publisher's interests are harmed
> by the infringement of the original edition.[59]

The court's reasoning diverges from a view of copyright as the proper reward for the author's creativity. Rather, the real party of interest was the one who financed and disseminated the work. The court may have perceived the publisher as the proper claimant of a right to compensation for its investment. But contemporary publishers did not directly claim such rights for themselves; they claimed to be the contractual beneficiaries of the authors' rights.[60] The court appears to identify the publisher as the "true owner" because, by funding and distributing the work of authorship, the publisher is the vital link between the work and its public.

## CONCLUSION

This examination of the French revolutionary sources of copyright law reveals that revolutionary legislators, courts, and advocates perceived literary property primarily as a means to advance public instruction. Contemporary authorities certainly also recognized authors' claims of personal rights arising out of their creations, but the characteristic modern portrayal of French revolutionary copyright as an unambiguous espousal of an authorcentric view of copyright requires substantial amendment. Similarly, this study has shown that familiar conceptions of early U.S. copyright also warrant reconsideration. If U.S. copyright's exponents sought to promote the progress of knowledge, they also recognized that the author's labors are due their own reward. The revolutionary French and American systems shared much not only in theory, but also in practice. In both systems, formalities encumbered, and sometimes defeated, the acquisition or exercise of copyright protection. And both systems primarily protected works useful to advancing public instruction.

## NOTES

A more extensive version of this article appeared in *Tulane Law Review* 64 (1990), p. 991. The French court decisions cited in the present version are summarized in an Appendix in *Tulane Law Review* 64 (1990), pp. 1024-31.

1. H.R. Rep. No. 2222, 60th Cong. 2d sess. (1909), quoted in, A. Latman, R. A. Gorman and J. C. Ginsburg, *Copyright for the Nineties*, 3d ed. (1989), p. 14.
2. H. Desbois, *Le Droit d'auteur en France*, 3d ed. (1978), p. 538 (describing 1957 French copyright law).
3. C. Colombet, *Propriété littéraire et artistique*, 4th ed. (1988), p. 8.

4. Cf. S. Ricketson, *The Berne Convention 1886-1896* (1987), pp. 5-6
& n. 11. "It will be seen that both these [French revolutionary] laws placed
authors' rights on a more elevated basis than the [English] Act of Anne had
done. There was a conscious philosophical basis to the French laws that saw
the rights protected as being embodied in natural law. Accordingly, the laws
were simply according formal recognition to what was already inherent in the
'very nature of things'." Quoting J. R. Kase, *Copyright Thought in Continental
Europe* (1971), p. 8.

5. See also C. Hesse, *Publishing and Cultural Politics in
Revolutionary Paris, 1789-1810* (Berkeley: University of California Press,
1991), for consideration of other primary sources supporting this conclusion.

6. On regulation of publishing under the ancien régime see e.g., R.
Birn, "The Profits of Ideas: Privilèges en librairie in Eighteenth-Century
France," *Eighteenth-Century Studies* 4 (1971), p. 131; M.-Cl. Dock, *Etude sur
le droit d'auteur* (Paris: LGDJ,1963); H. Falk, "Les Privilèges de librairie
sous l'ancien régime," Thesis, Paris 1906; Henrion, "Appoint à l'étude des
privilèges des librairies aux XVIe et XVIIe siècles," *RIDA* VI (January 1955),
p. 113; E. Laboulaye and G. Guiffrey, *La Propriété littéraire au XVIIIe siècle*
(Paris, 1859); Malapert, *Histoire abrégée de la legislation sur la propriété
littéraire avant 1789* (Paris 1881).

7. See, e.g., the 1777 petition of the advocate Cochu on behalf of the
Paris publishers, reprinted in E. Laboulaye and G. Guiffrey, supra note 6, pp.
159-220. Cochu contended, "If there is one property which is sacred, self-
evident, incontestable, it is doubtless that of authors in their works." This and
similar rhetoric would be echoed in the Revolutionary assemblies. See infra,
text at notes 34-35.

8. Edict of August 30, 1777 on *Privilèges*, reprinted in E. Laboulaye
and G. Guiffrey, supra note 6, pp. 143-147.

9. See Edict of August 30, 1777 on Infringement reprinted in E.
Laboulaye and G. Guiffrey, supra note 6, pp. 147-150.

10. On the rights of dramatic authors and the Comédie Française
under the ancien régime, see, e.g., J. Boncompain, *Auteurs et comédiens au
XVIIIe siècle* (Paris 1976); J. Bonnassies, *Les Auteurs dramatiques et la
Comédie Française aux XVIIe et XVIIIe siècles* (1874).

11. Statute of Anne, 1710, 8 Anne ch. 19, preamble, §§ 1, 3. Sec.
9 required deposit of copies to university libraries. On the Statute of Anne and
its history, see, e.g., H. Ransom, *The First Copyright Statute* (1956); L. R.
Patterson, *Copyright in Historical Perspective* (1968).

12. U.S. Const., art. I, § 8, cl. 8.

13. Act of May 31, 1790, 1 Stat. 124.

14. Act of May 31, 1790, 1 Stat. 124. § 3. Formalities often proved
fatal to U.S. authors' or publishers' claims. See, e.g., Wheaton v. Peters, 33
U.S. [8 Pet.] 591 (1834) (failure to comply with registration requirements0;

Clayton v. Stone, 5 F. Cas. 999 (C.C.S.D.N.Y. 1829) (No. 2872) (news bulletins held uncopyrightable because unamenable to compliance with formalities).

15. 1 Stat. 124 § 2. Neither the English nor the U.S. laws provided in the eighteenth-century for a right of public performance.

16. "Resolution passed by the colonial Congress, Recommending the several States to secure to Authors or Publishers of new books the copyright of such books," May 2, 1783, reprinted in T. Solberg, ed., *Copyright Enactments of the United States* (1906), p. 11.

17. Reprinted in T. Solberg, supra note 16, p. 14. See also New Hampshire, Act of Nov. 7, 1783, Solberg, p. 18; Rhode Island, Act of December 1783, Solberg, p. 19.

The organization of the Connecticut statute places the author's personal rights before the public's. It states: "Whereas it is perfectly agreeable to the principles of natural equity and justice, that every author should be secured in receiving the profits that may arise from the sale of his works, and such security may encourage men of learning and genius to publish their writings; which may do honor to their country, and service to mankind." Connecticut, Act of January 1783, Solberg, p. 11. The wording of the North Carolina, Georgia, and New York statutes closely resembles the Connecticut statute's. See North Carolina, Act of November 19, 1785, Solberg, p. 25; Georgia, Act of Feb. 3, 1786, Solberg, p. 27; New York, Act of April 29, 1786, Solberg, p. 29. Francine Crawford, "Pre-Constitutional Copyright Statutes," *Bulletin of the Copyright Society* 23 (1975), p. 15 concludes from this organization that "even though encouragement of learning was included as a reason for these four statutes, the primary purpose seemed to have been the enforcement of a pre-existing right--a property right in intellectual works." See also L. R. Patterson, supra note 11, p. 188 ("The dominant idea of copyright underlying the state statutes was the idea of copyright as an author's right.") But see J. Tebbel, *A History of Book Publishing in the United States: The Creation of an Industry, 1630-1865* (1972), 1: 139 (pointing out that the Connecticut statute "gave the Superior Court the right to withdraw the copyright if the author 'did not furnish the public with sufficient Editions' of a book").

18. See "Proceedings in Congress During the Years 1789 and 1790, Relating to the First Patent and Copyright Laws," *Journal of the Patent Office Society* 22 (1940), p. 243 (reproducing the text of the petitions). Morse's work became the first to be deposited for federal copyright pursuant to the 1790 statute in the state of Massachusetts. J. Tebbel, supra note 17, p. 196, states that Morse's and Pike's works "may safely be said to be 'first' among [American] schoolbooks."

19. J. Gilreath, ed. and E. C. Wills, comp. *Federal Copyright Records, 1790-1800* (1987).

20. J. Tebbel, supra note 17, p. 142.

21. These works are cataloged as nos. 265 and 267 in Gilreath and Wills supra note 19, p. 74. I have taken the title of Webster's work from the entry in Evans's *American Bibliography*, No. 23050.

22. T. Jefferson, *The Writings of Thomas Jefferson* (1903), 15: 166 quoted in Gilreath, supra note 19, p. xxii.

23. Nichols v. Ruggles, 3 Day 145 (Conn. 1808) and Ewer v. Coxe, 8 Fed. Cas. 917 (No. 4584) (C.C.E.D. Pa. 1824), cited in L. R. Patterson, supra note 12, p. 207 (1968). Wheaton v. Peters is reported at 33 U.S. [8 Pet.] 591 (1834). I have found one other federal copyright decision predating Wheaton v. Peters. However, it postdates the French Revolution. The case, Clayton v. Stone, 5 Fed. Cas. (No. 2872) 999 (C.C.S.D.N.Y. 1829), nonetheless is worth signalling for its restrictive interpretation of the term "book" in the 1790 copyright act. The court denied copyright protection to market reports published in daily newspapers on the ground that "books" imply some permanent contribution to knowledge; newspapers are too "ephemeral." Moreover, stressed the court, the daily publication of newspapers makes them ill adapted to compliance with the extensive statutory formalities. It followed that Congress could not have meant to include newspapers.

24. In English copyright decisions predating the French revolutionary laws useful works also predominate. See, e.g., Gyles v. Wilcox, 2 Atk 141, 3 ATK.296, 26 Eng. Rep. 489, 957; Barn. Ch. 368, 27 Eng. Rep. 682 (Ch. 1740) (law books); Sayre v. Moore, 1 East 361n, 102 Eng. Rep. 139n (K.B. 1785) (maps); Trusler v. Murray, 1 East 362n, 102 Eng. Rep. 140n (K.B. 1789) (chronologies); Carnan v. Bowles, 2 Bro. C.C. 80, 83, 29 Eng. Rep. 45, 47 (Ch. 1786) (road atlases).

25. The Comédiens had indicated their willingness to relinquish monopoly rights in the works of *living* authors but invoked the principle of nonretroactivity of new laws to insist on their continuing rights in long-deceased playwrights, such as those mentioned in text (who, not incidentally, constituted the core of the repertory). See Report of Le Chapelier, *Moniteur Universel*, January 15, 1791, p. 116.

26. See, e.g., E. Pouillet, *Traité théorique et pratique de la propriété littéraire et artistique*, 3d ed. (Paris, 1908), p. 26, n. 1; M.-CL. Dock, *Etude sur le droit d'auteur* (1963), p. 152; A. Françon, *Cours de propriété littéraire, artistique et industrielle* (1980), pp. 14-16.

Pouillet may have relied on several earlier treatise writers, whose incomplete quotations from Le Chapelier supply apparent evidence for an author-oriented concept of copyright. See, e.g., A. Nion, *Droits civils des auteurs, artistes et inventeurs* (Paris, 1846), pp. 39-40; M. Gastambide, *Historique et théorie de la propriété des auteurs* (Paris, 1862), p. 47, n. 1.

27. *Le Moniteur Universel*, January 15, 1791, p. 117.

28. Le Chapelier's remark that "in the nature of things" publication marks the demise of authors' and publishers' rights thus rejects assertions of an inherent post-publication property right in literary works. Others would echo this position. See, e.g., Court of Cassation, decision of January 20, 1818, Chaumerot c. Michaud; pleading of defendant's advocate quoted in P. A. Merlin, *Recueil de Questions de Droit*, 4th ed. (1828), pp. 340-42. Defendant argued that neither natural law nor customary law accord to authors the exclusive right to reproduce their published works, but rather a "specific law grants this right which derogates from the natural right acquired by all [to copy] as of the first publication of the work."

Eighteenth-century English copyright case law construing the Statute of Anne also ultimately distinguished between published and unpublished works. See Donaldson v. Beckett, 4 Burr. 2408, 98 Eng. Rep. 257 (H.L. 1774).

29. The sanction for unauthorized performances was confiscation of all revenues from the performances, and their award to the authors. Article IV stated the extent of the new law's retroactive effect. Article V covered a five-year post mortem right on the dramatists' heirs or grantees.

30. The text of the 1792 law printed in the collected laws from June 1789 to August 1830, *Bulletin annoté des lois, décrets et ordonnances* (Paris, 1834), does not include the preamble. It is set forth in Baudin, "Rapport et projet de décret sur la propriété des auteurs dramatiques, preséntés au nom du comité de l'instruction publique," in *Procès verbaux du Comité d'Instruction Publique de la Convention Nationale*, ed. M. Guillaume (1891) 1: 349, 353 [hereinafter *Procès verbaux*].

31. The 1792 law thus harks back to the *règlement* of 1723 governing publishing and bookselling: Art. 103 conditioned issuance of printing privileges on publication of the text of the privilege at the front or back of each copy; Art. 108 required deposit of copies in the royal libraries.

32. This decree, voluably resented by dramatists, was repealed by the decree of September 1, 1793. See *Procès verbaux*, supra note 30, 2: 353 (1894). Concerning the dramatists' efforts before the revolutionary legislature, see generally Anon., "Fragments d'histoire de la protection littéraire, la lutte entre les auteurs dramatiques et les directeurs de théâtres sous l'Assemblée législative Française (1791-1792)," *Le Droit d'auteur*, Oct. 15, 1890, pp. 105-110.

33. See *Procès verbaux*, supra note 30, 1: iv. For a more detailed account of the shifts in committee responsibility in the revolutionary legislature over copyright legislation, see generally Hesse, "Enlightenment Epistemology and the Laws of Authorship in Revolutionary France, 1777-1793," *Representations* 30 (1990), p. 110.

34. The assertion is Diderot's, made at the behest of his publisher. See Birn, supra note 6, pp. 152-153, quoting D. Diderot, *Sur la liberté de la presse*.

35. *Le Moniteur Universel*, July 21, 1793, p. 176.

36. Interestingly, Pouillet's highly influential copyright treatise quotes this text quite selectively, removing the more insecure passages, those which claim that copyright will not harm the Republic; see E. Pouillet, supra note 26, p. 14. Many leading subsequent authors appear to resort to Pouillet's rendition, rather than to the original text; see, e.g., A. Françon, supra note 26, p. 15; C. Colombet, supra note 3, p. 7, thus propagating the view that the Revolution perceived copyright as "un véritable *droit naturel*," A. Françon, p. 16.

37. E. Laboulaye, *Etudes sur la propriété litteraire en France et en Angleterre* (1858), p. xi.

38. This observation is shared by R. Crouzel, "Le Dépot légal at 31," Thesis, Toulouse, 1936. See also A. Vaunois, "Le Dépôt légal des imprimés en France," *Droit d'auteur* (1916), pp.125, 126.

39. Court of Cassation, decision of 23 oct. 1806, Bruysset c. Albert Joly, L.-M. Devilleneuve & A.-A. Carette, *Recueil général des lois et des arrêts, lère série, 1791-1830* (Paris, 1840-) [hereafter, Dev. & Car.] vol. AN XIII-1808.1.299; Paris Court of Appeals, decision of Nov. 26, 1828, Troupenas c. Pleyel et Aulagnier, Dev. & Car. 1828.2.159.

The Court of Cassation's decision of January 20, 1818, in Chaumerot c. Michaud, Dennevers, ed., *Journal des audiences de la Cour de Cassation depuis 1791* (Paris, 1808-) [hereafter, Den.], vol. 1818, at 193, appears to consider compliance with formalities as giving rise to exclusive rights: the court states the plaintiffs "published the work in 1816 and fulfilled all the formalities prescribed for acquiring the exclusive right to sell." Plaintiff's advocate seems to make the same assumption: he contended that a French national first publishing abroad could nonetheless obtain copyright protection in France "by completing the formalities to which the privilege is subject" (1818: 198).

40. The Cour de Cassation's decision of March 1, 1834, Terry c. Marchant, Dev. & Car. 1834, Part I, p. 65, both state that the 1793 law "guarantees literary property, upon condition of deposit of two copies with the Bibliothèque nationale" and refers to the "loss of that property right through failure of deposit." As a result of this decision, the question whether deposit under the 1793 law created, perfected, or merely served to prove, the copyright became moot: the court held that subsequent enactments (in 1810, 1814, and 1828) had substituted a different deposit requirement for that set forth in Art. 6 of the 1793 law.

France required pre-suit deposit of copies of works of authorship until the beginning of the twentieth century.

41. E. Laboulaye, supra note 37, p. xii.

42. France, Law of 19-24 July 1793, Arts. 1, 7.

43. See, e.g., Paris Court of Appeals, decision of 12 ventôse Year IX, Chenier c. Gratiot, Dev. & Car. 1791-An XII Part 2, p. 17 (discussed infra note 51); Court of Cassation, decision of 29 thermidor Year XI, Buffon c. Behemer, Dev. & Car. 1791-An XII Part 1, p .818 (reviewing the genesis of copyright law, defendant's advocate states "to advance the sciences it was necessary to encourage the savants; a very appropriate encouragement would be to assure them a private right over the printing and sales of their works").

44. Jefferson and the French revolutionaries agreed to this extent: In France too, novels, it seems, were a disfavored form of literary expression. See infra note 46.

45. For example, daily reports in *Le Moniteur Universel* often included listings of plays in current performance in various theaters. The *Feuille de correspondence du libraire*, a biweekly listing of works published in France from 1791-92, lists many dramatic works, many of these on republican or revolutionary themes. See, e.g., No. 56, *Les Citoyens français, ou le triomphe de la Révolution*," prose drama in five acts by Pierre Vaque.

46. Bureau Criminel, No. 5380.D.3, Paris, 21 Nivôse, year VII, excerpted in *RIDA* IV (July, 1954), pp. 98-99.

Not all literary expressions, however, won revolutionary approbation. Drama might help spread the Enlightenment, but novels, apparently, were considered retrograde and useless. See, e.g., Lefebvre de Villebrune, *Considérations sur le commerce de la librairie*, March 19, 1794, quoted in Hesse, "The Dilemmas of Republican Publishing, 1793-1779" (this book), p. 69.

47. See, e.g., Cass. 2 juill. 1807, Clémendot c. Giguet et Michaud, Dev. & Car. An XIII-1808 Part 1. p.406, (poem and critical essay, "L'Imagination" by Delille); Cass. 2 déc. 1808, Guillaume c. Stapleaux, Dev. & Car. An XIII-1808 Part 1, p. 609 (works of Florian, including *romans pastoraux Estelle* and *Galatée*; in his introduction to *Estelle*, the author claims to have "given a degree of usefulness to the pastoral novel").

48. Bibliographic records for the revolutionary period are incomplete, but information identifying published books and pamphlets may be garnered from *Feuille de correspondence du libraire* (1791-92); *Journal typographique et bibliographique* (from 1797); see also Adrien Jean Quentin Beuchot, *Bibliographie de la France* (Paris, Pillet, 1811-56).

49. Trib. ler arr., 19 nivôse II, Latude c. Bossange, reported in Douarche, ed., *Les Tribunaux civils de Paris pendant la Revolution (1791-1800), documents inédits recueillis avant l'incendie du Palais de Justice de 1871* (Paris 1905) [hereafter Douarche and a volume number] vol. I, p. 657. This decision was affirmed by the Trib. ler arr. 13 floréal II (Douarche I: 658 n. 2), and by the Trib. 4e arr. 8 therm. II (Douarche I: 794).

50. Cf. Trib. 3e Arr., 25 mai 1793, Douarche I: 471, Bernardin de St.-Pierre c. Prieur (infringement of *Paul et Virginie*; validating seizure, and condemning defendant to payment of the fine "prononcée par la loi," court does not state what "law" is at issue).

51. Cass. 29 therm, XI, Dev. & Car. 1791-An XII. Part 1, p. 851.

52. But the 1793 law did not alter the terms, duration, or protection for works governed by the 1777 decree. See Judgment of 16 brum. an 14, Cass. crim., [1808] 2 Dev. & Car. Part 1, p. 177; Judgment of 27 prair. an 11, Cass. crim. [1791] 1 Dev. & Car. Part 1, p. 818 (both holding that works whose 1777 decree term of protection had run were not entitled to new protection under the 1793 law).

53. See, e.g., Paris, 21 nivôse VII, Bureau Criminel No. 5380 D.3, *RIDA*, dramatic work discussed supra at n. 46; Paris, 12 vent. IX, Chénier c. Gratiot, Dev. & Car. 1791-An XII, Part 2, p. 17, (author's interest in publicly delivered speech: Chénier's advocate asserts that were speeches made in public part of the public domain, all authors would be compromised because publishers would rely on free public sources rather than paying authors for new written works); Cass. 29 therm. XII, Veuve Malassis c. Busseuil, Dev. & Car. 1791-An XII. Part 1, p. 1023, (recognizing copyright in works by clerics because of the works' value to public education).

54. Bossange c. Moutardier, Cass. 7 prair. XI, Dev. & Car. 1791-An XII. Part 1, p. 806; Cass. 28 flor. XII, Dev. & Car. 1791-An XII. Part 1, p. 971; Cass. 6 floréal XIII, Dev. & Car. An XIII-1808. Part 1, p. 103.

55. Law of July 19, 1793, Arts. 1 and 3.

56. Ibid, Art. 4 ("véritable propriétaire").

57. See France, Code of Intellectual Property, Art. L. 111-1. But see in the same Art. L. 113-5 (initial title to copyright in collective works belongs to persons or entity organizing the work's assemblage and publication).

58. 17 U.S.C. sec. 101 (1976). See Varmer, "Works Made for Hire and on Commission," in *Studies on Copyright* (Arthur Fisher mem. ed. 1963) (discussing 1909 Copyright Act and its judicial interpretation). But see in Varmer, p. 721 (asserting that older cases vested initial copyright ownership, but not authorship status in employer, citing Colliery Eng'r Co. v. United Correspondence Schools Co., 94 F. 152 (C.C.S.D.N.Y. 1899); Atwill v. Ferrett, 2 F. Cas. 195 (C.C.S.D.N.Y. 1846) (No. 640) (both vesting initial copyright ownership in employer or commissioning party).

59. Cass. 7 prair. XI, Dev. & Car. 1791-An XII. Part 1, p. 806; Bossange c. Moutardier (emphasis in original). In a later stage of the proceeding, the court rejected defendants' assertion that their edition did not infringe plaintiff's because they had not copied plaintiffs' new material, but had added their own new articles. Citing both the 1793 law and the 1777 decree, the court held that copying and revising the underlying work was also infringment. Cass. 28 floréal XII, Bossange c. Moutardier, Dev. & Car.

1791-An XII. Part 1, p. 971.  A final, procedural, aspect of the case was decided in Cass. 6 floréal XIII, Moutardier c. Bossange, Dev. & Car.  An XIII-1808. Part 1, p. 103.

60. See Birn, supra note 6.

# READING

# BOOK MARKETS AND READING IN FRANCE AT THE END OF THE OLD REGIME

*Roger Chartier*

(Translated by David Skelly and Carol Armbruster)

Historians long considered the French Revolution a result of the Enlightenment. The corpus of philosophical ideas--condemnation of fanaticism, demand for tolerance, refusal of despotism, definition of a secular morality, and reformulation of the social bond--was presented as the matrix of the revolutionary event, its necessary condition. Then, the connection between Revolution and Philosophy, political breach and intellectual innovation seemed less clear. Other phenomena were credited for inspiring the Revolution: the weak and then critical state of the economy, the bitter antagonism between a prosperous yet frustrated bourgeoisie and a nobility that obstinately maintained its privileges, or even state resistance to reforms proposed by a coalition of elites. All these theories challenged both a strictly ideological interpretation of the Revolution, that the Revolution was caused by new thoughts which appeared during the eighteenth century, and a naively teleological one, that the Enlightenment inevitably led to the Revolution.

Research on the cultural origins of the Revolution, or rather, on the conditions that made the break with an absolute monarchy and a hierarchical society conceivable and possible, is currently the dominant research on the origins of the revolutionary upheaval. When, how, and why could the beliefs that formed the foundation of the Old Regime--from reverence of the sanctity of the king to respect for the hierarchy of orders and estates, from accepting government by secrecy and councils to loyalty to the Church--be weakened and then destroyed? Were books responsible for this change of thought and sensibility? Or, more generally, was it all the printed materials denouncing the fundamental myths of monarchy that were circulated throughout the kingdom? Which texts were most frequently read? Which had the widest distribution? The eighteenth-century Enlightenment has long been understood as the canon of French writers from Montesquieu to Voltaire, from Diderot to Rousseau.

But contemporary readers liked other writers as well.  They liked popularizers who are completely unknown to us today and pamphleteers who were as fierce as they were marginalized in the great Republic of Letters.  Wasn't frequent contact with these writers more responsible for the new defiance of authority, for demanding freedom, and for giving primacy to self-cultivation and the common good?

This chapter will examine the hypothesis that prerevolutionary shaping of public opinion should be conceived as the internalization by ever more numerous readers of the ideas, images, and criticisms contained in philosophical texts.  Such is the classic model we know from Tocqueville,[1] Taine,[2] and Mornet.[3]  It suggests that the French of the eighteenth century brought on the Revolution because what they read profoundly transformed their ways of thinking and living.  By spreading an abstract discourse far removed from practical affairs and everyday living, by violently denouncing authority in all its manifestations, by submitting religion and politics to public debate, where previously they had always been exempt from rational examination, it is assumed that the new books freed their readers from the old order and made it possible for them to conceive of a new one.

This theory implies that the act of reading transforms the reader into what the text wants him or her to be.  A philosophical text is thus presumed capable of inscribing, or perhaps we should say "imprinting," new, subversive, and destructive ideas onto the mind of the reader.  Recent scholarship that proposed to reevaluate the connection between the circulation of printed materials and the mythic and symbolic disenchantment with the monarchy appears to be based on the same premise.  By broadening the definition of "philosophical" books, describing them as they were understood by eighteenth-century publishers, police, and readers, and by discerning a radicalization of clandestine literature during the last two or three decades of the Old Regime, as well as an increase in its general distribution throughout the kingdom, Robert Darnton has accustomed us to relate the undoing of the whole monarchical propaganda machine to the critical effectiveness of texts circulating covertly but on a very broad scale.  We would like to discuss here the concept of reading implied by such a hypothesis, starting with the conflict that is at the very core of the history of books and reading in the Age of Enlightenment.  How can we understand reading as a free, creative activity, in no way subject to the text in hand, and maintain that reading philosophical books was the major cause of throwing off old habits of obedience and formulating wholly new aspirations?

A large body of data clearly indicates three different book markets in eighteenth-century France.  The first market was for rare and unusual books, and it functioned much like the art market.  There were multiple public sales, and certain dealers specialized in the trade.  Sales catalogs gave precise information about the rarity, state, and provenance of the works up for auction.

Collectors valued books differently than scholars and men of letters, who (following the humanistic and encyclopedic traditions of the great libraries of the legal professions) valued editions according to their texts, commentaries, manageability, and legibility.

Rather than on the intellectual value of a book, the value of rare and unusual books was based on particular characteristics of a book, its age, origin (Elzevir or Aldine editions), subject matter (Gothic antiquities, tales of chivalry, or heterodox writings, particularly prized by eighteenth-century collectors), or material (books printed on vellum). Individual copies were distinguished by their bindings, especially embellished or well-preserved binding. A primary book market was established to cater to an aristocratic and wealthy clientele who wished to build special collections unlike the working libraries used by men of letters. This market expanded throughout the century.[4] Reading the text in this book market was only one way, and often a less important one, of relating to the book.

The second book market, based on new books, was much broader in scope. The lack of change in the book manufacturing process, however, the "typographical Old Regime," worked against the expansion of this market. At the end of the eighteenth century, the basic structure, if not the size, of the printer's workshop was much the same as it had been in the fifteenth century. It depended on the same technology (composition in movable type and printing with the hand press), and it had the same problems of paper supply (still the single largest expense in the printing of a book), hiring enough workers for a job, and coordinating the work of the typesetters with that of the pressmen. Innovations that might have modified the organization of composition ("concurrent output" at the end of the sixteenth century, where typographers and pressmen worked on several works at the same time independently of one another, then the companionship system *(paquet)* in the eighteenth century, which joined the work of a team leader, responsible for the definitive makeup, and that of a team of workers who simply supplied him with the raw sheets) had no profound effects on either the manner or the efficiency of the work.

In addition, from the mid-fifteenth century to the beginning of the nineteenth publishing was controlled by commercial capital. Publishers-booksellers *(marchands-libraires)* sought, and frequently obtained, the protection of officials who granted *permissions*, monopolies and patronage. They controlled the master printers, ordering them what to print, and they developed a book trade based on selling their own publications as well as those of their colleagues which they acquired by exchange, a *librairie d'assortiment*.

The lack of technological development and the domination of publishing by the demands of book trade capitalism allowed for a very limited number of copies in a pressrun, usually between one and two thousand copies. Fonts were expensive, and publishers could ill afford to leave the few they owned idle for any length of time. Inventory was also expensive to maintain. Increasing the number of copies using the technology of the time reduced only to a negligible degree the cost per page. These factors may explain the long-term small runs, a prime obstacle to the diffusion of books.[5]

There is some indication, however, of an expansion in the market for new books. First, there was an annual increase in the number of French-language works published, legally or illegally, within and outside the kingdom. From the beginning of the eighteenth century, when about a thousand books were published, until 1765 or 1775 production increased three, perhaps four, times.[6] Increased production was in response to increased demand. In the course of the century the percentage of book owners, particularly among urban artisans and small merchants, increased, as did the size of private libraries at all social levels. In Paris, for example, 40 percent of the domestics and 35 percent of the craftsmen and day laborers owned books in 1780, as opposed to 30 percent and 13 percent respectively at the beginning of the century. In cities in the west of France from the late seventeenth to the mid-eighteenth centuries, the percentage of estate inventories listing books, increased from 10 to 25 percent for legacies of less than 500 livres tournois and from less than 30 percent to more than 40 percent for legacies of between 500 and 1,000 livres tournois. These figures illustrate the increase in secular ownership of the privately owned book.[7]

Buying books was not the only means of access to them. Readers who could not afford books had access to them in two types of institutions. The great libraries (royal, religious, university, academic, or private) were open to varying degrees to scholars and men of letters. Beginning in 1760, bookshops created more and more lending libraries where, for an annual subscription of 10 to 12 livres, newspapers and gazettes, large and expensive reference works, and the most recent philosophical and literary works could be read or borrowed. These lending libraries left very few records, but a preliminary survey lists 49 of them between 1759 and 1789. These popular libraries seemed to attract a large clientele from among the liberal professions, as well as among businessmen, students, teachers, and even artisans. By acquiring multiple copies of the most popular works and offering their subscribers between one and three thousand titles, lending libraries constituted an essential relay station in the book market at the end of the Old Regime. They were able to satisfy the demands of readers unable to afford the costly subscriptions of newspapers or to buy all the books they wanted to use.[8]

For the more famous books of the century, there were two ways in which the printer-bookdealers worked against the constraints on production. They increased the number of editions, either authorized or pirated, and published more than the usual number of copies. The publication of the *Encyclopédie* is an example.[9] Between 1751 and 1782 there were six editions of the original text on the European market. There was the Paris edition begun in 1751 and not completed until 1772; the two pirated Italian editions from

Lucca and Leghorn; the Geneva edition printed by Cramer for a consortium centered around Panckoucke (all folio editions); the quarto edition printed in 1777 by Panckoucke, the Société Typographique de Neuchâtel, and a bookseller from Lyons, Joseph Duplain; and, finally, the octavo edition announced for the same year, 1777, by the typographical societies of Lausanne and Bern (Sociétés Typographiques de Berne et de Lausanne). All in all--and not counting F.-B. de Félice's "protestantized" edition published in Yverdon, nor the *Encyclopédie méthodique* put in the works by Panckoucke in 1782-- there were about 24,000 copies of Diderot and d'Alembert's book circulating in eighteenth-century Europe, about half this number in the Kingdom of France.

If the number seems high, it is because there was an unusually large number of printings of several of these editions. Of the Paris folio, 4,225 copies were printed, 5,500 to 6,000 of the Lausanne/Berne octavo, and 8,525 of the Neuchâtel quarto. Taking into account losses and defective copies, there were 8,011 sets available of this last edition issued in 36 volumes. A printing of that size, spread out over two or three editions, requires a considerable initial investment (covered in part by subscriptions), mobilization of about 20 printshops in Geneva, Neuchâtel, and the area around Lyons, and the use of 100 printing presses. The enterprise stood a chance of succeeding only under condition of receiving licenses (protections) and privileges. It was thanks to the powerful support that Panckoucke had in the ministry, the Direction de la Librairie, and in the offices of the lieutenant general of the police, and even in Lyons that the quarto edition was printed in France with complete impunity, even though the *permission* for the work was withdrawn in 1759, and the commercial threat represented by the cheaper octavo edition could be averted. The publishers, suffering losses from official confiscations, preferred to abandon the market in France before dealing, in 1780, with the quarto consortium. This "War of the *Encyclopédies*" and the large number of printings amply attest to the expansion of the French book market and its avid search of new titles. Format reduction allowed the publishers of the quarto edition to lower the subscription price of the work from 980 livres, the price of the Paris edition, to 394 livres. This gave them a large clientele among the traditional elites (military nobles, justice/police officials, clerics, men of law and government), and also encouraged book dealers to purchase copies for literary lending libraries. A market was thus created for the *philosophical* book, and this, in turn, assured the success of these large publishing speculations. A third book market reached an even wider public. Inexpensive editions of texts first published for a more moneyed and therefore more limited clientele were made available. Printed with worn-out and ill-matched types, illustrated with worn-out woodcuts, bound with blue, black, red, or marbled paper, these cheap editions were invented by provincial book dealers in the second half of the sixteenth century, for example, Benoît Rigaud of Lyons and Claude Garnier of Troyes.[10]   As of the early seventeenth century, first of all in Troyes, then in Rouen, and later, in several provincial cities and in Avignon, printer-booksellers specialized in this sort of trade, without, however, totally abandoning the more traditional book trade.

Although there was more than one way to distribute these works, colportage was by far the most effective.  Malesherbes, in the fourth of his five *Mémoires* on the book trade written between 1758 and 1759, notes colportage among the dangers and the usefulness of all trade in printed material that exceeded the fundamental principle of the February 28, 1723, Réglement du Conseil (known as the Code de la Librairie):  "It is forbidden to any person, of whatever profession or social status, other than book dealers and printers, to trade in books."  Malesherbes, who was directeur de la Librairie at the time, lists four classes of book dealers not conforming to the regulations. The first two were subject to the rules and regulations set down in the Code de la Librairie, which was drawn up for the capital, but extended in practice to provincial cities as well.  There were first the "sack carriers," or so-called "notions merchants," "vulgar persons from the city of Paris," whose trafficking was limited to "abc books, almanacs, and small devotional books printed outside said city."  There were secondly the "peddlers and billposters," listed in the registry of the community of book dealers and printers.  They were identified by a "leather badge or shield pinned to the front of their clothing and on which shall be written the word: colporteur," and who are authorized to sell "edicts, declarations, ordinances, rulings, or other legal mandates whose publication shall have been decreed, almanacs, and tariffs, and also small books not to exceed eight sheets, paperbound, and sewn/tied with string, printed with permission and privilege by printers in Paris only, with the name of the dealer."

The last two categories are not specifically mentioned in the regulations, but they were nonetheless tolerated by the police.  In Paris there were "booksellers who go from house to house and are commonly called colporteurs."  Since bookstores had to be established near either the university or the Palais Royal, Malesherbes notes that "we have been unable to prevent a large number of people of no rank from getting involved in the sale of used books."  In the provinces there were large numbers of "itinerant merchants displaying books at fairs, in markets, and on the streets of small towns.  They sell on the great highways; they even get into the châteaux and display their wares there.  In short, they trade so openly that you would hardly believe they have no licence."  These "stallkeepers" were no more specialized in specific types of book than were the secondhand dealers in Paris.  We can assume that both supplied their customers with the same titles as did the bookdealers (of new books).[11]

This study, which Malesherbes concludes by stating the need to licence all forms of book peddling, reveals two important facts.  First, book peddling was overwhelmingly, if belatedly, an urban phenomenon. For all books and printed material, the primary market was the urban populations, where literacy was more widespread and of longer tradition. Before they were distributed in any great number in the countryside, the cheaper editions of Troyes were first sold in cities, and, first and foremost, in the biggest city of all: Paris. The Oudot and Garnier families, major publishers of these editions, established members of their families in Paris and maintained close relations with their fellow bookdealers. Secondly, Malesherbes's inventory underscores the great variety of printed materials that was hawked from the sacks and trunks of these itinerant merchants. There were almanacs, abcs, small paperbacks (eight sheets in octavo format yielding 128 pages), official items, and what the 1723 Code de la Librairie calls "defamatory pamphlets, articles against the government and religion."

Book colportage dealt in more than just the *livres bleus* of a Garnier or an Oudot, and it was not oriented exclusively toward a popular or rural public. It had two markets. One market was made up of notables who could not, or would not, buy the very latest work from bookdealers. The other was made up of people who were less skilled, had less money, and whose abilities and expectations could only be satisfied by publications specifically, but not exclusively, intended for them. These editions were inexpensive, easy to handle and to understand. The *marchands forains*, equipped with cart and horse, were the privileged agents in the first market. During the 1770s Noël Gille, nicknamed La Pistole, went around in his two-horse wagon selling to the notables of town and country (or resold to a whole swarm of fellow colporteurs) philosophical books that he ordered from, among others, the Société Typographique de Neuchâtel. These included the works of Helvétius, d'Holbach, Voltaire, and Rousseau, anti-religious satires, and politico-pornographic lampoons.[12] The *merciers*, with their packs on their backs or slung across their shoulders attended to a more working-class clientele. They offered a mélange of chapbooks and white linens, ribbons and cloth, gifts and necessities. Just as Autolycus in *The Winter's Tale* mingles notions and ballads in his pack,[13] the merchants who went to Troyes for supplies stocked up on cheap editions and sewing needs. By way of defending the printshop that was being threatened by the widow of Jean Oudot IV, the city aldermen declared that "the greater part of the notions trade in Troyes is done by back packers who come to supply themselves with Bibliothèque bleue."[14]

For all these readers, book production changed in the most basic ways. Records of the requests for public licenses *(permissions* or *permissions simples)* indicate the decline and then collapse of the market for religious works. Whereas religious titles of all kinds constituted half the printed production in Paris at the end of the seventeenth century, and still a third of it in the 1720s, they amounted to only about a fourth of the titles in the early 1750s and a mere tenth in the 1780s. Other large subject categories such as law, history, and belles-lettres retained throughout the century the same percentage of the production. The arts and sciences, however, benefitted the most from the decrease of theological, liturgical, and devotional works, doubling their percentage between 1720 and 1780. The majority of the *permissions tacites* were granted for the arts and sciences, increasing from only one fourth of the requests in the 1750s to more than 40 percent in the early 1780s. They were surpassed by the sciences for *permissions du sceau* and by politics for *permissions tacites* (permissions granted by the directeur de la Librairie without involving the chancellor's authority and registered under the false rubric: "works printed abroad whose distribution in France is not prohibited"). The arts and sciences offered its readers accumulations of knowledge, but also critical perspectives and reformist viewpoints.[15]

Books published under the protection of a *permission*, whether *publique* or *tacite*, constituted, however, only part of the books offered to the French public in the eighteenth century. Philosophical books, printed by typographical societies in Switzerland or the German principalities on the periphery of France and smuggled in and sold under the cloak, were widely circulated throughout the kingdom. Works designated as *philosophical* in business correspondence and secret catalogs were something of a mixed bag, but can be divided into three groups. First, there were texts that were philosophical in the sense in which we usually understand the term, that is, those which submit morality and political beliefs and authority to critical analysis. Second, there was pornographic literature, still offering a strong traditional fare as well as new titles. Finally, there was a whole series of satires, *libelles*, and *chroniques scandaleuses* whose sensational and often salacious accounts denounced the arbitrariness and corruption of the establishment. These philosophical books, known to the police as *harmful books*, were a dangerous business. Anyone caught carrying them, stocking them, or distributing them ran enormous risks: confiscation, imprisonment in the Bastille, or being sent to the galleys. Publishers outside the jurisdication of French authorities ran the risk of calling down the wrath of the Protestant authorities who governed them. Hence the ruses required either to elude surveillance or to corrupt the authorities, and hence, as well, the high price of philosophical books, which were generally twice as expensive as others.[16]

The size of this illicit output has long been underestimated in studies aimed at reconstructing book circulation by quantitative treatment of administrative archives--the lists of actual permissions to print--or library inventories compiled by lawyers when they were evaluating bequests. The first excluded all titles for which publishers would not have dreamed of requesting a *permission* (even a tacit one). The second never included certain titles, zealous heirs having expunged them before the inventory was even done to preserve the reputation of the deceased.

Records of public permissions thus indicate only a part of what eighteenth-century readers could have read. For the year 1764, for example, of some 1,548 titles published in French that year and still preserved today, only 40 percent are listed in the requests for permission to publish--*permission de sceau* or *permissions tacites*--addressed to the directeur de la Librairie. Nearly two thirds of the books, therefore, were printed with a secret or verbal authorization, with no authorization at all, or in violation of the law.[17] Publishers outside the kingdom took the lion's share of the market for illicit books, and, according to Robert Darnton, "it is quite possible that the majority of French books produced during the second half of the century came from presses outside France."[18]

There were two kinds of illegal publications--prohibited and pirated-- and the authorities distinguished between them when they confiscated materials entering Paris. Prohibited materials were confiscated and later destroyed. Pirated editions, defined in the *Encyclopédie* as "printed by one person to the detriment of another to whom had been ceded the right of ownership by the author; property made public and authorized by the King's privilege, or equivalent judicial authorization" were either returned to sender or remanded to the publisher holding the privilege to be sold for his own profit. The distinction between the two categories was well known in the book trade. Foreign publishers compiled two sales catalogs, an openly circulated catalog for pirated editions and a clandestine one for philosophical books. Smugglers knew that they ran different risks for different publications. And readers certainly knew the difference between pirated editions--illegal reprints of books that had been officially sanctioned--and prohibited books, which circulated in defiance of the board of censors.[19]

The question arises as to whether the large quantities of illegal publications brought into France consisted mainly of lampoons and pamphlets that are today entirely forgotten or of the texts which tradition has considered the very heart of Enlightenment philosophy. Until the end of the Old Regime philosophical treatises and pornographic-political writing were associated with each other in the booktrade and its official control. The *Livres philosophiques* catalog offered by the Société Typographique de Neuchâtel in 1775 includes among its 110 entries numerous titles of licentious satire as well as political pamphlets and chronicles.[20] It lists 15 pornography titles, including all the ancient and modern classics of the genre from the translation of Aretino's *La Putain errante* to *Thérèse philosophe*, from *Venus dans le cloître, ou la religieuse en chemise*, to the *Histoire de dom B\*\*\*, portier des chartreux*, to its pendant, the *Histoire de la tourière des carmélites*. In the political satire category, the *Mémoires authentiques de Mme la comtesse Du Barry* (London, 1772) is listed with multivolume series such as the six volume *L'Espion chinois* or the *Journal historique de la révolution opérée dans la constitution de la monarchie française* by M. de Maupeou, by Pidansat de Mairobert and

Mouffle d'Angerville (three volumes listed in the catalog; it was later completed in seven).

What is most striking about the catalog is how well represented the philosophes are. The whole foundation for the new thinking is there, with Fontenelle (if the work offered under the title *La République des incrédules* is the same as *La République des philosophes*, one of Fontanelle's posthumous works), Boulainvilliers, Hobbes (d'Holbach's translation of Hobbes's *Essay on Human Nature*), and Bayle (the eight-volume *Analyse raisonnée* of his works by François-Marie de Marsy and Jean-Baptiste-René Robinet). Also listed are Diderot (the *Lettre sur les aveugles*, the *Lettre sur les sourds et muets*, and *Les Bijoux indiscrets*), Rousseau (*Du Contrat social* and *Oeuvres diverses*), the popularizers of the Enlightenment (Raynal, Du Laurens, Mercier, Bordes), as well as the materialist current (four titles by Helvétius, including *De l'Esprit*, La Mettrie's *Oeuvres philosophiques* and, most important, 14 works written or translated by d'Holbach). But the author who dominates the catalog with 31 titles is Voltaire, from the *Lettres philosophiques* of 1734, the *Romans et contes philosophiques*, and the *Questions sur l'Encyclopédie* published in the early 1770s.

Voltaire is also the best represented author in the the catalog compiled by the Parisian bookdealer Poinçot between June and September of 1790. Poinçot had been commissioned to inventory the books remaining in the Bastille after the last official pulping of books in the Old Regime in 1785.[21] Poinçot was commissioned to do the inventory after he pointed out that it "was possible for the City to profit from that heap of printed materials, piled up in no order whatsoever and which would be ruined by the humidity and dust if someone did not get them out of there quickly."[22] The catalog consists of four inventories listing 564 entries corresponding to 393 different titles. The list includes books confiscated during the five years preceding the Revolution as well as a number of new titles. In the pornography category, for example, there is *La Foutromanie, poème lubrique* by Sénac de Meilhan (Sardanapolis, 1780), Mirabeau's *Errotika Biblion* (Rome: Vatican Press, 1783), or *Le Rideau levé, ou l'éducation de Laure*, (Cytheria, 1786). In the pamphlet category, there are the *libelles* aimed at the queen (*Les Amours de Charlot et de Toinette*, 1779, or the *Essais historiques sur la vie de Marie-Antoinette d'Autriche, reine de France*, 1781).

As in the catalog of the Société Typographique de Neuchâtel, the works of the Philosophes found in the Bastille were classified with the more scandalous books. At the top of the list is Voltaire, who had 18 works impounded in the Bastille in 1790, followed by d'Holbach with eight titles, Rousseau with four titles (among them *Du Contrat social*, the *Discours sur l'origine et les fondements de l'inégalité parmi les hommes*, and *Emile*) and Helvétius, Diderot, Condorcet, Raynal, and Mercier, each with one or two titles. There may have been only seven prisoners in the Bastille on July 14,

1789, but all the classics of the Enlightenment were there--all victims of the board of censors and the royal police.

Literary production was basically divided into two categories. As in Voltaire's diatribes, authors considered worthy of the name were distinguished from hacks belonging to that "unfortunate species who write in order to live." The distinction was not always obvious in the kinds and quality of their publications, but it allowed the disdain for "gutter literature" to serve as the very symbol of a writer's quality. It also gave a writer the upper hand in literary rivalries, by contrasting the frustrated ambitions of the "gutter Rousseaus" with the comfortable situations enjoyed by established philosophes.[23]

Philosophical works, on the other hand, were considered a sort of special literary corpus existing within the total literary production, and either sold or suppressed, they were all valued equally. They were either profitable or met with an unfortunate end. Their censure made them appealing; their irreverence and disobedience made them seductive. The grouping into one category of a quite varied corpus of material was not only a phenomenon imposed by the trade, the police, or readers. It began in the writing of them. Even the most esteemed authors thought nothing of using the most common forms of gutter literature. Voltaire, for example, was an old master in both using and subverting the defamatory lampoon, the antireligious satire, and the political pamphlet, and used pseudonyms, false attributions, and false signatures. Genres intermingled. A philosophical discourse could include pornography, sometimes even in the title as in *Thérèse philosophe*, or the *Mémoires pour servir à l'histoire du P. Dirrag et de Mlle Eradice*. The *genre licencieux* was also not beneath the philosophes, as we see in Voltaire's *Maid of Orleans* and Diderot's *Les Bijoux indiscrets*, published in Monomotapa in 1748. The very free use of forms and motifs undoubtedly reinforced the habit of categorizing together different philosophical books. Should we, then, consider them all torches that lighted the revolutionary conflagration?

Most assuredly, according to Robert Darnton. He believes that the large-scale distribution of this critical, denunciatory literature, whose flow and violence grew in the last two decades of the Old Regime, had an indisputably profound effect on the portrayal of the monarchy, undermining its founding myths, mocking the rituals which were its expression, and accustoming the French to thinking of themselves as victims of an arbitrary and debased government. The philosophical books would thus have produced a veritable "ideological erosion," which, no matter what their intent, laid the groundwork for the revolutionary breach: "The political tracts worked a dozen variations on a single theme: the monarchy had degenerated into despotism. They did not call for a revolution or foresee 1789 or even provide much discussion of the deeper social and political issues that were to make the destruction of the monarchy possible. Inadvertently, however, they prepared for that event by desacralizing the symbols and deflating the myths that had made the monarchy appear legitimate in the eye of its subjects."[24]  In other words, there was a direct link between the deep interpenetration of these prohibited, scathing, and defamatory works and the depletion of the belief systems that had guaranteed the king the love and respect of his people.

This theory seems to attribute a questionable power to literature.  The contemporary observations of Louis-Sébastien Mercier, whose *L'An 2440* and *Tableau de Paris* were included on the list of prohibited authors, seriously question the role of denunciatory writings.  He notes, first of all, the limited social milieux in which these writings were circulated, milieux that were much narrower than for, say, obscene prints.  "Philosophical books have been dealt with quite harshly, although they are read by a very small number of people and the masses are quite incapable of understanding them.  It is pornographic prints that are carrying the day with the public.  The eye is immediately arrested by them: innocence is disturbed, modesty blushes."[25]  The interest they inspired was very short-lived: "What lampoon has not been condemned by public opinion after two weeks and abandoned to its own infamy?"[26]  Finally, there was public reaction, far from willing to take the literature seriously.  "Formerly it was common enough to find posters criticizing current affairs. . . . Caricatures of this type are no longer put up on the walls, they have gone into pamphlets which are distributed clandestinely. . . .  The only satire is now to be found in these pamphlets; high society is amused by them, without, however, placing too much credence in them."[27]  Far from postulating that readers of philosophical works accepted completely the perceptions that the texts were intended to impose, Louis-Sébastien Mercier describes the act of reading them in terms reminiscent of the categories set up by the English sociologist Richard Hoggart.  Hoggart characterizes the ambiguities of contemporary popular reading, which believes without believing, maintains a skeptical distance even while giving support, and loves to be persuaded without wanting to rely on anything too seriously.[28]  The images conveyed by lampoons and pamphlets were not engraved in readers' minds as if these were so much soft wax, and reading does not necessarily imply believing.  If a link exists between the wide distribution of an aggressively disrespectful satirical literature and the ruin of the monarchy's image, it is neither direct nor inevitable.

Readers who were to make very different choices during the Revolution read many of the same philosophical texts.  Rousseau, for example, was avidly read by all social classes.  He was well known and loved by the urban lower classes.  In his *Journal de ma vie*, the journeyman glazier Jacques-Louis Ménétra cites only six works.  Three of them were written by Rousseau: *Du Contrat social*, *Emile*, and *La Nouvelle Héloïse*.  Ménétra claimed to have been one of Rousseau's friends during his last stay in Paris between 1770 and 1778: "We go to the Café Régence He asked for a pitcher of beer He asks me if I know how to play chess I reply no He asks me if I know how to play checkers I say yes a little he says well you're young We play I lose I hear and I see the people around us who never stop saying Why it's Rousseau and that must be his brother."[29]  The fervent Rousseauism of Parisian sans-culottes, fed by jacobin speeches, the radical press, and the deification of the author has its roots in the preferences of some of the most working- class readers of the Old Regime.

Readers at the other end of the social ladder, the aristocracy, were equally enthusiastic about Rousseau.  Nobles at court, in the military, and in the provinces represented 36 percent of Rousseau's correspondence, the same percentage represented by the third estate.[30]  Rousseau was memorialized in the Ermenonville gardens, where, at the invitation of the Marquis de Girardin, the most brilliant names in the French and European aristocracy came to pay homage.  Even counter-revolutionary émigrés were devoted to him, in spite of the Revolution and in spite of the *Contrat social*.[31]  In the letters written by La Rochelle merchant Jean Ranson to Ostervald, a director of the Société Typographique de Neuchâtel, we see that Rousseau was also the favorite author of the commercial bourgeoisie.[32]  Rousseau was considered a guide in intellectual matters and in life.  The same Rousseau--his works and even more, his person, guarantor of the truth he proclaimed--was read in different, often contradictory, ways and led to opposing commitments during the Revolution.

The *Encyclopédie* offers a similar example.  When subscribers can be identified (as they can in Besançon or the Franche-Comté for the Neuchâtel quarto edition), we can see two things.  First, it is obvious that the high price, even for the smaller format, limited sales to the well-to-do.  The real buying public for the *Encyclopédie* was the traditional elites--the clergy, military, nobility, parliamentary magistrates, the law, and the liberal professions.  Merchants constituted only a small minority.    Second, although some purchasers were resolutely committed to the Revolution, the majority was undoubtedly indifferent or even hostile to it.[33]  Buying a subscription to the book which was emblematic of the Enlightenment did not necessarily imply any community of choice or action among its readers.  Its great presence in the circles most intimately connected to the government of the Old Regime signified to no greater degree any radical break with their traditional way of thinking their social world.

The books of the émigrés and those who were sentenced to death, confiscated by the revolutionary authorities after 1792, bear witness to the strong, if belated, adherence to the philosophical corpus on the part of those who were victims or enemies of the Revolution.  Their reading was not fundamentally different from that of the most committed revolutionaries.  When he went to prison, Maréchal de Broglie took Buffon and the *Encyclopédie* with him.  In the Temple, Louis XVI read Montesquieu and Voltaire as much as he did Corneille and La Fontaine.[34]  This confirms

Toqueville's intuition ("basically, all those placed above the masses are alike; they have the same ideas, the same habits and tastes; they indulge in the same pleasures, *read the same books*, speak the same language,"[35] and keep us from attributing too much of a direct power to books. New ideas are not imprinted all by themselves in the reader's mind. They can be used and interpreted differently. It is thus too risky to credit the indisputable success of the philosophical books with alienation from the king and the monarchy.

Moreover, disaffection with the sovereign did not necessarily result from intellectual activity. More common phenomena, such as popular gestures, words, and expressions may have played a greater role. Mercier points out that because such phenomena were widespread and used unconsciously, even by him, they were all the more effective. An example is the use of the expression *à la royale*. "A common expression, frequently used. Boeuf *à la royale*, cakes *à la royale*, doormats *à la royale*; restauranteurs put the expression in gold letters above the doors of their establishments, the butcher sells hams and sausages *à la royale*, everywhere you see fleur-de-lys crowning *chickens, gloves, boots,* and *booties,* the tea sellers cry '*à la royale!*'" Hostility toward the monarchy is not conveyed in these examples. On the contrary, as Mercier remarks, "*à la royale* is a figurative way of saying *good, excellent, superb,* because the masses cannot conceive that anything mediocre, of whatever kind, could be so bold as to approach the court."[36] It is the common use of the attributes and symbols of royalty that strips them of any transcendent meaning.

"At the ironmongers on the Quai de la Mégisserie there are shops selling *old signs*, suitable to decorate the entrances of all the inns and smoke-filled bars in all the working-class districts and outlying suburbs of Paris. There, all the kings on earth repose together: Louis XVI and George III embrace fraternally; the King of Prussia sleeps with the Empress of Russia, the Emperor is at the same level as his electors; there, at last, the crown and the turban mingle. The proprietor of a bar comes on the scene, moves all these crowned heads around with his foot, examines them, takes at random the image of the King of Poland, carries it off, hangs it up and writes underneath: 'au Grand Vainqueur.'"[37] This act, real or imagined, shows how the image of royal majesty no longer required any particular reverence, elicited no awe. It leads us to suggest another relationship between changes in sensibility and large-scale circulation of texts which weakened royal authority.

From 1750 at the latest, harmful discourses had proliferated attacking the king, his person, his authority, his physical body as much as his body politic. In Paris, journalists and police agents collected large numbers of spontaneous remarks, handwritten posters pasted to walls, all the rebellious gestures attesting that old representations of the sacred and revered king had lost their efficacy. The process of symbolic disenchantment with the monarchy begun during periods of high emotion, such as immediately after the kidnappings in 1750, or the liberalization of the grain trade in 1768, and fueled by the Jansenist message progressively damaged the royal image. Conduct showing respect to or love of the king faded with the unpopular Louis XV, and the habit spread of talking and acting with no reverence at all for the mysteries of monarchy.[38] The success of the philosophical books may be attributable to an affective rift between the king and his people which made them not only acceptable but expected. We may need to look at these books as the result rather than the cause of such a breach.

That is the main reason for questioning the power so often attributed to philosophical writings. There is, however, a second one. Although these texts, particularly the political lampoons, were actually machines producing effects, the manner in which they worked is always explained in terms of expectations, interpretive tools, and levels of comprehension. These can vary from reader to reader or cause one and the same reader to respond to the same text in different and contradictory ways. There is the danger of reading philosophical literature *backward*, reading it retrospectively of the revolutionary event, and attributing to it an unequivocal meaning, either denunciatory or persuasive. Eighteenth-century readers did not necessarily believe everything they read, such as the arbitrariness of a monarchy which had become despotic or the depravity of the king and his court. Nor did their suspension of belief diminish in any way their appetite for forbidden books.

Pornographic lampoons, for example, depicted people in high places, the court favorites, and the king and queen. Such texts speak on several levels and call for multiple interpretations. First of all, they follow the traditional conventions of erotica: the use of a codified vocabulary to describe sexual pleasure, the play with the literary forms of the age--although with rather startling contents--and a point of view presumed to be that of the reader. In the political lampoon, however, these recognizable devices are used to transcend them. The message is, nevertheless, not immediately clear. For example, the first lampoons of Marie-Antoinette (*Les Amours de Charlot et de Toinette* or the *Essais historiques sur la vie de Marie-Antoinette d' Autriche, reine de France*), which like the *mazarinades* of more than a century before,[39] were not necessarily meant to persuade the reader to believe that the queen was really what they said she was, but rather, in discrediting her, to justify her adversaries at court. For readers who knew about the struggles in the court, the significance of such texts was not to be found in what they said literally, but in the effects they were intended to produce on court politics. Other readers might be more easily led to believe accusations brought against a queen who had been described as being ruled by her senses and negligent of her duties. A set of themes was thus established which revolutionary pamphleteers were to amplify after 1789, tirelessly merging the image of a rapacious and bloodthirsty queen with that of a lascivious and depraved woman.[40] These different perspectives, conferring a different status on the same text were in some respects set up by the philosophical books themselves. Different genres, motifs, and registers (political denunciation, pornographic description, philosophical reflection) were intermingled. Plurality was written into the texts, a fact that makes it difficult to believe that all readers read the texts in the same way, or that the reading of them can be reduced to one simple ideological statement.

What importance should be attributed to the circulation of printed material in the intellectual and affective changes that made the radical break with absolute monarchy and hierarchical society possible and comprehensible? Should we not focus on the changes that profoundly modified ways of reading rather than on the numerous critical and denunciatory attitudes expressed in such a variety of philosophical books? For Germany of the second half of the eighteenth century, the hypothesis of a *Leserevolution* has been proposed.[41] A new manner of reading could be recognized by several outward signs: a more mobile reader confronted with more numerous and less durable texts, the individualization of reading, reading in silent and solitary privacy, the divestment of reading of its religious overtones. A freer, more casual and critical reading succeeded the communal and respectful relation to books, which had been sustained by reverence and obedience.

This thesis is debatable. The traditional way of reading did not disappear in the age of "extensive" reading. The most common reader, accustomed to the colporteur's books, was still dominated by traditional habits: the same books, few in number, were read and reread, memorized and recited, and were often shared in group reading. Also, the French love of sentimental novels and the German vogue of pre-Romantic works conferred upon the reading of a literary work some of the traits characteristic of the reading of a sacred text. The book, read over and over again, is in the end known by heart. It is reading for sociability as well as for solitude; it overwhelms and transforms all who approach it.[42]

Reading practices definitely changed in France during the eighteenth century at least in the cities. With the tripling or quadrupling of book production between the turn of the century and the 1780s, the proliferation of institutions that permitted reading without having to purchase, and the proliferation of short-lived printed commodities such as periodicals, lampoons, and pamphlets, a new way of reading became widespread which took away from books their status as authorities. A motif popular with writers and painters toward the end of the century depicting a peasant family, patriarchal and biblical, being read aloud to at eventide by the head of the household expresses nostalgia for a way of reading. In this representation of an idealized peasant existence, a favorite of the educated elite, communal reading represented a world in which the book was revered and authority respected. This image seemed to denounce a way of reading that was urban, insatiable, negligent, and skeptical.[43] Readers of the *Nouvelle Héloïse* who wrote to

Rousseau to tell him that they were indeed the kind of readers that his works required and deserved, show that their kind of reading was not communal, that in the midst of hurried and skeptical readers, they knew how to summon up attentiveness and emotion.

By entering the most ordinary situations in life, and by greedily appropriating texts quickly cast aside, reading lost the religious reference that it had long had. A new relationship to the text was established. It was disrespectful of the authorities, alternately seduced and disappointed by novelty, and, most of all, little inclined to religious belief or obedience. It was a new way of reading, rather than the contents of philosophical books, which developed a critical attitude freed of the dependency and obedience that were the basis of the traditional way of thinking. This way of reading affected all texts, even those upholding the views of the traditional political and religious establishments. The relationship between books of any kind and the Revolution is far from direct, immediate, or obvious. We must consider how an overall change in habits--including reading--and perceptions--due to reading but not exclusively--made the radical rejection of the old order of things not necessary or ineluctable, but possible and conceivable.

## NOTES

1. Alexis de Tocqueville, *L'Ancien Régime et la Révolution*, (1856) Book II, Chapter 1, "Comment vers le milieu du XVIIIe siècle, les hommes de lettres devinrent les principaux hommes politiques du pays, et les effets qui en resultèrent" (Paris: Gallimard, 1967), pp. 239-240.

2. Hippolyte Taine, "La Propagation de la doctrine" in *L'Ancien Régime*, vol. 1, book 4 of *Les Origines de la France contemporaine*, (1876; Paris: Robert Laffont, 1966), p. 205.

3. Daniel Mornet, *Les Origines intellectuelles de la Révolution française (1715-1787)* (1933; Paris: Armand Colin, 1967), p. 432.

4. Jean Viardot, "Livres rares et pratiques bibliophiliques," in *Le Livre triomphant, 1660-1830*, vol. 2 of *Histoire de l'édition française*, ed. Henri-Jean Martin and Roger Chartier (Paris: Promodis/Cercle de la Librairie, 1984), pp. 446-467; and "Naissance de la bibiliophilie: les cabinets de livres rares," in *Les Bibliothèques sous l'Ancien Régime, 1530-1789*, ed. Claude Jolly, vol. 2 of *L'Histoire des bibliothèques françaises*. Sous la direction d'André Vernet (Paris: Promodis/Cercle de la Librairie, 1988), pp. 268-289.

5. Roger Chartier, *Frenchness in the History of the Book: From the History of Publishing to the History of Reading*, The James Russel Wiggins Lectures in the History of the Book in American Culture (Worcester, Mass.: American Antiquarian Society, 1988), pp. 20-22.

6. Henri-Jean Martin, "La Librairie française en 1777-1778," *Dix-Huitième Siècle* 11 (1979), pp. 87-112, (reprinted in his *Livre français sous l'Ancien Régime* (Paris: Promodis/Cercle de la Librairie, 1987), pp. 113-129.

7. Roger Chartier, "Du livre au lire. Les pratiques citadines de l'imprimé 1660-1780," in his *Lectures et lecteurs dans la France d'Ancien Régime* (Paris: Seuil, 1987), pp. 165-222 (English trans., "Urban Reading Practices 1660-1780," in his *Cultural Uses of Print in Early Modern France*, trans. Lydia G. Cochrane [Princeton: Princeton University Press, 1987], pp. 183-239).

8. Jean-Louis Pailhès, "En marge des bibliothèques: l'apparition des cabinets de lecture," in *Les Bibliothèques sous l'Ancien Régime*, ed. Jolly, pp. 414-421.

9. Robert Darnton, *The Business of Enlightenment: A Publishing History of the Encyclopédie, 1775-1800*, (Cambridge, Mass. and London, England: Harvard University Press, 1979).

10. Jean-Paul Oddos, "Simples notes sur les origines de la bibliothèque dite bleue," in *La 'Bibliothèque bleue' nel Seicento o della Letteratura per il Popolo*, (Bari, Adriatica, Paris: Nizet, 1981), pp. 159-168; and Roger Chartier, "Livres bleus et lectures populaires," in his *Livres et lecteurs dans la France d'Ancien Regime*, pp. 247-270 (English trans., "The Bibliothèque bleue and Popular Reading," in his *Cultural Uses of Print in Early Modern France*, pp. 240-264).

11. Malesherbes, *Mémoires sur la librairie et sur la liberté de la presse*, Introduction and Notes by Graham E. Rodmell (Chapel Hill: North Carolina Studies in the Romance Languages and Literatures, 1979). (Quotations from 1973 Code de la Librairie are on p. 346 and p. 365; quotations from Malesherbes on p. 160).

12. Robert Darnton, "Un Colporteur sous l'Ancien Régime," in *Censures: De la Bible aux larmes d'Eros*, (Paris: Editions du Centre Georges Pompidou, 1987), pp. 130-139, that completes Anne Sauvy, "Noël Gille dit La Pistole, marchand forain libraire roulant par la France," *Bulletin des Bibliothèques de France* 12 (May 1967), pp. 177-190.

13. Margaret Spufford, *The Great Reclothing of Rural England: Petty Chapmen and their Wares in the Seventeenth Century* (London: Hambledon Press, 1984), pp. 8-10, 88-89, 145.

14. Quoted from Robert Mandrou, *De la Culture populaire aux XVIIe et XVIIIe siècles: La Bibliothèque bleue de Troyes* (1964, new ed.; Paris: Flammarion, 1975), pp. 41-42.

15. François Furet, "La 'Librairie' du royaume de France au 18e siècle," in *Livre et société dans la France du XVIIIe siècle*, ed. Geneviève Bollème (Paris and The Hague: Mouton, 1965), pp. 3-32 et Henri-Jean Martin, "Une Croissannce séculaire," in *Les Bibliothèques sous l'Ancien Régime*, ed. Jolly, pp. 94-103.

16. Robert Darnton, "Philosophy under the Cloak," in *Revolution in Print: The Press in France 1775-1800*, ed. Robert Darnton and Daniel Roche (Berkeley: University of California Press, in collaboration with the New York Public Library, 1989), pp. 27-49.

17. Jacqueline Artier, "Etude sur la production imprimée de l'année 1764," *Position des thèses soutenues par les élèves de la promotion de 1981*. Ecole nationale des chartes. (Paris, 1981), pp. 9-18.

18. Robert Darnton, "Le Livre prohibé aux frontières: Neuchâtel," in *Les Bibliothèques sous l'Ancien Régime*, ed. Jolly, pp. 342-359 (quotation on page 343).

19. Silvio Corsini, "La Contrefaçon de livres sous l'Ancien Régime," and Jeanne Veyrin-Forrer, "Livres arrêtés, livres estampilles: traces parisiennes de la contrefaçon," in *Les Presses grises: La contrefaçon du livre (XVIe-XIXe siècles)*, ed. François Moureau (Paris: Aux Amateurs de Livres, 1988), pp. 22-38 and pp. 101-112.

20. Robert Darnton, "Livres philosophiques," in *Enlightenment Essays in Memory of Robert Shackleton*, ed. Giles Barber and C. P. Courtney (Oxford: The Voltaire Foundation, 1988), pp. 89-107.

21. Bibliothèque de l'Arsenal, MS 10 305, "Etat des livres des pausés a St. Louis de la cultur mit en ordre par ordre de m.m. les commissaires commancé le 14 juillet 1790 par Poinçot."

22. Report sent to the mayor of Paris on October 19, 1790, quoted in Frantz Funck-Brentano, *Archives de la Bastille* vol. 1 (Paris, 1892-1894), p. xlv.

23. Robert Darnton, "The High Enlightenment and the Low-Life of Literature in Pre-Revolutionary France," *Past and Present* 51 (May 1971), pp. 81-115.

24. Robert Darnton, "A Clandestine Bookseller in the Provinces," in his *Literary Underground of the Old Regime* (Cambridge, Mass. and London, England: Harvard University Press, 1982), pp. 122-147 (quotation on page 147).

25. Louis-Sébastien Mercier, *Tableau de Paris*, vol. 6, new ed., revised and expanded (Amsterdam, 1782-83), "Estampes licencieuses," pp. 92-94, (quotation on page 94).

26. Ibid., vol. 7, "Libelles," pp. 22-28 (quotation on pp. 22-23).

27. Ibid., vol. 6, "Placards," pp. 85-89.

28. Richard Hoggart, *The Uses of Literacy: Aspects of Working-Class Life with Special Reference to Publications and Entertainments* (London: Chatto and Windus, 1957).

29. *Journal de ma vie. Jacques-Louis Ménétra, compagnon vitrier au 18e siècle*, introduction and commentary by Daniel Roche, (Paris: Montalba, 1982), pp. 218-222 and p. 300 (English trans., *Journal of My Life*, by Jacques-Louis Ménétra, with an introduction and commentary by Daniel Roche, trans.

Arthur Goldhammer, foreword by Robert Darnton, [New York: Columbia University Press, 1986], pp. 181-184 and 255).

30. Daniel Roche, "Les Primitifs du rousseauisme. Une analyse sociologique quantitative de la correspondence de J.-J. Rousseau," *Annales E.S.C.*, 1971, pp. 151-172.

31. Jean Biou, "Le Rousseauisme, idéologie de substitution," *Roman et Lumières au XVIIIe siècle* (Paris: Editions Sociales, 1970), pp. 115-128.

32. Robert Darnton, "Readers Respond to Rousseau: The Fabrication of Romantic Sensitivity," in his *Great Cat Massacre and other Episodes in French Cultural History* (New York: Basic Books, 1984), pp. 214-256.

33. Robert Darnton, *The Business of Enlightenment*, pp. 287-294.

34. Agnès Marcetteau and Dominique Varry, "Les Bibliothèques de quelques acteurs de la Révolution, de Louis XVI to Robespierre," in *Livres et Révolution*, ed. Frédéric Barbier, Claude Jolly, and Sabine Juratic, pp. 189-207. *Mélanges de la Bibliothèque de la Sorbonne* 9 (Paris: Aux Amateurs de Livres, 1989).

35. Alexis de Toqueville, *L'Ancien Régime et la Révolution*, p. 153.

36. Louis Sébastian Mercier, *Tableau de Paris*, vol. 5, "À la royale," pp. 148-149.

37. Ibid., vol. 5, "Vieilles enseignes," pp. 123-126, (quotation on p. 123).

38. Arlette Farge, *La Vie fragile: Violence, pouvoirs et solidarités à Paris au XVIIIe siècle* (Paris: Hachette, 1986), pp. 201-258; and Arlette Farge and Jacques Revel, *Logiques de la foule: L'Affaire des enlèvements d'enfants Paris 1750*, (Paris: Hachette, 1988), pp. 121-137.

39. Christian Jouhaud, *Mazarinades: La Fronde des mots* (Paris: Aubier, 1985), pp. 37-39.

40. Jacques Revel, "Marie-Antoinette," in *Dictionnaire critique de la Révolution française*, ed. François Furet and Mono Ozouf (Paris: Flammarion, 1988), pp. 286-298.

41. Rolf Engelsing, "Die Perioden der Lesergeschicte in der Neuzeit. Das statistische Ausmaß und die soziokulturelle Bedeutung der Lektüre," *Archiv für Geschichte des Buchwesens* 10 (1970), pp. 945-1002.

42. See examples from Rousseau's correspondence collected by Claude Labrosse, *Lire au XVIIIe siècle: La Nouvelle Héloise et ses lecteurs* (Lyon: Presses universitaires de Lyon, 1985).

43. Roger Chartier, "Représentations et pratiques: lectures paysannes au XVIIIe siècle," in his *Lectures et lecteurs dans la France d'Ancien Régime*, pp. 223-246 (English trans., "Figures of the 'Other': Peasant Reading in the Age of the Enlightenment," in his *Cultural History: Between Practices and Representations*, (Ithaca: Cornell University Press, 1988), pp. 151-171.

# MALE AND FEMALE: WORDS AND IMAGES IN THE FRENCH REVOLUTION

*Lynn Hunt*

This chapter is a series of invitations to reflection about the relationship between the verbal and the visual orders of representation and their possible connection to a parallel, sometimes overlapping set of gender categories. I start with the observation that the French Revolution fostered a proliferation of signs, in which the political and the artistic were interwoven. I move from there to an examination of the implicit hierarchy of orders of representation and then to a brief consideration of the role of gender in helping to establish or at least solidify this hierarchy.

Every great revolutionary upheaval has its semiotic side in which art and politics are mixed. We need think only of the films of Eisenstein or Chinese revolutionary posters to make the point. But there are significant ways in which the French Revolution inaugurated the modern revolutionary obsession with the sign, especially the visual sign. The American Revolution, its contemporary counterpart, did not foster the same kind of proliferation of the sign. Admittedly, this is a comparison that is very difficult to quantify, and one might want to argue on ontological grounds that life everywhere is always in the same degree semiotic because it is always every instant permeated by signs and symbols. I am not being less symbolic here writing in the familiar, all too dry academic tones, than the French were when they were celebrating the Festival of Reason. Symbolic is not synonymous with interesting or even artistic! Nevertheless, both for contemporaries caught up in it and for those who tried to make sense of it afterward, the French Revolution had the effect of making the importance of the sign more conscious, more visible, as it were. This self-consciousness about the sign was related to a greater and more general self-consciousness about the organization of society and social relationships.[1]

The Americans did invent a seal for their new republic, and they had to put something on their money. Yet, the American symbolic effort was different in character from the French. First of all, much of the American concern with symbolism was tied up in the nearly simultaneous mythologizing of George Washington and the Constitution, that is, with the investment in a person and a document, but most of this came after the war of independence was won.[2] The American republic devoted relatively little of its official energy to propaganda through symbols and signs; in France, in contract, one of the most important revolutionary committees, the Committee on Public Instruction, was devoted to devising new ways of mobilizing the population to support the republic.[3]

There was, then, something uniquely self-conscious about the French obsession with the sign. No one captured this better than the abbé Grégoire, who was at the forefront of the Republic's republicanizing mission:

> When one reconstructs a government anew, it is necessary to
> republicanize everything. The legislator who ignores the
> importance of the language of signs will fail at his mission;
> he should not let escape any occasion for grabbing hold of
> the senses, for awakening republican ideas. Soon the soul is
> penetrated by the objects reproduced constantly in front of its
> eyes; and this combination, this collection of principles, of
> facts, of emblems which retraces without cease for the citizen
> his rights and his duties, this collection forms, in a manner
> of speaking, the republican mold which gives him a national
> character and the demeanor of a free man.[4]

It is not surprising, that the French gave the modern meaning of the words *propaganda* and *vandalism*. They first had previously referred to the *propaganda fide*, a special religious congregation established in Rome in the seventeenth century to oversee missionary work; in 1792, French radicals began to call for *Apostles* and *Propagators* of Reason who would be the foot soldiers of *revolutionary propaganda*. The term *vandalism*--meaning the destruction of the artistic patrimony--was introduced by the ubiquitous abbé Grégoire in January 1794 and used generally thereafter.[5]

These two new words are especially significant because they capture the two sides of the revolutionary politicization of the sign: the effort to reconstitute the semiotic system in entirely new and secular terms and the concomitant endeavor to root out the old one. The emphasis on the secular distinguished the French Revolution from the English Revolution 140 years before, and the emphasis on breaking completely with the French past distinguished the French Revolution from the American Revolution. The Americans were trying to recapture a golden era of British liberties and the purer moment of their own Puritan past. The French wanted to start all over in year I of the French Republic. In other words, then, propaganda and vandalism in their new incarnations defined the very modernity of the French revolutionary experience, and they had at their center the relationship between politics and the arts, or to put it more generally, the relationship between political meaning and its possible forms of representation.

No one has done more to highlight the semiotic revolution than François Furet. Furet's influential views are not easy to outline schematically. He tries to offer what Tocqueville himself could not, an analysis of the Revolution as a process with its own distinctive mode of functioning. We might take as his point of departure, Tocqueville's own confession of defeat: "I sense where the unknown object is, but try as I might, I cannot lift the veil which covers it." What was behind the veil of revolutionary ideology and rhetoric was what Furet calls, following Marx, the "illusion of politics," that is, the belief that politics could be used to refashion society. Rather than expressing the conflict of interests within society, revolutionary politics was used to reshape society itself. Central to this "illusion" was the use of language to get and maintain power; language had this centrality because "it was the sole guarantee that power would belong only to the people, that is, to nobody."[6]    Rather than establishing representative institutions, the revolutionaries, according to Furet, constantly repeated formulaic expressions of their willingness to do the people's will; they used the illusion of consensus to hold power.

Thus, in Furet's analysis, the Revolution was semiotic because it was democratic; democratic ideology made language the centerpiece of the revolutionary process because language was the one political vehicle sufficiently general to be available to everyone (and no one in particular). Because the Revolution was democratically semiotic, it also had inherent totalitarian or totalizing tendencies: "The Revolution was a collectively shared symbolic image of power, which broke continuity and drifted toward pure democracy only the better to appropriate, albeit at a different level, the absolutist tradition."

> The Revolution thus experienced, in its political practices, the theoretical contradictions of democracy, . . . because it ushered in a world where mental representations of power governed all actions, and where a network of signs completely dominated political life. Politics was a matter of establishing just *who* represented the people, or equality, or the nation: victory was in the hands of those who were capable of occupying and keeping that symbolic position.[7]

It is apparent, even from these brief quotes, that Furet has put the relationship between political meaning and the process of representation or signification at the heart of the revolutionary experience. In the Revolution, "a network of signs completely dominated political life." Thus, though one might argue that signs always dominate political life in some fashion, Furet clearly wants to argue that there was something unique about the revolutionary impact of the network of signs.

Furet does not simply call attention to the revolutionary concern with signs. He makes the semiotic character of the Revolution its defining quality: in his terms, "The Revolution was a collectively shared symbolic image of power." The "competition of discourses" no longer reflected "the conflict of interests"; the semiotic no longer simply expressed the social; rather, "language was substituted for power."[8]     Indeed, the Revolution was totalitarian, according to Furet, precisely insofar as it was driven by a kind of asymmetry between words and things, an asymmetry between the normal functioning of social relationships and the politicized processes of signification.     The Revolution was totalitarian because the revolutionaries tried to make social life conform to the language of democracy rather than the other way around.

I see this semiotic revolution in somewhat different terms, but I have the space to insist on only two points: 1) that the semiotic has to be viewed in much broader terms than just words, language, the verbal expression; and 2) that the proliferation of signs could be either democratic or authoritarian, but the fact that this proliferation could be either does not mean that the democratic tendency of the Revolution was necessarily also always authoritarian. Signs multiplied and became so important because the revolutionary leadership wanted to effect a complete break with the past. As Grégoire said, it was necessary to republicanize everything. The democratic thrust of the Revolution certainly affected the content of signs, but signs could be multiplied with the intention of opening up the political arena or with the intention of closing it down; after all, a government can use signs to occupy all the political space for itself.

I want to make these two points in a more indirect way by focussing on two polarities of the revolutionary semiotic system that are completely overlooked by Furet: (1) the visual versus the verbal, and (2) masculine versus feminine in the gendering of signs. Attention to these two polarities will show that the semiotic system was much more complicated than Furet makes it out to be, that it was not inherently or monolithically democratic, that its democratic content did not lead ineluctably to authoritarianism, in short, that the sign system was a source of conflict as much as it was a source of control. In other words, signs were unstable and susceptible to reinterpretation and conflict.

The visual and the verbal were often associated with each other in the Revolution, especially in revolutionary engravings, but the visual and the verbal were also often at odds. In a brilliant and still too little appreciated analysis, Judith Schlanger has shown how the revolutionaries tried to insert words everywhere. Not only were words meant to capture the charisma of the revolutionary experience and thus be "full at every moment", they also invaded other kinds of representation. Musical creations were often chanted, and the plastic arts were most often subtitled, inscribed upon, or surrounded with banners or placards. But this very invasiveness of words shows that the visual was thought to be potentially threatening; it had to be circumscribed by the verbal to keep it under control. So, in paradoxical fashion, I want to use Schlanger's analysis of the importance of the verbal to make the point that the visual continued to haunt the revolutionary imagination. She argues that "the verbal is then globally the base of vision and in some sense its building blocks and its finality," but this analysis is really a projection of the wish of the revolutionaries rather than the reality of their situation.[9] The word may have been best suited to create and recreate what I have called elsewhere the "mythic present" of revolutionary discourse--that will to break with the past and continually reinscribe the moment of revolutionary communion--but the visual image nevertheless--or perhaps because of this--retained its power to capture the suppressed and the repressed of the political imagination.[10]

In his analysis of the "Rhetoric of the Image," Roland Barthes made this kind of argument in a more general mode. He claimed that all images are polysemous, and that linguistic messages are used to fix what he called "the floating chain of signifieds in such a way as to counter the terror of uncertain signs." He concluded that "with respect to the liberty of the signifieds of the image, the text has thus a *repressive* value and we can see that it is at this level that the morality and ideology of a society are above all invested."[11] The repressive value of the text can be seen at work in the seal of the Republic, for the words, "In the Name of the French Republic: Liberty, Equality," make it clear to the viewer that what is at issue is not female power but rather the allegorized power of the body politic. But repression did not always work, or rather, it always worked incompletely. The text, or linguistic message as Barthes termed it, could never entirely control the meaning of the visual image. Thus the issue of female power could not be entirely contained, as many revolutionary and counterrevolutionary caricatures make apparent.

The polarity or tension between the visual and the verbal is itself suggestive of the second polarity between the masculine and the feminine in revolutionary imagery. In many ways, the verbal was associated with the masculine and the visual with the feminine. On the masculine, verbal side was clarity of intention, transparency of meaning, and control over what Barthes called the "terror of uncertain signs." As Schlanger explained it, but without reference to gender, the verbal was meant to circumscribe the visual, be both its building blocks and its teleology. The verbal was to be a kind of "final cause" of the visual much in the same way that male sperm was commonly thought to be the final cause of reproduction. There is no better example of the latter than Madame de Saint-Ange's physiology lesson in the Marquis de Sade's *Philosophy in the Bedroom*. As she explaines to Eugénie, her pupil:

>it is proven that the fetus owes its existence only to the
>man's sperm . . . that which we women furnish has a merely
>elaborative function; it does not create, it furthers creation
>without being its cause.[12]

In the same way, the verbal was imagined as providing the true, core meaning
of any representation, whereas the visual provided only an elaboration, not its
essence.  But as we have seen, the visual was always escaping the control of
its verbal text just as women's bodies were always escaping the control of the
semiotic system that men wanted to put in place.

This analogy between the visual/verbal // feminine/masculine should
not be pushed too far, for men and women appear in both forms all the time.
Yet, it is striking that the visual imagery of the Revolution introduced the
problem of women over and over again, while the verbal forms largely
excluded them.   Since men excluded women from political office and
eventually from all public political arenas altogether, women's speech was very
rarely heard.  Women's actions and the representation of women in imagery
were much harder to repress.

Visual imagery constantly reintroduced the issue of women.  There are
many reasons for this.  The visual often relied on the human figure, and almost
ineluctably included women with all that they could represent in terms of
family relationships, domination and subordination, humor, and pornography.
Iconographic tradition had it that abstract qualities were best represented by
women, even including Reason itself, and not even excluding Force, by the
way.  In France and other Latin countries, this was reinforced by the simple
grammatical fact that abstract qualities were feminine nouns: *La Raison*, *La
Victoire*, *La Fraternité* [an interesting contradiction], and, of course, *La Liberté*
and *La République*.  This femininization of abstract qualities was reinforced no
doubt by the Catholic veneration of the Virgin Mary, intercessor for all true
believers.[13]   The founding of the Republic required not only the destruction
of everything associated with monarchy but also a system of signs that was as
distant as possible from monarchy.   Since only men could rule directly in
France--there was no equivalent to Elizabeth the First in England--there was
an obvious virtue in representing the Republic by a female allegory; she could
not be confused with the king.  Perhaps even more significant, however, was
the way in which French democracy operated to make the representation of
individual political leaders quite problematic.   There was no equivalent to
George Washington in France; no living political leader was able to establish
a cult of personality with the representational strategies that would inevitably
accompany such a cult.  Marat was memorialized as a dead martyr to the
cause, not, as in Washington's case, as a living symbol.  Only Napoleon was
able to change this state of affairs and make his own body the center once
again of the representational system of political meaning.

This resistance to the fixing of charisma on any individual male leader made feminine allegories all the more attractive. The female figure could stand above politics precisely because women were not meant to act politically. No individual male leader could be singled out because charisma was now located in the people as a whole body, not in the body of any leader or sacred figure. The only sacred figure for the Republic was the goddess of Liberty, who seemed not only above politics but also above familial obligations. She has an impassivity and stolidity of countenance that distinguished her from any living mother.

Yet even the feminine allegory was subject to reinterpretation and conflict. Maurice Agulhon has shown that the meaning of the Republic could vary depending on the kind of woman who was chosen to represent it. She could be standing as opposed to sitting, active or passive, she could hold a sign of aggression or something more pacific, the symbolism could be accessible or esoteric, and it could require long textual explanations.[14]

In my own work, I have shown that Liberty, first known in derision and then in affection as Marianne, was not in fact the only seal of the Republic during the revolutionary years.[15] In October 1793, after the arrest of Girondin deputies and in the midst of desperate efforts to recast the Republic in a more radical mold, the National Convention decreed that the seal and the coins of the Republic would henceforth carry the ark of the constitution and the fasces of their emblem. Within a month, the Convention changed its mind again. In early November 1793 the artist and Jacobin deputy David proposed that the Convention order the erection of a colossal statue to represent the French people. Ten days later the Convention voted to make the statue the subject of the seal of state. The deputies had chosen a giant Hercules as the emblem of the radical Republic.[16]

The choice of Hercules can be explained in various ways, but we cannot be entirely sure about any explanations because the deputies were very reticent about the reasons for their symbolic choices. In a conventional political explanation, it might be argued that Marianne had come to be associated with the moderate Republic and had to be superseded in order to announce the new, radical direction that had taken shape when in September the Terror had been made the "order of the day," a general maximum on prices was declared, and the workings of the revolutionary tribunal were accelerated. At the same time, de-Christianization was reaching its peak and a new calender had just been introduced. Significantly, David proposed that the statue of Hercules be made out of the debris from the statues of kings knocked off the porticos of Notre Dame cathedral. At 46 feet in height, Hercules would overshadow memories of even the most popular kings, such as Henry IV, whose merely life-size image he would replace on the Pont-Neuf. Hercules represented the Jacobin alliance with the people: Hercules was the people, as one radical newspaper cartoon made clear. The Jacobins were showing that they valued their reliance on the people, that direct popular action was essential to the success of the Revolution.

According to an iconographic explanation, it might be argued that the people, being a masculine noun, *le peuple*, needed a masculine representation. Hercules had been the mythological representation of French kings from at least the mid-sixteenth century. Under the Republic, he would become the representation of a collective, popular power. David made the point clear by insisting that the statue of Hercules be made up of the stone bodies of former kings. David was taking the emblem of royalty and transforming it into the emblem of popular power.

But there is also a gender explanation: the giant, virile Hercules was chosen for the seal just after Queen Marie-Antoinette was executed and all women's clubs were suppressed. Hercules put the women back in their place; the official engraving showed him carrying the tiny female figures of Liberty and Equality in his hand. They are now entirely dependent on him, just as the Republic is dependent on the people, defined as the male people. The queen had been denounced for her meddling in politics; "a woman who becomes queen changes sex," warned one militant.[17] And the women's clubs were suppressed because women's participation in politics would lead to "the kinds of disruption and disorder that hysteria can produce." Hercules cleared up the ambiguity that might have been left by the female allegory of the Republic; now it was evident that only men were to do the work of politics.

There is also what might be termed a representational explanation. Hercules was chosen because he was the most "transparent" possible representation of popular power. He could be imagined as a nearly literal translation of the people since he was a male figure and hence a political actor, unlike female figures, who were assumed to stand for abstractions, not actual actors. At least one popular newspaper printed an engraving that transformed the Hercules figure on the seal into a sans-culotte, one of the militant men of Paris. The choice of Hercules thus encapsulated the various revolutionary tensions about the visual and the verbal, the masculine and feminine, and indeed, most fundamentally, about the need to represent anything in the new political order. Hercules was meant to be immediately apparent; his meaning was not supposed to be difficult to decipher. He was not as much an allegory as Marianne.

The story of the reinvention of Hercules tells us a great deal about the revolutionary hierarchy of the orders of representation. Hercules appeared first in David's Festival of Unity on August 10, 1793. There he was a kind of papier-maché figure who served as one of several stations for a fairly typical festival procession. Afterward, David proposed him as a colossal statue, and then he was proposed for the seal. The progression went from life-sized figure in a tableau vivant to monumentalized, classicized, and fixed-in-stone nude to textualized and textualizing seal, imprimatur, printed thing--a transition, in

other words, from a more strictly visual figure to a visual image that was
virtually verbal.   Yet even the Hercules of the original festival required
explanation in speech and writing; he required a verbal frame.   In the festival
of August 10, 1793, when the procession arrived in front of the figure, the
president of the Convention had to explain what the people were to see in him:

> French people!  Here you are looking at yourself in the form
> of an emblem which is rich in instructive lessons.  The giant
> whose powerful hand reunites and reattaches in one bundle
> the departments which make up its grandeur and its strength,
> that giant is you.

David's plan for the monumental statue called for the engraving of several key
words on the giant's body.  "Light" would appear on his brow; "nature" and
"truth" on his arms; and "work" on his hands.  The statue had to be inscribed
in order to control its signification.  The people had to be taught to recognize
itself and to recognize the proper attributes of popular sovereignty.  The visual
could not be expected to accomplish this alone.

   Even this brief review of revolutionary imagery shows that the
semiotic revolution went far beyond the verbal.  The Revolution was not
simply a competition between discourses, and it was not just language that was
substituted for power.  Power was the control over symbolic practices of many
kinds.  The Revolution was not really "a collectively shared symbolic image
of power," as Furet put it.  It was rather a set of mutually linked struggles
over representational practices: who would represent the people, yes, but also
how, in what form, allegorical or transparent, feminine or masculine, visual
or verbal.  The new semiotic system was meant to take the place of the old
one, but it was not invented all at once by a government that was clear as to
its aims.  The new semiotic system was continually in the process of creation
and reshaping.  The government did try to get control over its manifestations,
but it constantly came up against the fact of reinterpretation, misinterpretation,
and conflict.  Catholics paraded their Black Virgins and derided Liberty as a
common whore; counterrevolutionaries tore out Liberty Trees; and well-
meaning locals set up unofficial festivals with manikins and donkeys.
Democracy was more than a question of the right to vote; it included a
fundamental contest about the place and control of signs.   And though a
government could inscribe words all over its visual representations, it could not
completely control the way people saw them.  Between intended meaning and
the viewer, there was always a gap left by the polysemous sign, a gap of
freedom and subversion.

   It is more difficult to demonstrate that the revolutionaries had an
implicit hierarchy of the orders of representation.  The revolutionary leadership
valued the verbal over the visual because it considered the verbal more reliable

both as a representational medium and as a political instrument.[18]    The hierarchy that the revolutionaries developed over time ran something like this: at the top were the verbal forms of speeches in the assembly and printed decrees and reports.    Included in the latter category were the newspapers, which could be censored or closed down.    Then came those visual forms that were clearly framed by the verbal: seals and festivals that were programmed (that is, had printed programs prepared before the event) by the national government.    Visual forms that characteristically stood alone, such as paintings and sculptures, might be framed by the verbal in the way that David proposed to write on his gigantic Hercules or might be divided along the lines of narrativity: the revolutionary government encouraged, for example, the production of paintings that would tell well-known stories of revolutionary episodes.    At the bottom of the hierarchy were those visual forms that threatened to get out of control, that is, outside the verbal frame and beyond national political constraints.    The most menacing were the ad hoc or "wild" festivals that popped up in villages and towns without government authorization.    The presence of living or papier-maché figures--actresses playing the goddess of Liberty or manikins representing nobles and kings-- served as a kind of red light of warning to government officials.

Only the most extreme materialists were willing to express forthrightly iconoclastic views.    The best-known of these is Jean-Baptiste Salaville, who attacked the cult of Reason in a series of articles in the *Annales patriotiques et littéraires* in the fall of 1793.

> if we want to lead the people to the pure cult of Reason, rather than encouraging its penchant for concretizing abstractions [*son penchant à réaliser des abstractions*], for personifying moral beings, we should cure it of this mania, which is the principal cause of human errors; it is essential that the metaphysical principles of Locke and Condillac become popular, and that the people get used to seeing in a statue only a stone and in an image only a canvas and paints.[19]

A few days later, Salaville made the connection with gender explicit:

> it seems to me, first of all, that the meaning and the conception of the philosophers are equally outraged by the idea of a *woman* representing *Reason* and by the youth of this woman.    In women, this faculty, which is so pure, is identified so to speak with *weakness*, with *the prejudices*, with *the attractions* even of this enchanting sex.    With the man, its empire is disengaged from all error: *force, energy,*

*severity* line up in a series in the man. But especially, reason
is *mature*, it is *serious*, it is *austere*, qualities which are
developed weakly in a young woman.

And even the representational argument, as I have been calling it, was clearly
suggested by Salaville:

I wonder if even the idea *of a temple of Reason* doesn't
contrast fundamentally with the idea that we have of Reason
itself? Isn't every man himself the temple of Reason? Isn't
its cult that of study? . . . At least this temple, which should
only resound with the measured accents of Reason, must be
entirely free of superfluous ornamentation. We should only
read emblems there [*Qu'on n'y lise que des emblèmes*]. We
should say to the people: 'Do not look here for a statue in
gold, silver or marble erected to Reason, nor expect to
contemplate it on a speaking canvas [*une toile parlante*].'[20]

There is much to be disengaged analytically even from these few short
passages, but at the very least they show that the revolutionary program of
political re-education involved nothing less than a complete rethinking of the
relationships between psychology, art, gender, and politics. Condillac and
Rousseau provided important tools for the revolutionary packaging of this
complex of problem, but the actual experiences of revolutionary re-education
took the problems much further than they had been by the eighteenth-century
predecessors.[21] Gender was not a peripheral issue in this search for
democratic representational politics. It was an absolutely central category,
which shaped in the most fundamental ways the revolutionary reconsideration
of the role of images and the role of words.

## NOTES

1. Brian C. J. Singer, *Society, Theory, and the French Revolution:
Studies in the Revolutionary Imaginary* (New York: St. Martin's Press, 1986).
2. For an emphasis on the early process of mythologizing
Washington, see Paul K. Longmore, *The Invention of George Washington*
(Berkeley: University of California Press, 1988).
3. Unfortunately, Emmet Kennedy does not specifically address the
role of the Committee on Public Instruction in his useful overview, *A Cultural
History of the French Revolution* (New Haven and London: Yale University
Press, 1989).

4. *Rapport faut au Conseil des Cinq-Cents, sur les sceaux de la République, par Grégoire* (Séance du 11 pluviôse an IV-31 January 1796).

5. Serge Bianchi, *La Rèvolution culturelle de l'an II* (Paris: Aubier, 1982), p. 168; on the origins of revolutionary words, see Ferdinand Brunot, *La Révolution et l'Empire*, vol. 9 of *Histoire de la langue française des origines à 1900* (Paris: Armand Colin, 1967).

6. François Furet, *Interpreting the French Revolution*, trans. Elborg Forster (Cambridge: Cambridge University Press, 1981), pp. 163, 48.

7. Ibid., pp. 78, 48.

8. Ibid., pp. 49, 48.

9. Judith Schlanger, *L'Enjeu et le débat: les passes intellectuels* (Paris: Denoel/Gonthier, 1979), p. 159.

10. Lynn Hunt, *Politics, Culture, and Class in the French Revolution* (Berkeley: University of California Press, 1984).

11. Roland Barthes, *Image, Music, Text*, trans. Stephen Heath (New York: Hill and Wang, 1977), pp. 39-40.

12. Marquis de Sade, *La Philosophie dans le boudoir* (Paris: Gallimard, 1976), p. 306.

13. On female imagery in the Republic, see Maurice Agulhon, *Marianne au combat: L'Imagerie et la symbolique républicaines de 1789 2 à 1880* (Paris: Gallimard, 1979).

14. Ibid.

15. Hunt, *Politics, Culture, and Class.*

16. For my previous discussion of Hercules, see Hunt, *Politics, Culture, and Class*, pp. 87-119.

17. Louise de Keralio [attributed to Louis Prudhomme], *Les Crimes des reines de France depuis le commencement de la monarchie jusqu'à la mort de Marie-Antoinette; avec les pièces justificatives de son procès.* Publié par L. Prudhomme, avec Cinq gravures. Nouvelle édition corrigée etaugmentée. (Paris: Au Bureau des Révolutions de Paris, an II), p. vii.

18. My analysis of the verbal/visual as paralleling the masculine/feminine should be compared to Joan B. Landes's analysis of the shift away "from the motivated, iconic imagery of the father-king and toward an abstract system of representation in which the impersonal order of law, writing, speech, and its proclamation prevailed." Landes seems to see the shift as one within male forms of representation. *Women and the Public Sphere in the Age of the French Revolution* (Ithaca, N.Y., and London: Cornell University Press, 1988), p. 41.

19. François Victor Alphonse Aulard, *Le Culte de la raison et le culte de l'être suprême (1793-1794)*, Essai historique par Alphonse Aulard, 2d ed., rev. (Paris: F. Alcan, 1904), p. 87.

20. Ibid, p. 89.

21.    Lynn Hunt, "The Political Psychology of Revolutionary Caricatures," in *French Caricature and the French Revolution, 1789-1799*, published in conjunction with an exhibition co-organized by the University of California, Los Angeles, and the Bibliotheque Nationale de France (Los Angeles, 1988), pp. 33-40.

# THE POLITICS OF WRITING AND READING IN EIGHTEENTH-CENTURY AMERICA

*David Hall*

Responding to a fellow minister who accused him of being too puristic in his conception of church membership, Jonathan Edwards undertook to expose his opponent's inconsistencies. At one point Edwards paused to explain, for the benefit of those he characterized as "illiterate" readers, the expression "begging the question."[1]   He had in mind the many men and women who, in mid-eighteenth-century America, were strangers to the Latin-based world of academic learning.   That world was second nature to Edwards and his opponent; both had graduated from Yale College, and in keeping with their education both writers drew on the resources of logic, rhetoric, and the classical languages in debating one another. Yet Edwards realized that the subject of church membership engaged the interests and attention of a far wider audience, the thousands of lay members who, according to the rules of "congregational" ecclesiology, were empowered to participate in church governance. Thus it happened that he found himself immersed in a complex politics of culture, a politics of privilege (the special discourse of the "literate") and a politics of what, for want of a better term, we may term an inclusive culture that required him to reach out to the common reader.

The purpose of this chapter is to reflect on this politics of culture and its relationship to the practices of writing and reading in eighteenth-century America. To simplify, I want to describe two different systems of cultural production that existed side-by-side. One of these systems presumed hierarchy and privilege: literacy in the sense of learnedness, and equivalent assumptions about writing and reading that stemmed from "genteel" culture. The other system operated quite differently, as in due course I hope to make clear.

My purpose is also to reflect on change and continuity. For a conference on the book in revolutionary France and America the question prompts itself, did a system based on hierarchy collapse as part of our war for independence?  The case for France is elegantly displayed in the catalogue entitled *Revolution in Print*.[2]  Similarly, some historians have argued that a "democratization of print" was occuring in post-revolutionary America.[3] I want to outline an alternative possibility, that most Americans[4] inherited a "revolution" that unfolded two centuries before the events of 1776. From this revolution sprang a literary culture premised on broad access to the Word in the vernacular; from it followed Edwards's effort to address a wider audience.

But let us start with the distinction between "literacy" and "illiteracy." Literacy connoted cultural authority; illiteracy, cultural inferiority and exclusion. This pattern of meaning was crucial to the world of cosmopolitan or genteel culture that emerged to supplement the world of learning in eighteenth-century America.[5] Via either of these systems, hierarchy imposed itself on the relationship between books and readers.

The colleges and the literary coteries that affirmed hierarchy as fact and value helped to convey the civilizing traditions of humanism and rationalism to a society that easily yielded to sectarian and interracial conflict. Hierarchy was a counterweight to decentralizing tendencies. Deferring to the authority of London, the Americans who styled themselves cosmopolitans relieved some of the provincialism of our new-world culture. They patronized what little there was of "literature" or literary activity; to the social worlds of genteel and learned culture we owe the earliest of our magazines and social libraries and the first of our writers to break free of didacticism.

Genteel culture came into being in the major coastal cities in the early decades of the century. The first such stirrings in Boston were centered on a coterie that wrote for James Franklin's weekly newspaper *The New England Courant* (1722-23). The writers who participated in this coterie specialized in verse satires on contemporary politics. Theirs was "insider" verse, made so in part by the abundance of pseudonyms and comic sallies meaningful only to those fully in the know. Not surprisingly, most of these writers knew their way around learned culture, which is to say that they were "literate" in the ancient languages and availed themselves of literary and rhetorical modes they learned from the classics. Their verse observed the conventions of the neoclassical tradition. It was customary to display a little Latin and to celebrate the ancients.[6] In these same years William Byrd (1674-1744) of Westover, Virginia, was keeping up with the classics in his private reading. Like the Bostonians to the north, he was playful in observing contemporary politics, changing every name in *A Secret History* to fanciful inventions that his twentieth-century editors must struggle to decode.

These practices signalled the emergence of new structures of literary production and consumption. The coterie or club, the gentlemen's library, and the periodical began to supplement the college as settings in which certain writers found a sympathetic audience.[7] In general, the persons who affiliated with such agencies thought of themselves as "gentlemen." Gentlemen writers in eighteenth-century America did not produce for the marketplace. Typically they shared their work with friends and allowed what they wrote to circulate in manuscript. Byrd was one such writer. Another was Alexander Hamilton (1712-56) of Annapolis, Maryland. Byrd circulated *A Secret History of the*

*Dividing Line* among a handful of fellow Virginians. Not until the nineteenth century would the manuscript be "published" for a wider public. Hamilton shared the manuscript of his *Itinerarium*, a narrative of his travels from Maryland to Massachusetts and back in 1744, only with his fellow members of the Tuesday Club in Annapolis. So too the club members kept an elaborate history of themselves that has also had to wait for publication; only now, at the close of the twentieth century, has it been published.[8]

Satire came easily to the gentlemen writers I have been describing. The structure of satire lent itself to voicing (and enhancing) the cultural distance they wished to impose between the rabble and themselves. Hence the famous passages in Byrd's *Secret History* in which he described certain North Carolinians as almost wholly without civilization. Alexander Hamilton was ever alert to exposing the difference between pretense and reality:

> Among the rest [in a tavern crowd] was a fellow in a worsted cap and great black fists. They stiled him doctor. Flat told me he had been a shoemaker in town and was a notable fellow at his trade, but happening two years ago to cure an old woman of a pestilent mortal disease, he thereby acquired the character of a physician, . . . laid aside his awls and leather, got himself some gallipots, and instead of cobling of soals, fell to cobling of human bodies.

The social ineptitudes of the "lower orders" served these writers well. So did the moral code of Puritanism. Inheriting from Dryden and other writers of the Restoration the theme of anti-Puritanism, Byrd and Hamilton mocked the mores of the Yankee and his Blue Laws.[9]

Byrd's well-known frankness about sex was another legacy from the Restoration. Genteel writers had an eye for the ladies and presented themselves as eager to make conquests.

> The character of a certain Church of England clergyman in Boston was canvassed, he having lost his living for being too sweet upon his landlady's daughter, a great belly being the consequence. I pitied him only for his imprudence. . . . As for the crime . . . it is but a peccadillo.

So too these cosmopolitans disdained "sectaries" and "enthusiastic" religion, Hamilton complaining at one point of a travelling companion who "kept poring upon Whitefield's sermons." Hamilton's own taste in writers ran to Fielding, Cervantes, Montaigne, and Rollins.[10]

In the first half of the eighteenth century coteries and clubs served as milieus in which writers exchanged work in manuscript. As David Shields is demonstrating, a substantial literary culture grew up around this apparently archaic process. Alternatively, literary culture revolved around the periodical, which drew its patrons and contributors mainly from the ranks of cosmopolitan gentlemen. When Benjamin Franklin took over the *Pennsylvania Gazette* in 1729, he appealed to "gentlemen" to send him "private letters" to print in the newspaper. Franklin was assuming that men of a certain social class would possess distinctive "Information." He wished, in other words, to link up with an existing network of exchanges that, occurring as they did among the members of an elite, bridged the public and the private.[11]

Benjamin Franklin may seem an improbable person to associate with genteel culture. Yet it was precisely the status of a "gentleman" who did not have to work for a living that Franklin adopted after handing over his printing business to his partner. He cut his literary teeth, moreover, on the coterie that nourished *The New England Courant*. From them he learned to admire *The Tatler* and *The Spectator*. From them he learned as well the literary mode of burlesque and that Boston variant, the mock-jeremiad.[12]

Perhaps more crucially, these writers encouraged in Franklin an anti-Puritanism that enabled him to break with his family culture, which was authentically Protestant and Nonconformist, and start down a different road. At the age of five he was sent a poem written by his uncle Benjamin counselling him on the way of "Duty." Duty for the elder Benjamin meant something different than what it would come to signify for a man of the Enlightenment:

> Mans Danger lyes in Satan, sin and selfe.
> In vertue, Learning, Wisdome progress make.
> Never shrink at suffering for thy saviours sake . . .
> In Heart with bended knee Alone Adore
> None but the Three in One Forevermore.[13]

Young Franklin rejected both the doctrines and the cultural style of pietistic Calvinism. When he began to contribute the "Silence Dogood" essays to his brother's paper, he filled them with mockery of that "pious rhetoric and somber world-view." A characteristic subject, then as later, was the war between the sexes, treated as a cause for humor. Franklin's cosmopolitan identity was masterfully displayed in "The Speech of Miss Polly Baker," which circulated in manuscript (a copy reached the members of the Tuesday Club) before being published in 1747 in a London newspaper. In Leo Lemay's summary, "this entertaining and complex hoax satirizes New England's blue laws, protests the double-standard for women, defends prostitution, ridicules traditional Christian morality . . . and elegantly but subtly advocates deism."[14] That Franklin expected his correspondents to share the letters they received with friends--thus again making "public" what seemed "private"--is a further clue to the literary practices and assumptions that made up this system.

Let me suggest that these writers were deliberately engaged in a politics of culture. Whatever their political allegiance in the struggle between royal government and local independence, all wanted to create a sphere that was liberated from the pulpit. The *Independent Reflector* was born in 1752 amid the intensely factionalized politics of colonial New York. Political historians regard it as signalling the transfer from England to America of "radical Whig" or "republican" ideas that would flower in an ideology of independence. But in representing themselves as friends of "free inquiry" or the "free exercise of thought," William Livingston and his fellow writers were also attempting to subvert the cultural role of the ministry. Hence they ridiculed the discourse of theologians as consisting of meaningless "metaphysical riddles." The history of Christianity was, for them, a babble of conflicting doctrines and ideas, none of which really mattered. A much-used epithet was "orthodoxy," which they construed as a system that the clergy sought to impose on the people. Mere riddles, senseless zeal, "enthusiasm"--all these Livingston contrasted to the "rationality" and "decency" of proper religion. More bluntly, he and his colleagues contrasted the "pulpit" with the "press," labelling the former an instance of "Tyranny" and identifying the press with freedom. This way of categorizing the press has much to do with the ideology of "republicanism" that Michael Warner describes elsewhere in this volume. But it also has to do with a specific politics of culture that, originating in the Anglican reaction to the English Civil War, deliberately misrepresented evangelical Protestantism and the relationship between the clergy and the people.[15]

This politics of culture was reprised in the 1790s as American writers turned to the genre of the novel.[16] An early example, Royall Tyler's *The Algerine Captive* (1797) extends the themes that I have been describing. The novel is a comedy of manners in which writer (a Harvard graduate) and reader amuse themselves at the expense of a naive rustic. Young Updike Underhill leaves the family farm to attempt a series of professions. His pious mother is confident that Updike will easily triumph as a minister: "she did not doubt, when he came to preach, he would be as much run after as the great Mr. Whitefield." To prepare himself for the right career Updike reads

> ten funeral, five election, three ordination, and seventeen
> farewell, sermons, Bunyan's Holy War, the Life of Colonel
> Gardner, and the Religious Courtship. In law, the Statutes of
> New Hampshire, and Burn's Justice abridged. In physic,
> Buchan's Family Physician, Culpepper's Midwifery, and
> Turner's Surgery.

As a doctor he turns out to be no more bumbling than his competitors.[17]

Having established that Underhill was a mere amateur, Tyler went on to contrast two modes of reading, the one he expected of his own readers and the unsophisticated alternative. The proper reader was someone who, having moved from sermons to fiction and the periodical essay, knew how to recognize the special rules and implicit epistemology of the novel. Updike Underhill did not have that skill. When he read *Pilgrim's Progress*, "he stuck a skewer through Apollyon's eye in the picture, to help Christian beat him."[18] As in this example, so in general Tyler differentiated writing, reading, and learning along an axis that at one end was labelled "country," and, at the other, "cosmopolitan."

Did Tyler realize that the naiveté of the Underhills threatened his own career as a novelist? His way out of this difficulty was to proclaim that Americans were entering on a new age of reading: the novel was triumphing over all of its rivals.

> When [Updike] left New England . . . certain funeral discourses, the last words and dying speeches of Bryan Shaheen, and Levi Ames, and some dreary somebody's Day of Doom, formed the most diverting part of the farmer's library. On his return from captivity, he found a surprising alteration in the public taste. In our inland towns...country booksellers, fostering the new-born taste of the people, had filled the whole land with modern travels, and novels almost as incredible.

As Tyler continued to explain,

> with one accord, all orders of country life forsook the sober sermons and practical pieties of their fathers, for the gay stories and splendid impieties of the traveller and the novelist.[19]

A veritable revolution in reading was carrying cosmopolitan culture to supremacy over "sermons" and "dreary somebody's Day of Doom."

This truth was slow to dawn on the man who printed *The Algerine Captive*. Certainly David Carlisle of Walpole, New Hampshire, could not have survived as a printer-publisher on the sales of Tyler's novel, of which he issued but a single printing. The meat-and-drink of his business were ordination sermons and tales of "wonders" of a kind that Tyler would have despised, like *A Wonderful Dream of Dr. Watts*. Country printers thrived on such ephemera. And if we look behind these publications and ask what they tell us about literary culture, a quite different structure comes into view, and with it a different politics of culture.

Isaac Backus, a New Light minister in the second half of the eighteenth century, was versed in a politics of culture that hinged on how to read and understand the Word of God. Backus was concerned with validating the authority of spiritual knowledge over against the authority of "learning." Were the "learned," with their esoteric knowledge of the ancient languages, the best interpreters of Scripture? On the contrary: echoing George Whitefield's critique of Harvard, Backus declared that a college education all too often introduced young men to the "corrupt principles" of "rank" Arminianism. The key qualification for interpreting Scripture was not learning, but "being internally called by the Spirit of God." Even more boldly, Backus asserted that *"every saint* now has the same way to know the truth and certainty of God's Word that his people had of old."[20]

Clergy such as Backus stepped outside of cultural hierarchy via their evangelical insistence on reversal. Whether Samuel Davies was preaching to the students of the College of New Jersey or to farmers and their families in Hanover County, Virginia, where he played a major role in inaugurating a revival, he contrasted "the irreligious world" and "the children of God." The comparison was prelude to an act of cultural reversal:

> O, sinners! could you but see in all his future glory, the
> meanest saint whom you now contemn and ridicule, how
> would it astonish you! . . . You will then see those whom
> you now account stupid, mopish creatures, that have no taste
> for the pleasures of life, shining more glorious than the sun;
> happy as their natures can admit, and in their humble sphere,
> resembling God himself.

The worldly dashed from their high places, and the meek of God rewarded with eternal life--this working of the divine will limited the authority of genteel and learned culture.[21]

Davies specified a literary consequence of this reversal. All learnedness, including his, would be displaced by the "humble language" God used in speaking to his children.[22] Humble speech was understood by everyone who felt the workings of the Holy Spirit. So too the Holy Spirit enabled the unlearned--as it once enabled a mere carpenter--to confound the worldly wise. A process of reversal thus functioned to eliminate the problem of illiteracy: the godly knew and spoke the truths of the gospel.

Jonathan Edwards joined Backus and Davies in acknowledging this displacement. For these evangelists in mid-eighteenth-century America, the spiritual preparation of a minister was ultimately more consequential than that person's skill in reading Greek and Latin. The true minister--and, for sure, the effective preacher--was someone who had undergone conversion, or "new birth," and who relied on the Holy Spirit in communicating the Gospel. Feeling himself infused with the Spirit, the evangelical preacher experienced what one such person imagined as a "divine power":

> The divine power seemed in some measure to attend this discourse, in which I was favored with uncommon freedom and plainness of address, and enabled to open divine truths and explain them to the capacities of my people in a manner beyond myself. . . . [And on another preaching day] the Word appeared to be accompanied with a divine influence, and made powerful impressions upon the assembly in general.[23]

This passage from David Brainerd's diary is laced with assumptions about literary production and literary consumption. Let me specify three of them.

1. The transparency of speech and writing. Brainerd spoke "beyond myself," and with "plainness." That is to say, once the Holy Spirit came to him, Brainerd was able to overcome the everyday limitations of speech and writing. His "people" understood him perfectly, indeed so well that they too became infused with the Spirit. It is as though the medium by which the Spirit moved has become transparent: Brainerd the person, and the human instrumentalities of writing and speech, vanish, leaving communication to occur between pure Spirit (the living Word) and the hearts of those who believe.

2. Speech and writing as spontaneous acts. A longstanding ethic in the world of radical Protestants was that ministers should never preach from a fully written text or (at an extreme) bring written notes of any kind into the pulpit. The essential preparation consisted of meditation, a process that involved the cycle of repentance and renewed commitment to the will of God. So cleansed, the preacher rose above the corruptions of the mundane world and spoke truth directly.

3. Interpretation is figural. All acts of speech and writing referred ultimately to the grand design of God's providence, the work of redemption. Hence the writer's task was to connect events in the everyday world, none of which had meaning in and of themselves, to Christ's mission of salvation. This master plot was revealed in the Bible, which laid out the types or figures to which all events thereafter were but antitypes.

These assumptions were consequential for the practice of reading, the relationship between writers and readers, and, more generally, for the meaning and distribution of cultural power. One immediate result was, as Isaac Backus indicated, to minimize the importance of the learned tradition. Less obvious, but in the long run of greater consequence, was how these assumptions worked against the "literary" concepts of style and genre.   Figural interpretation allowed no "description of random everyday life" or the varying of "style" to suit different occasions.  Comedy became irrelevant; there was nothing to satirize, since there was but one true version of the divine will, and one essential plot, the work of redemption.[24]   So too the assumptions I have outlined worked against the concept of authorship.  Samuel Davies and Isaac Backus participated in a wholly different system of cultural production from that of the genteel writers.   Evangelicals did not retreat into a coterie that sought distance from the rabble.  Nor did they elaborate a distinction between the "cultivated" and the everyday, or between the public and the private.  On the contrary, the sermons they saw through the press were always public in the sense of being instruments of persuasion aimed at a general audience.  Davies and Backus assumed the presence of an audience that wanted *repetitions* of a stock message--the permanent message of the gospel, not the ever-changing fashions of the moment. Consistent with this premise, evangelicals continued to recommend, and to read themselves, a stock of "steady sellers" that remained immune to the mutability of time.[25]

Notwithstanding the attention that our literary historians have lavished on the likes of Royall Tyler and his genteel predecessors, the actual production and consumption of print in eighteenth-century America was closely bound up with the religious culture I have sketched.  On a strictly quantitative basis, more "religious" books were printed than those in any other category (with the possible exception of schoolbooks), and most of the persons we in retrospect deem "writers" in eighteenth-century America were clergy who wrote only sermons.[26]  Within this system and its adjuncts certain kinds of books, or genres, sold consistently and widely. The better-selling religious books tended to be the work of English Nonconformists such as Isaac Watts.   Some contained an element of sensationalism--say, evoking the millennium and the threat of fiery hell. The cheapest form of print may have been the tales of "remarkables" or "wonders" of the kind that David Carlisle issued from his press. Similarly inexpensive and widespread were stories of conversion or extreme religious experience. Again, it is hazardous to generalize. But the genre of spiritual autobiography (or biography) was consistently important in eighteenth-century America, as were narratives of collective experience. A Boston minister's son established a magazine, *The Christian History* (1741-44) that filled its pages with such narratives.[27]  And in keeping with the tradition, Issac Backus inserted at the end of his pamphlet on the liberty of interpretation *An Apppendix Containing Some Short Account of the Experiences and Dying Testimony* of a fellow New Light minister, a man who credited his spiritual awakening to God's "dear servant Mr. Whitefield."[28]

This genre came easily to untrained writers who may have been "illiterate" in the learned disciplines but who knew the Bible closely.   The other genres to which these writers turned were the forms that Tyler mocked in *The Algerine Captive* and that Benjamin Franklin satirized in the "Silence Dogood" essays: the elegy, poems and prose describing the history of redemption, the narrative of God's remarkable providence. No learning or esoteric skill was required to produce such work, which in general drew its motifs from the Bible or from a long-established set of story frameworks-- deliverance from sin, the providential ordering of one's life, the passage of the saint or pilgrim to heaven from this weary world. Anyone immersed in Scripture, and who felt the stirrings of the Spirit, was apt to feel empowered as a writer. Such a writer was Franklin's uncle, and such were hundreds of others who will never figure in our literary history.

This empowerment extended to the act of reading. I have argued elsewhere that a majority of Americans became literate (in the sense of knowing how to read) in the context of a household system of instruction. Elsewhere, too, I have sketched a mode of reading that this household culture perpetuated, a mode that owed its structure and its rhythms to the practice of spiritual meditation.[29] We may trace this way of reading back to the very beginnings of the Protestant Reformation, and still further, to the medieval tradition of learning to read by memorizing a primer. As manifested in eighteenth-century America, this literacy went hand-in-hand with a limited supply of printed books. The common reader was easily satisfied; he or she owned at best but a handful of titles--perhaps a Bible, a steady seller, a psalm book--and with the probable exception of the yearly almanac, rarely added new books to this stock.

We are now in a position to appreciate more fully the cultural politics of *The Algerine Captive*. From Royall Tyler's vantage, Updike Underhill was a *retardaire*, or naive reader, someone so accustomed to "plain" or figural interpretation that he could not differentiate the "literary" from the true or real. From this vantage Underhill was also *retardaire* in continuing to fancy tales of "wonder" and "dreary days of doom." Interventions of the supernatural had ceased to interest the genteel writer; by the middle of the eighteenth century, genteel and learned culture were deeply marked by the disenchantment that followed on the heels of the new science and the reaction against "enthusiasm." The final expression of Tyler's politics is his picture of a revolution in reading, as though the genres long preferred by the common reader were suddenly abandoned and fiction of the kind that Tyler wished to write prevailed. As it happens, every detailed study of country booksellers and probate inventories contradicts this fable.[30] Instead it was the genteel writer who struggled in the marketplace. As one literary historian has noted, the aspiring men of letters in the new republic were unable to discover "the appropriate form for appealing to the widest possible audience."[31]

Those who did succeed in that endeavor were the writers who owed their understanding of writing and reading to the Protestant Reformation and the inclusive culture of the Word to which it gave rise. The persistence of this culture, together with the persistence of a decentralized social system that constrained the authority of urban, professional elites, stand in sharp contrast to the situation in eighteenth-century France. Consider, as illustration, the American printer-publisher and his allies. Versatile in moving back and forth between the roles of printer, writer, bookseller, and publisher, men like Benjamin Franklin (before he retired from the business) and Isaiah Thomas regarded themselves as of the "middling classes" and articulated the values of that social formation. In France, on the other hand, the press "did not routinely acknowledge [commercial expansion] or appeal to the professionals and tradespeople most affected by it. Rather, periodicals in France continued to present an aristocratic view of society."[32]

The more aggressive of our new-world printers worked closely with professional writers, the most famous of whom was Thomas Paine. Half a century earlier, Franklin had befriended James Ralph, who sailed with him in 1724 to England. There Ralph became a denizen of Grub Street--composing poetry and drama of his own, flourishing as a political writer in the pay of (mostly) opposition politicians, and finally being pensioned by the government in exchange for silencing his pen. Thomas Paine crossed the Atlantic in the opposite direction. Arriving in Philadelphia in 1774, he found work as a literary jack-of-all-trades, becoming the editor of the *Pennsylvania Magazine*. As Frank Luther Mott has observed, Paine was more properly a "contributing editor" who "wrote over several signatures" for the journal. His contributions included everything from "descriptions of mechanical devices" to "anecdotes, Addisonian essays, argumentative papers, and poems in some variety," the latter including "Cupid and Hymen," printed the month that the minute men of Lexington and Concord repelled a British expedition, and "reflections on Unhappy Marriages."[33]

Paine's versatility was in keeping with the cultural position of printer-publishers in colonial and revolutionary America and those in their employ. Such men were comfortably at home with the "popular" literary culture that encompassed almanacs, simple schoolbooks, the hoax, and certain forms of journalism. Yet they were equally at home with the modes of genteel culture. Affiliating with those who were socially superior as well as reaching out to "country" readers, these printers were uniquely situated when the movement for independence reached the point of crisis. It was at that moment that Paine wrote *Common Sense* (1776), the *only* pamphlet on the constitutional issues of the period that reached the common reader.[34] Himself a child of religious Nonconformity in England, Paine harnassed certain motifs of the culture of the word to his attack on the British monarchy.

Protestantism, and especially the kind of Protestantism that came with the early colonists, made a difference. Yet it has been argued that in the first half of the eighteenth century the clergy in America grew apart from the people--that hierarchy imposed itself on what once had been a common culture.

The remark I quoted at the outset of this essay is perhaps a case in point. Many clergy were unwilling to concede the limitations of learnedness, and some began to prefer the world of the cosmopolitans. Accordingly, it may have taken something like a "revolution" to reaffirm the premises of the culture of the Word, and especially its latent egalitarianism. Historians have pointed to the New Lights of the Great Awakening as the group that, repudiating hierarchy, moved in this direction.[35] Granting this possibility, it must also be recognized that in the long run the New Light movement was secondary or subordinate to the Reformation as a time of cultural change. Either way, we end up acknowledging a fundamental transformation that occurred prior to the movement for American independence.

The "revolution in print" that erupted in France after 1789 destroyed a centralized system of patronage for writers and a centralized system of control over the book trades. In their place the Revolution swept into power the elements of a "literary underground."[36] But our Revolution did not have these consequences. The patriots forced a few printers to stop doing business. But since most printers did not depend on the royal government for their work, and since an opposition press had operated openly for several decades, the passage from colonies to nation was marked by continuity. Like other institutions in the wider society, the business of printing was as decentralized and entrepreneurial before the Revolution as it remained in the early republic.

The agitation that preceeded the outbreak of war in 1775 was innovative in certain respects, but traditional in others. In 1772 the more "radical" patriots in Boston organized a Committee of Correspondence. The goal of the committee was to sustain the momentum of the protest against British power. To this end the Committee, having commissioned and paid for a print run of 600 copies of *The Votes and Proceedings of the Town of Boston*, sent a single copy to each of the 260 towns in Massachusetts, and others to "four fifths of the Gentlemen Selectmen in the Country, the Representatives of the several Towns, the Members of his Majesty's Council and others of Note." In doing so, the Committee expected that a public reading of the text, followed by discussion, would occur in most of these communities.[37] Such moments had been characteristic of the civic culture of Massachusetts from the outset of colonization in the seventeenth century. Then as later, the government often paid the cost of distributing election sermons and codes of law to every town. Thus in Springfield when a printed copy of the code of laws of 1648 arrived in 1649, it was promptly "published," that is, read aloud to a gathering of the townspeople.[38] In this one example, as in others, the revolutionaries relied on a structure of communication that arose within the culture of the Word.

What may have made the revolution distinctive was a momentary convergence of the two cultures I have sketched. For sure, the vernacular culture entered into the making of the "myth" of American "liberty" on which the leaders of the revolutionary movement played. These leaders appropriated the Reformation motif of the freeing of the Word of God from Catholic tyranny and enlarged it into a vision of exceptionalism: Americans were entitled to liberty because they had always been distincively free. This was the argument of John Adams's *Dissertation on the Feudal and the Canon Law* (1765-66). Adams imagined the Puritans as animated by "a love of universal liberty" that included a commitment to general education and the freedom of the press. Two centuries before him, John Foxe the martyrologist had linked the coming of the Reformation to the invention of printing. Extending that association, Adams celebrated the literacy of the colonists: "All Ranks and orders of our People, are intelligent, are accomplished--a Native of America, especially of New England, who cannot read and write is as rare a Phenomenon as a Comet."[39] In effect, the hierarchy of "ranks and orders" gave way for the moment to the values of a different cultural system.

The same accommodation occurred in the thinking of a Maryland man who came under pressure to demonstrate his support for the patriot cause. In his own defense he quoted from a letter he had written an Englishman about the common people of America. Describing them as "a well-informed, reasoning commonality, too, perhaps the most of any on earth," this erstwhile patriot anticipated Tocqueville in saluting "the freedom and general circulation of newspapers, and the eagerness and leisure of the people to read them, or to listen to those who do."[40]

Could it be that, somehow, Americans were accustomed to a democratic world of print without having to experience a democratic revolution? To acknowledge the element of ideology in these statements, as we must, and to suggest that they partake of the mythic, does not exhaust their relevance. They underscore anew the differences between revolutionary France and revolutionary America: in the former, printing, writing, and reading were closely bound up with a centralized aristocracy, while in the latter, printing, writing, and reading were far more open-ended and inclusive. It took 1789 to break open the French system. But not so in America, where 1776 may be understood as the outcome of existing structures.

## NOTES

1. Jonathan Edwards, *Misrepresentations Corrected* (Boston: S. Kneeland, 1751), p. 115. Elswehere in his writings Edwards referred to "the common people," and "the common, and less considerate and understanding sort of people." *A Treatise Concerning Religious Affections*, ed. John L. Smith (New Haven, Conn.: Yale University Press, 1959), pp. 210, 212.

2. Robert Darnton and Daniel Roche, eds., *Revolution in Print: The Press in France, 1775-1800* (Berkeley and Los Angeles: University of California Press, 1989).

3. Gordon Wood, "The Democratization of Mind in the American Revolution," in *Leadership in the American Revolution* (Washington: Library of Congress, 1974), pp. 68-71; Nathan Hatch, *The Democratization of American Christianity* (New Haven, Conn.: Yale University Press, 1989).

4. Especially in the middle colonies and New England; the southern colonies were less affected by the transformation I describe.

5. See Richard L. Bushman, "American High-Style and Vernacular Cultures," in *Colonial British America*, ed. Jack P. Greene and J. R. Pole (Baltimore, Md.: Johns Hopkins University Press, 1984), pp. 345-383.

6. David S. Shields, "Nathaniel Gardner, Jr., and the Literary Culture of Boston in the 1750s," *Early American Literature* 24 (1989), pp. 196-216.

7. The preceding description is indebted to Larzer Ziff, "Upon What Pre-text? The Book and Literary History," *American Antiquarian Society Proceedings* 95 (1985). The role of the salon in eighteenth-century France was partly replicated by the "club" in colonial and revolutionary America, but with the interesting difference that the latter were male institutions; to the best of my knowledge, no women in eighteenth-century America ran a literary salon.

8. *Gentleman's Progress: The Itinerarium of Dr. Alexander Hamilton, 1744*, ed. Carl Bridenbaugh (Chapel Hill, N.C.: University of North Carolina Press, 1948).

9. *Gentleman's Progress*, ed. Bridenbaugh, p. 91; Richard Beale Davis, "William Byrd," in *Major Writers of Early American Literature*, ed. Everett Emerson (Madison, Wis.: University of Wisconsin Press, 1972), pp. 169-171.

10. *Gentleman's Progress*, ed. Bridenbaugh, pp. 123, 129, 79, 75, 23. 70. "Whitefield" refers to the famous English evangelist George Whitefield.

11. *The Papers of Benjamin Franklin*, ed. Leonard Labaree et al. (New Haven, Conn.: Yale University Press, 1962-), vol. 1, p. 161. See also Jurgen Habermas, *The Structural Transformation of the Public Sphere: An Inquiry into a Category of Bourgeois Society*, trans. Thomas Burger (Cambridge, Mass.: M.I.T. Press, 1989).

12. Leo Lemay, "Benjamin Franklin," in *Major Writers of Early American Literature*, ed. Emerson, p. 210 and passim.

13. *Papers of Benjamin Franklin*, ed. Labaree et. al., vol. 1, pp. 4-5.

14. Lemay, "Benjamin Franklin," p. 233.

15. William Livingston (and others), *The Independent Reflector*, ed. Milton M. Klein (Cambridge, Mass.: 1963), pp. 90, 271, 339.

16. It was also reprised as professional theatre spread to cities such as Boston.

17. Royall Tyler, *The Algerine Captive*, with an introduction by Jack B. Moore (Gainesville, Fla.: Scholars' Facsimiles, 1967), pp. 32, 55.

18. Tyler, *Algerine Captive*, pp. 32, 55.   Compare the scene in Tyler's play *The Contrast* in which the country bumpkin attending the theatre mistakes a sword fight for the real thing.

19. Ibid., pp. vi-ix.

20. Isaac Backus, *All true Ministers of the Gospel, are called into that Work* (1754), repr. in *Isaac Backus on Church, State, and Calvinism*, ed. William G. McLoughlin (Cambridge, Mass.: Harvard University Press, 1968), pp. 74, 72, 77, 103 (emphasis added).

21. Samuel Davies, *Sermons on Important Subjects* (New York: Dayton and Saxton, 1841), vol. 3, p. 135.

22. Ibid., p. 127.

23. Jonathan Edwards, *The Life of David Brainerd*, ed. Norman Pettit (New Haven, Conn.: Yale University Press, 1985), pp. 343-344.

24. Erich Auerbach, *Mimesis: The Representation of Reality in Western Literature*, trans. Willard Trask (New York: Doubleday Anchor Books, 1957), pp. 39-43, 63-65. Auerbach notes that "the true heart of the Christian doctrine . . . was, as we have previously noted, totally incompatible with the principle of the separation of styles. Christ had not come as a hero and king but as a human being of the lowest social station. His first disciples were fishermen and artisans. . . . That the King of Kings was treated as a low criminal, that he was mocked, spat upon, whipped, and nailed to the cross--that story no sooner comes to dominate the consciousness of the people than it completely destroys the aesthetics of the separation of styles." (p. 63).

25. David D. Hall, "The Uses of Literacy in New England, 1600-1850," in *Printing and Society in Early America*, ed. William L. Joyce et al. (Worcester, Mass.: American Antiquarian Society, 1984), pp. 1-47.   These clergy-writers were like the genteel amateur in rejecting money as a rationale for writing. But on the other hand they hoped to reach as many readers as possible.

26. This statement is based on the data in *American Writers Before 1800: A Biographical and Critical Dictionary*, ed. James A. Levernier and Douglas R. Wilmer (Westport, Conn.: Greenwood Press, 1983).

27. It is characteristic of our secularist bias that even so great a work as Frank Luther Mott's *A History of American Magazines* fails to include an entry for *The Christian History*.

28. *Isaac Backus on Church, State, and Calvinism*, p. 123.

29. David D. Hall, *Worlds of Wonder, Days of Judgment: Popular Religious Belief in Early New England* (New York: Alfred Knopf, 1989), chap. 1.

30. I review this evidence in an essay to be included in a forthcoming collection of essays on the "commercialization of culture" in eighteenth-century America, edited by Cary Carson and Ronald Hoffman.

31. Emory Elliott, *Revolutionary Writers: Literature and Authority in the Early Republic* (New York: Oxford University Press, 1982), p. 69.

32. Stephen Botein, Jack Censer, and Harriet Ritvo, "The Periodical Press in Eighteenth-Century English and French Society: A Cross-Cultural Approach," *Comparative Studies in Society and History* 23 (1981), p. 490.

33. Frank L. Mott, *A History of American Magazines, 1741-1850* (Cambridge, Mass.: Harvard University Press, 1930), pp. 88-89.

34. The statistics on editions compiled by Thomas R. Adams in *American Independence: The Growth of an Idea. A Bibliographical Study of American Political Pamphlets Printed Between 1764 and 1776* (Providence: Brown University Press, 1965) indicate a sharp drop in the number of printings (editions) after *Common Sense*; of the 220 pamphlets in the bilbiography, only 5 had as many as 7 printings and but 1 as many as 12.

35. Harry S. Stout, "Religion, Communication, and the Ideological Origins of the American Revolution," *William and Mary Quarterly*, 3d ser., 34 (1977), 519-541.

36. Robert Darnton, *The Literary Underground of the Old Regime* (Cambridge, Mass.: Harvard University Press, 1982).

37. The episode is described in Richard L. Bushman, "Massachusetts Farmers and the Revolution," in *Society, Freedom, and Conscience: The American Revolution in Virginia, Massachusetts, and New York*, ed. Richard M. Jellison (New York: W. W. Norton, 1976), pp. 78-79.

38. Hall, *Worlds of Wonder*, p. 45.

39. *The Adams Papers: Diary and Autobiography of John Adams*, ed. L. H. Butterfield et al. (Cambridge, Mass.: Harvard University Press, 1962), vol. 1, p. 257.

40. Peter Force, *American Archives*, 4th ser., vol. 3 (Washington, 1840), p. 54. The reach and influence of the colonial newspaper is unclear. Robert M. Weir is notably reserved in describing "The Role of the Newspaper Press in the Southern Colonies on the Eve of the Revolution: An Interpretation," in *The Press & the American Revolution*, ed. Bernard Bailyn and John B. Hench (Worcester, Mass.: American Antiquarian Society, 1980), pp. 99-150.

# PUBLICATION AND THE PUBLIC SPHERE

*Michael Warner*

In *The Structural Transformation of the Public Sphere* (1962) Jürgen Habermas made a powerful version of the argument that printing changed the political life of the West. Unlike many who have made the connection, Habermas does not see printing as directly causing democratization or modernization. Instead he describes a set of institutions that he calls the bourgeois public sphere, developed in the West beginning late in the seventeenth century. An arena of discourse came to be separated both from the state and from civil society, the realm of private life (including economic life). This new public discourse could therefore regulate or criticize both. Because of its autonomy, the separateness that allowed critical regulation, the bourgeois public sphere played a key role in bringing about both the democratic revolutions of the eighteenth century and the modern nation-states that followed. Habermas argues that the independence of the public sphere has since eroded; the media of publicity, in his view, have become increasingly colonized and have lost their critical relation to both the state and civil society. From the beginning, however, reading holds the key play in his narrative. Habermas tells the story of an interesting differentiation of a public sphere from state and civil society as primarily a story about new uses of texts. Newspapers, literary salons, coffeehouses, novels, art criticism, and magazines all play an important role in his account of how the fundamental structure of politics changed.[1]

If Habermas is correct, then the spread of new reading practices of the late seventeenth and early eighteenth centuries were an epoch-making event. Once a public discourse had become specialized in the Western model, the conventions of the public sphere became an inescapable but always unrecognized political force, governing what is publicly sayable. Inescapable, because only when images or texts can be understood as meaningful to a public rather than simply to oneself, or to specific others, can they be called public. Unrecognized, because this strategy of impersonal reference--in which the subject might say, "The text addresses me" *and* "It addresses no one in particular--is a ground condition of intelligibility for public language.

The public sphere therefore presents problems of rhetorical analysis. The "public" in this new order has no empirical existence, and cannot be objectified. When we understand images and texts as public, we do not gesture to a statistically measurable series of others. We make a necessarily imaginary reference to the public *as opposed to* other individuals. Public opinion, for example, is understood as belong to a "public" rather than to scattered individuals. Opinion polls in this sense are a performative genre. They do not measure something that already exists as *public* opinion; but when they are reported as such, they are public opinion. So also it is only meaningful to speak of public discourse where it is understood as the discourse of a public rather than as an expansive dialogue among separate persons.

Because the moment of special imaginary reference is always necessary, the publicity of the public sphere never reduces to information, discussion, will formation, or any of the other scenarios by which the public sphere represents itself. The mediating rhetorical dimension of a public context must be built into each individual's relation to it, as a meaningful reference point against which something could be grasped as information, discussion, will formation. To ask about the relation between democracy and the rhetorical forms of publicity, we would have to consider how the public dimension of discourse can come about differently in different contexts of mediation, from official to mass-cultural or subcultural. There is not simply "a" public discourse as a "we" who apprehends it. The rhetorics that mediate publicity have undergone some important changes, of which the "structural transformation" that Habermas speaks of is the most far-reaching.

To the extent that publicness is a convention of imaginary reference, it raises an important problem for historians. For it could not have come about simply by the spread of printing. If new reading practices enabled the bourgeois public sphere, as Habermas argues, then those practices must have involved making the imaginary reference we now call "public." They would thus have required a special cultural interpretation of printed discourse. In the eighteenth century, as I have argued elsewhere, that is exactly what came about.[2] At least in the Anglo-American world, a new style of thinking about print, a tacit symbolic vocabulary for print, appeared in which printed discourse was linked to a special understanding of the public.

The scale of the shift is difficult to apprehend, since we still take for granted the assumptions that emerged in the period. To us, for example, it seems merely definitional to speak of printing as "publication." But the publicness of a court or a civic pageant and the publicness that we now associate with printed works are not the same. For Cotton Mather, the printing of a sermon was no more a publication of it than its preaching had been. He referred to his printed sermons as being "Preached a Second Time in the way of the Press."[3] All of his activities as a minister were, for him, public in the same way, and publicness was not a distinctive feature of print. Mather in this respect shared the notion of publicity involved in court society. In either case, being public involved one's own person. Whether you were a minister or a queen, your person represented your station, and your public activity was part of your visible presence. Printing was at best secondary-- public only as an extension of its author's visible station. "Remember," Mather used to say when giving away his tracts, "that I am speaking to you, all the while you have this Book before you!"[4] In Habermas's terms, this was the world of the representative public sphere.

During Mather's lifetime, however, a different imaginative scenario came to be applied to the reading of books. It increasingly became possible to consume printed goods with an awareness that the same printed goods were being consumed by an indefinite number of others. This awareness came to be built into the meaning of the printed object for both readers and writers. Readers began understanding their reading activity as making them members of an active public. Authors began understanding their writing as a way of abstracting away from their private persons to an impersonal discourse. In print, understood this way, one surrendered one's utterance to an audience that was by definition indefinite. Earlier writers might have responded with some anxiety to such mediation, or might simply have thought of the speaker-audience relation in different terms. In the eighteenth century the consciousness of an abstract audience became a badge of distinction, a way of claiming a public disposition.

This is not to say that the reading public had not been previously noticed in the history of printing. It is to say that sustaining an awareness of a necessarily abstract public became part of the distinctive value of print. As one Maryland writer put it in 1727, "I am very glad that a Gentleman who is a Friend to his Country, (as I am firmly persuaded the Author of the late *Letter to the Printer* really is) has communicated his Thoughts to the Publick, concerning a thing so much desired and so much wanted as a Tobacco-Law. . . And I am in Hopes that others, excited by the same generous Motive, will follow so laudable an Example, that by the Communication of Mens Thoughts and Sentiments to each other, such Methods may be taken for the Regulation of our Staple of Tobacco."[5] For this anonymous writer, responding to another anonymous writer, it is self-evident that the public is a general public, that it weighs "Thoughts and Sentiments" without caring especially whose they are, and that herein lies the utility of printed discourse. So although his pamphlet is nominally en epistle, the rhetoric of disinterested general debate means that both the freeholder-author and his representative-addressee must sustain an awareness of the limitless others who may be reading. They implicitly recognize the reproduction of printing as an important feature of their relation to each other. To the extent that assumptions such as these came to dominate the uses of print in the late seventeenth and early eighteenth centuries, printing became publication in a newly special way.

The transformation was a cultural rather than technological one. Printing was scarcely new, and no major technological improvements occurred in the period.  But different assumptions were brought to bear on the cultural meaning of printedness.  Their chief effect in the printing trade was to attach a higher social value not only on the genres of debate--pamphlets, broadsides, and the like--but also on new genres, especially the newspaper.  Moreover, since the assumptions in question were the basis on which to decide who speaks, to whom, with what constraints, and with what legitimacy, they had profound consequences for the nature of power.  Such important but silent decisions could be called the metapolitics of speech.  They are always linked to whatever passes for common sense about the medium in use.  In the case of the shift I have described, the consequences were profound and complex, but they can only be grasped when historians of print begin to think about the assumptions governing the conditions of utterance in a cultural context, about the tacit force of what I would call the dominant metalanguage.

By "metalanguage," I mean something more than the express opinions people held about printing, or what is usually called their "attitude" toward print, or even the lexical categories for speaking about print (such as "publication" or even "print" itself), though the latter are an important part of it.  Printing, like any mediating context, is also governed by special discourse rules that can only be inferred from practice.  These also appear to have changed considerably in the early eighteenth century.  Even personal pronouns come to be used in a different way in print contexts.  Here, for example, is how the Spectator, in 1712, describes the advantage of being realized in the medium of print:

> It is much more difficult to converse with the World in a real than a personated Character.  That might pass for Humour, in the *Spectator*, which would look like Arrogance in a Writer who sets his Name to his Work.  The Fictitious Person might condemn those who disapproved him, and extoll his own Performances, without giving Offence.  He might assume a Mock-Authority, without being looked upon as vain and conceited.  The Praises or Censures of himself fall only upon the Creature of his Imagination, and if any one finds fault with him, the Author may reply with the Philosopher of old, *Thou dost but beat the Case* of Anaxarchus.[6]

The Spectator's attitude of conversing with the world is emphatically public and disinterested.  But it could not come about without a value placed on the anonymous subjectivity here associated with print.  The Spectator's point about himself is that he is different from the person of Richard Steele.  Just as the Spectator here secures a certain liberty in not calling himself Richard Steele, so it would take a certain liberty for us to call the author of this passage Richard Steele--all the more so since the pronoun reference begins to slip around the third sentence ("those who disapproved *him*"). The ambiguous relation between Spectator and Writer, Steele says, liberates him. The Spectator is a prosthetic person for Steele, to borrow a term from Lauren Berlant--prosthetic in the sense that it does not reduce to or express the given body.[7] By making him no longer self-identical, it allows him the negativity of debate--not a pure negativity, not simply reason or criticism, but an identification with a disembodied public subject that he can imagine as parallel to his private person.

In a sense, however, that public subject does have a body, because the public, prosthetic body takes abuse for the private person. The last line of the passage refers to the fact that Anaxarchus was pommelled to death with iron pestles after offending a despotic ruler. In the ventriloquistic act of taking up his speech, therefore, Steele both imagines an intimate violation of his person and provides himself with a kind of prophylaxis against violation (to borrow another term from Berlant). Anaxarchus himself was not so lucky as to be fictitious. Despite what Steele says, the privilege that he obtains over his body in this way does not in fact reduce to the simple body/soul distinction that Anaxarchus, in the quoted speech, invokes. Instead, it allows him to think of his public discourse as a routine form of self-abstraction, quite unlike the ascetic self-integration of Anaxarchus. When Steele impersonates the philosopher to have the Spectator (or someone) say, "Thou dost but beat the case of Anaxarchus," he appropriates an intimate subjective benefit of publicity's self-abstraction.

Part of the metalanguage governing print in the period of the Spectator--the same period as Cotton Mather's late career--is the convention that persons who speak in printed discourse are only persons in a special way. The contemporary obsession with anonymity and pseudonyms indicate the appeal of this discourse convention. Although pseudonyms had of course been known before, to use them now became a way of implicitly asserting that one's thoughts and sentiments should be judged by impersonal public criteria, that one had no special private warrant or interest in them. Whether speaking as the Spectator or as Richard Steele, Richard Steele found that in print he could speak differently than in other mediating contexts. He acquired, in the very generality of first-person pronouns, an abstractness that was part of the new meaning of being public.

The conventions about public speech involved in such a passage could hardly be inconsequential where they were widely accepted. Whatever the dominant metalanguage might be for a discourse medium in a given context, its ways of uttering or ways of comprehending will necessarily be linked to assumptions about what persons should be, whom they address and how, what a legitimate audience would be, and what the social environment of the discourse might be. In this case, Steele's way of making himself abstract elaborates specific republican assumptions about the citizen's exercise of virtue. The distance between Steele and his persona is understood as a version of the disinterest of the freeholder. Steele does not need to make that link explicit. He takes it as a natural feature of printed discourse, as does the Maryland author quoted earlier. To them, one who speaks in print is one who speaks to an indefinite and impartial public, and therefore one who speaks in a voice that is in some measure impersonal.

From such an apparently innocent notion about the character of print discourse, a great many assumptions about the social world could be extrapolated. Why, for example, does Steele's understanding of print have so much to do with *criticism*? The advantage of a fictitious character in print, he thinks, is the ability to criticize (and be criticized). He speaks of "contemning," "disapproving," "extolling," "giving Offence," "praising," "censuring," and "finding fault." In what social context is it valuable for a great many anonymous people to be able to do these things? Steele does not answer that question. He takes the utility of criticism to be axiomatic. Yet we can easily imagine other contexts, including the entire public order of court society, in which it would be anything but valued. That print should enable a routinely critical discourse is the ground assumption of the bourgeois public sphere as Habermas describes it. That is why, as he shows, there was considerable continuity between the contexts of art criticism, music or literary criticism, science, and political debate. Each elaborated the notion of a critical public as well as the notion of impersonally expressed opinion.

How were these notions established as values intrinsic to printed discourse? I have elsewhere argued that the metalanguage of this public discourse was from the beginning linked to the relatively specific political language of republicanism.[8] It was in the culture of republicanism--with its categories of disinterested virtue and supervision--that a rhetoric of print consumption became authoritative, a way of understanding the publicness of publication. A critical, evaluating public is desirable if you think of the political world as requiring citizens to be ever vigilant against the encroachment and corruption of power. That link could be made explicit, as it often was in debates about freedom of the press in the late seventeenth and early eighteenth centuries. But where it was not explicitly made, the metalinguistic assumption that printed discourse addresses an abstract critical public confirms and extends a republican assumption about the social world. The Anglo-American strand of republicanism allowed people to think of the mediation of print as enabling rather than compromising. It was both a political vocabulary and a vocabulary for thinking of the routine use of print as valuable--something that is not, after all, naturally or universally true.

A complex body of assumptions underlies any notion that a specialized, critical, public printed discourse is desirable, but for this period we could boil them down to two related principles. The first is what

Habermas calls "the principle of supervision": "that very principle which demands that proceedings be made public."[9]  When the public is treated as intrinsically critical, having a right to censure with impunity, having a duty to read critically, having an active involvement in ongoing debate, then it is assumed that the public essentially supervises the public world.  This role for the public is radically different from that of the public before which power displayed itself in the representative public sphere of court society.  In the context of printed discourse, it makes the reader a citizen, and vice versa.  (Interestingly, *The Spectator* plays on this shift in its very title: nominally the passive observer of spectacle, the Spectator in fact emerges as an active critic in a supervising public that the essay serial helps to create.)

The second principle of the public sphere is what I have called the principle of negativity, by which I mean that in public printed discourse the evaluation of opinion is separated from the evaluation of persons.  What you say in public is valid not because of who you are but despite who you are.  This is both your privilege--since it allows you to get away with things, as Richard Steele points out--and your obligation.  You are expected to speak impartially, setting aside personal motives, personal history, personal particularities.  You enter into a negative relation to yourself in the self-abstraction of public discourse.  Such a posture is not valuable in all cultural contexts.  It is the very thing that Cotton Mather denies when he asks his reader to consider him as speaking ministerially through the text.  It was made valuable in large part because of the republican opposition between general and private interests and the corresponding notion that the virtuous citizen is capable of a disinterested regard for the general good.  Many writers of the period were capable of making explicit links between their pseudonymous printing and their disinterested virtue, but once print began to be understood as the impersonal discourse of an abstract public, it was not necessary to make that link, nor to write with a pseudonym, in order to trade on the controlled depersonalization of print.

The two principles, supervision and negativity, are my way of describing the metalanguage of publication.  They were not articulated as such but were implicit in commonsense perceptions and uses of print.  The act of reading a newspaper, or nailing up a broadside, already implied these basic discourse conventions of the public sphere.  The same principles could be expressed in the republican political vocabulary, as the need for the vigilance of the disinterested and virtuous citizen against the corruptions of office and power, and so forth.  But the point of calling them a metalanguage is to point to the mutually determining force exercised between a culture of discourse and political culture.  Assumptions about the political world imply conventions of discourse and vice versa.  My empirical claim would be that around the early eighteenth century these linked sets of assumptions went through a significant transformation, accounting for the emergence of the public sphere that

Habermas describes. But a point of more general significance for the history of print is that the medium itself cannot be studied or even defined apart from a cultural metalanguage that both makes it intelligible and immerses it in the whole web of social and political relations.

## NOTES

1. Jürgen Habermas, *The Structural Transformation of the Public Sphere*, trans. Thomas Burger (Cambridge, Mass.: MIT Press, 1989).

2. The arguments condensed here can be found in their full form in *The Letters of the Republic: Publication and the Public Sphere in Eighteenth-Century America* (Cambridge, Mass.: Harvard University Press, 1990).

3. Mather, *Utilia* (Boston, 1716), iv.

4. Quoted in Kenneth Silverman, *Life and Times of Cotton Mather* (New York: Columbia University Press, 1985), 198.

5. Anon., *A Letter from a Freeholder, to a Member of the Lower House of Assembly* (Annapolis, 1727).

6. [Richard Steele], *The Spectator*, no. 555, in *Selections from "The Tatler" and "The Spectator"*, ed. Angus Ross (New York: Penguin, 1982), 213.

7. Lauren Berlant, "National Brands/National Body: *Imitation of Life*," in *Comparative American Identities: Race, Sex, and Nationality in the Modern Text*, ed. Hortense J. Spillers (New York and London: Routledge, 1991), pp. 110-140.

8. *Letters of the Republic, op. cit.*

9. Jürgen Habermas, "The Public Sphere: An Encyclopedia Article," trans. Sarah Lennox and Frank Lennox, *New German Critique* 3 (1974): 49-55.

# COLLECTING AND USING MATERIALS

# THE FRENCH REVOLUTION AND BOOKS: CULTURAL BREAK, CULTURAL CONTINUITY

*Henri-Jean Martin*

(Translated by David Skelly and Carol Armbruster)

On the eve of the French Revolution there were several major categories of libraries in France.[1] The Bibliothèque du Roi (The King's Library) was the largest library in Europe. It held approximately 300,000 printed volumes; 30,000 Greek, Latin, French, and Oriental manuscripts; and extensive collections of prints and medals. Numerous ecclesiastical libraries held a good part of our national heritage. Most of these libraries maintained a certain kind of humanistic, classical tradition, but the more active, namely those that belonged to the Benedictines of Saint-Maur, were veritable centers of learned activity. Of special note were the ecclesiastical libraries belonging to the *collèges*, which collected more contemporary literature, featuring, for example, some of the works of Montesquieu. Toward the end of the Old Regime, however, two important factors adversely affected church libraries: the increasing rarity of religious vocations and the expulsion of the Jesuits from France (1764). During this period church libraries were not maintained as well as others, and they failed to keep pace.

Members of the old French aristocracy and wealthy private citizens, such as the farmers general, on the other hand, had built up large libraries in conjunction with their private museums, or cabinets of curiosities, or with their scientific "studies," reflecting the owners' openness to the ideas of the Enlightenment. Concurrently, a certain "bibliophilia" had evolved in these circles. Priceless manuscripts, documents pertaining to French history, and rare and early printed books were eagerly sought. A mere fad may have been at the origin of the large-scale book trade that developed, but amateurs, many well-informed, as well as people simply wishing to display their wealth, suddenly found themselves surrounded by book dealers, librarians, and scholars. Many members of the clergy figured among the book professionals. They were well aware of the great value of collections, and many wished to take advantage of them, either for personal benefit or for that of their monasteries. A Benedictine from Metz, Dom Maugérard, for example, became famous during the last years of the Old Regime by scouring religious institutions across the Rhine and bringing back, notably from Mainz, two particularly precious 42-line editions of the Bible, one on paper and the other on vellum. Both of these Bibles found their way into the Bibliothèque du Roi just before the Revolution.[2]

Networks of book dealers and peddlers were responsible for a wide dissemination of new titles--forbidden books as well as those published with royal consent. Books, however, remained expensive items. Public libraries and lending libraries had been developing in France for several decades but were in my opinion unable to provide readers with the complete range of works they might have wanted to consult.[3] "Gifted people," without personal fortune or the help of a patron, could familiarize themselves thoroughly with Enlightenment literature only by asking permission of a rich or prominent person to consult the volumes in his collection or by requesting books through the active social networks of those days. Revolutionaries expressed frustration about the difficult access to books and other literature, especially scientific studies.[4]

The French Revolution was most certainly the revolution of the book par excellence. In face of the great diversity of local customs and privileges in existence throughout France, the French Revolution was first of all the Revolution of the Written Law, a law before which everyone was equal. In addition, the revolutionaries were educated to the point of saturation in the tradition of classical books. Most importantly, though, the revolutionaries considered themselves products of the Enlightenment, which was disseminated by print. We can thus understand why freedom of the press was written into the Declaration of the Rights of Man and why, on September 9, 1792, the Legislative Assembly passed a bill proposed by Anacharsis Clootz, the "orator of the human race," approving the removal of Gutenberg's ashes to the Pantheon. Unfortunately, these were lost during the siege of Mainz.[5]

There was a great respect, even a passion, for books. Many political men, commissioners of the Republic, even generals of the Empire, proved to be good bibliographers, even bibliophiles, as demonstrated, for example, by the books that some of them wrote on the history and invention of printing. Certain passages in their memoirs show that they, too, had succumbed to the "bibliomania" in vogue in France since the end of the Old Regime.[6]

French revolutionaries wanted to preserve the book heritage of France. They wanted to preserve even the books that had spread and sanctioned the errors that the revolutionaries denounced. As heirs of the Enlightenment, they intended to spread its ideas and preserve the evidence of past erring ways to serve as a lesson to posterity. To justify their policies about books, the revolutionaries often evoked the idea of "public instruction." They did not, however, promote any immediate increase in literacy amongst the masses, who were still in part illiterate.

Under such conditions, revolutionary policy concerning libraries remained above all a matter of circumstance.  After the property of the clergy was put at the disposition of the nation (1789), that of the émigrés and those condemned to death seized (1790), and, finally, when the academies and learned societies were suppressed and their collections confiscated, (1793),[7] the question naturally arose as to what to do with all the various art works and "monuments" that had thus accrued to the nation.  Particularly at stake was the disposition of the innumerable volumes that had become state property.  The Constituent Assembly set up a committee to determine what should be done.  This committee, which survived in one form or another throughout the Revolution, and which we shall simply refer to here as the Committee of Scholars, was composed not only of scholars and artists but also of librarians, clergymen, learned persons in general, and antiquarian book dealers, all admirably well-informed about the contents and value of the manuscripts and printed materials.[8]  Of particular note here is Anne-Louis-François de Paule Lefèvre d'Ormesson de Noyseau, a former president of the parliament who became the king's librarian on December 23, 1789.  First a member of the Constituent Assembly and then a member of the Committee of Scholars, he found himself out of favor and sent to the scaffold during the Terror.[9] Hubert-Pascal Ameilhon, the librarian and historiographer of the City of Paris, was a royal censor and a member of the Académie des Inscriptions et Belles-Lettres under the Old Regime.  A patriot from the very first moments of the Revolution, although somewhat compromised with the Jacobins, Ameilhon played such an important part in the revolutionary confiscations of books and materials that he was elected librarian of the Commune of Paris.  He retained the trust of the Commune for a long time.[10]  Another member of the Committee of Scholars was Guillaume de Bure, a book dealer for the Académie des Inscriptions et Belles-Lettres, for the Bibliothèque du Roi, and for the library of the count of Provence.  He signed numerous prestigious sales catalogues.[11]  Other members of the Committee included Barthélémy Mercier, known as Mercier de Saint-Léger, former librarian for the Abbey of Sainte-Geneviève, bibliographer and bibliophile emeritus.[12]  Dom Germain Poirier was archivist of Saint-Germain des Prés[13]  We must note especially Gaspard-Michel Leblond, member of the Académie des Inscriptions et Belles-Lettres and librarian of the Collège des Quatre Nations (that is, the Mazarine Library), beginning in 1791.  He was the secretary for the Committee for many years and a frequent opponent of Ameilhon.[14]  Antoine-Alexandre Barbier, a former ecclesiastic, eventually joined the Committee and in 1798 became the librarian of the Council of State.  He distinguished himself later as librarian for the Emperor Napoleon and as the author of a *Dictionnaire des ouvrages anonymes*, which has remained a classic.[15]  All of these people had been trained in scholarly bibliography under the Old Regime. Most of them had been close to the great bibliophiles of that time, especially to the most famous of them all: the Duc de la Vaillière.[16]

It remains to determine what policy was for the confiscated materials. As a rule, the Committee of Scholars struggled long to win acceptance over the vacillations of Assemblies and the vicissitudes of time, of certain general principles: the deposit of all impounded volumes into "book warehouses," where the integrity of individual collections was to be carefully maintained; and the compilation of a *Bibliographie générale de la France*, intended as a huge inventory of all confiscated books. They thus gave priority to safeguarding and inventorying the seized material--a sign of their good sense considering conditions in France at the time. They struggled ceaselessly to prohibit materials from being sold or liquidated without authorization. At the same time, however, they were forced to delay indefinitely setting up a program to create a network of public libraries. In the end this network never did materialize.[17]

The most important matter long remained the compilation of a *Bibliographie générale de la France*. The *Bibliographie* was to enumerate the some 5 million volumes seized from ecclesiastical institutions, plus those taken from collections belonging to émigrés and various academies and learned societies, a total of roughly 10 million at least.[18] Everything seems to point to d'Ormesson's having been the one to propose this huge enterprise in the first place, as he obviously wanted to seize the opportunity to complete the collections in the Bibliothèque du Roi, in order to gather everything that had ever been published in France as well as the most important works of the foreign production.[19]

The bibliographers on the Committee of Scholars, all thoroughly competent, sent very precise instructions to the provinces regarding the preservation of the nation's newly acquired books and the catalogs they were expected to create. A memorandum prepared and circulated under the direction of Mercier Saint-Léger prescribed using the backs of playing cards for cataloging and culling data from them to prepare summary statements. Beginning June 24, 1792, these statements were presented to the members of the Committee, who in turn marked the entries either *G* or *V*, according to whether the works in question were to be kept (Fr. *gardés*) or sold (Fr. *vendus*).[20]

Unfortunately, preserving and cataloging such an enormous mass ran up against insurmountable practical and psychological obstacles. For one thing, the former owners of the libraries, or their agents, had little enthusiasm for being stripped of their possessions. There was a great deal of dissembling and hurrying about to sell the most valuable pieces before they could be inventoried. Subsequently, those books which had been seized, often poorly guarded, as well as pictures and art objects, became part of intense commercial activity, in which foreigners seem to have played a major role.[21]  It was thus that a certain Pierre Dubrowsky, an attaché of the Russian minister plenipotentiary in Paris, misappropriated, after 1789, it would seem, more than 700 manuscripts, not counting whole series of documents of all kinds, including part of the archives of Chancellor Séguier.  Half the collection he had thus put together was left with d'Ormesson when Dubrowsky had to leave Paris after the events of August 10, but he was able to recover at least a part of it at the auction following d'Ormesson's execution.  Once in Russia, he offered this veritable treasure to the czar, who made him conservator of the Imperial Library of St. Petersburg.  Appointed senior member of the Council of State when he retired in 1812, he died in 1816.  The czar contributed 2,000 rubles for his burial.[22]  A shady affair, indeed, where espionage, the passion for great collections, and *raison d'état* became entangled, but where the roles played by dom Poirier and d'Ormesson--and, through them, by the Committee of Scholars--remain to this day ambiguous, to say the least.

The Committee of Scholars was able to supervise and direct the moving of books and their inventory only in Paris.  In the provinces everything depended on those whose task it was to gather the books into warehouses and inventory them.  In addition to librarians and former clergy, there were many book dealers and ruined aristocrats among these people.  Many of them were, of course, competent, but those who oversaw the richer collections were often inclined to obstruct an operation that threatened to despoil their own districts for the benefit of the National Library, or even for the benefit of regions less well endowed according to the new scheme of distribution, arrangements that were periodically the subject of rumor.  Moreover, everyone was all the more tempted to misappropriate valuable works because they were paid so poorly for their jobs.  In some cases, they were not paid at all.[23]

Moreover, orders from Paris to preserve countless copies of the same editions of books of "mysticism," as well as works tainted by "superstitions" or "feudalism," could hardly fail to antagonize officials recruited from "activist" circles.  These officials, furthermore, considered themselves perfectly capable of implementing the necessary sorting and selecting procedures without having to call on a handful of Parisian scholars for advice.  Several famous texts amply attest to this feeling.[24]

One can easily imagine why, in such an atmosphere, authorities responsible for liquidating the property of the émigrés and, more generally, agents of the financial services would insist that confiscated libraries be sold.[25]  It is well known that the revolutionaries were inordinately fond of bureaucratic paperwork, and ran out of paper regularly.  Works piled up in the literary warehouses, often dirty and deteriorated as a result of their tribulations, would thus be very tempting prey, both because people had learned how to reuse old paper and because such documents were frequently suspected to contain feudal titles that did not merit preservation in any event.[26]  Finally, the troops of the Republic demanded parchment or paper to make charges for their cannons. Many liturgical books met their end in this way. This was especially the case for the antiphonaries, which were printed on parchment, and devotional works, whose pages were much sought after to make cartridges.

All in all, if archival documents and especially feudal titles often fell victim to burnings and blatant acts of vandalism, very few such occurrences involving books have been uncovered. At the most we could mention the ceremony that took place in Verdun in front of the whole town and district and department representatives. All the books were burned, along with cult objects and works of art dragged out of the cathedral. The constitutionally appointed bishop of the district was forced to dance around the bonfire.[27] On the other hand, defenders of our book heritage managed to keep the coats of arms from being cut off bindings when the Convention decreed that all royal and aristocratic insignia were to be removed from all monuments, no matter what they were.[28]

Finally, let us note in passing that people's interest in manuscripts and early printed books during this period often stimulated French occupying forces during the revolutionary and imperial wars to pick up precious books intended to make Paris and the National, later Imperial, Library a sort of enormous mausoleum. Here they intended to gather together testimonies to the progress of the human spirit for the glory and instruction of the Grande Nation, which they had promoted to the rank of guide for other nations in their march toward Liberty.[29] Let us simply note that although the tactics employed might today raise a few eyebrows, nevertheless, the creaming of the cream of French libraries--in Lyons, for example, where revolt had just been put down--and especially of Belgian, German, and Italian collections, mainly by a certain Henri Beyle, Daru's nephew (better known under his pen name: Stendahl) was carried out with the most consummate skill and impeccable taste. It was what we might perhaps refer to as the "liberation" of a heritage.[30]

One ought not, however, underestimate the work carried out by the catalogers of the Republic. The accounts and reports that have survived show that the Paris office of the *Bibliographie générale de la France* received at least 3 million catalog cards. The catalogers undertook not only the compilation of an author catalogue of the works preserved in the collections concerned, but also made tables according to place of printing and printer and an inventory of incunabula.[31] Unfortunately, all this took longer than foreseen. The abbé Grégoire was still defending the vast undertaking shortly after the 9th of Thermidor (July 27, 1794) in his famous report on vandalism.[32] Day by day, however, and despite so much good will, the ambitious plan laid out during the heady days at the beginning of the Revolution proved to be more and more utopian. The *Bibliographie générale de la France*, which employed so many people and which was so labor intensive was not abandoned until 1796, but by that time, the game was already over.

In fact, the financial services considered it increasingly urgent to get rid of those books whose upkeep and cataloging were so very expensive. The members of the Committee of Scholars tried to throw out some of the ballast by authorizing sales and signing export permits, chiefly to Zurich and Lausanne.[33] After that there was nothing else but to sort them out cursorily on the spot and discard anything deemed unworthy of being kept.

The situation of the impounded materials seemed all the more precarious in that pieces had been long removed from them regularly. Very early, it seems, administrative officers and diplomats of the Republic had demanded that libraries be set up for them in keeping with the dignity of their functions. This trend grew to such an extent that even today you may still find scraps, often precious ones, of our heritage in many administrative offices and bureaus.[34] In addition, after the 9th of Thermidor the government began to return books to prisoners who had been freed, or to the families of the unjustly condemned, such as Lavoisier.[35] After this, it became necessary to return loads of books to the clergy, as Catholicism was being restored.[36]

The liquidation of these literary depositories took a long time--at least until the Restoration. The Republic's great mistake was the continual postponement of the key element: setting up a sensible plan for French libraries.[37] The absence of this plan did not unduly affect Paris. The selections and allocations carried out in the depositories in the capital by two particularly competent bibliographers, Leblond and Barbier, made it possible to gather the essential part of the confiscated holdings into organized institutions. The Bibliothèque Nationale was given priority in selections. Three other libraries of the Old Regime survived perhaps because they were classified national depositories: one was the former library of the Abbey of St. Geneviève--where Mercier Saint-Léger had been active, and which was still being very well directed by Pingré. Not even Ameilhon had dared to touch it. Then there was the Bibliothèque des Quatre Nations--that is, the Bibliothèque Mazarine--which Leblond was protecting, and, finally, the Bibliothèque de l'Arsenal, which held the very rich collections of Paulmy d'Argenson. These collections had been purchased by the Duc d'Artois shortly before the Revolution. The Bibliothèque de l'Arsenal was enriched by the remains of the Bastille archives and many other priceless items. Ameilhon was appointed head librarian. He was forced to abandon his directorship of the Bibliothèque de la Ville de Paris, which became the library of the Institut de France after the Republic restored the academies. To these we may add a small number of specialized libraries, the principal ones being those belonging to the Museum, Arts et Métiers, and the Faculté de Médécine, not counting, for example, those belonging to the countless administrative offices and bureaus just mentioned above, or to those belonging to military schools and institutions or to posts scattered throughout the country.[38]

In Paris, the greater part of the collections seems to have been saved, in spite of rather frequent depredatory sales and vandalism. The provinces, on the other hand, suffered a great deal from the government's hesitations. Following a number of requests and intervention by Convention members at the very highest level (e.g., Lakanal, Coupé, and Grégoire) a decree dated the 8th of Pluviôse in the Year II (January 27, 1794) determined that public libraries in the large communes would be maintained and that in each district a library would be established to house the books from the literary depositories in their area. Application of this measure, however, was delayed, mainly because of the lack of action on the part of the financial services. Subsequently, a bill dated the 7th of Ventôse in the Year III (February 25, 1795) decreed that each department should have a central school with a library whose holdings were to be drawn from the literary depositories. This brought about more moving of materials and the affixing of highly unaesthetic stamps to large numbers of volumes. This all came to an end on May 1, 1802, when the central schools were abolished and replaced by lycées. It was decided that the lycées would not have libraries. The library materials were put at the disposition and made the responsibility of the municipalities by order of the consul dated 8 Pluviôse in the Year XI (January 28, 1803). In this way Napoleon rid himself of the burdensome custodial responsibility of these books, while maintaining them as state property. The books became the foundation for the municipal libraries that we know today. Many of those books remained forgotten in the attics or cellars of public buildings, chiefly city halls, where sometimes even today valuable works still turn up.[39]

Can we give a brief assessment of this whole business? The moderate revolutionaries whom we saw intervene on the side of books were part of an Old Regime tradition. Disciples of the Enlightenment that they were, they wanted to preserve what they could of our written heritage. They saved the major part of a prestigious literary heritage. However, the proliferation of great bibliographers between 1760 and 1830 (I am thinking here not only of Ameilhon, DeBure, Mercier de Saint-Léger, or Barbier but also of their successors: Nodier, Peignot, Brunet, Quérard, etc.) would appear, aside from the revolutionary phenomenon as such, to correspond to a time when France began to see in certain aspects of her cultural heritage what Michel de Certeau called "the beauty of death."[40]

The Nation thus inherited a huge supply of books from the Revolution, all the more difficult to administer in that the volumes in question arrived at their new destination without being completely registered or marked as to ownership. It still remains to find out how the state administered this patrimony.

On the whole, despite the return to their owners of books confiscated outside France--ostensibly in 1815--the Bibliothèque Nationale was unable to manage effectively the flood of materials brought in by the Revolution. This eminent institution, while never totally supported, was also never totally neglected by the government and was able to go on adding to its treasures throughout the 19th and 20th centuries thanks to legal deposit and sometimes substantial allocations for acquisitions. This was not the case for other institutions in Paris. These institutions became a sort of necropoli unfunded by the government. Throughout this period most of the municipal libraries, often still prey to sales and excessive depredations throughout the 19th century, were used mainly by "enlightened" middle-class readers and scholars. Municipal libraries were also understaffed and lacked sufficient funding. Drowning in a sea of documents, they were neither able to catalog the treasures accumulated as a result of the Revolution, nor even physically to maintain the collections. They were in no position to replenish their holdings. Nonetheless, the new university, a completely novel creation from beginning to end, cut off from any kind of scholarly tradition and lacking a library, remained for years the refuge of a kind of neoclassical rhetorical tradition. There is a singular contrast here between the American collections, esteemed objects of value because of their high cost, and the revolutionary confiscations, acquired for nothing and hence neglected by their new owners. We must admit that even after the Republic was finally in place, it honored the Revolution's commitments to safeguard the heritage it had nationalized no more than did any of the other later regimes in France.

If we wish to extend the field of our reflections, we might point out that the actions of the revolutionaries were in line with a certain national attitude. In point of fact, the revolutionaries nationalized French heritage not only because they were in the grip of circumstances, but because they acted according to a certain logic that dictates that anything relating to the common interest is the responsibility of public authorities. This constitutes a major difference between Anglo-Saxon and French practices. While English or American libraries, established as a rule by citizens' groups joining together for a common purpose, have never stopped growing, so, naturally, French libraries seem to be abstract creations decreed by the state. This has been the inevitable cause of much concrete neglect.

It would be wrong to begrudge the revolutionaries for a failure to develop what we might call "public reading." Traditional French weakness in this area is above all, it would seem, due to a certain mentality: as a Catholic country, France reveres the cleric, the possessor of a learned culture, who likes to consider himself the country's mentor, while the Anglo-Saxons, who have mainly a Protestant culture, have regarded private reading as something sacred. The disappearance of the old clientele and the former collections doubtless provided the stimulus for nineteenth-century efforts to renew the French book trade, without, however, reviving the custom of patronage.

Let us add in closing that the violence with which the revolutionaries denounced the "opulence" of the Old Regime collectors and condemned the institution of patronage reminds us that the French have traditionally scorned certain kinds of private wealth. In turn, the wealthy French are not too fond of contributing to enterprises for the common good: that seems to them to be the responsibility of the public sector. All this augurs poorly for current efforts to revive certain forms of cultural patronage based on the Anglo-Saxon model in a society that has changed greatly over the last two centuries. But these are all just so many attitudes and ways of thinking: they vary from country to country and doubtless deserve to stimulate some comparative studies.

## NOTES

1. Simone Balayé, *La Bibliothèque nationale des origines à 1800* (Genève: Droz, 1988); Claude Jolly, ed. *Les Bibliothèques sous l'Ancien Régime*, vol. 2 of *Histoire des bibliothèques françaises* (Paris: Promodis/Cercle de la Librairie, 1988).

2. *1789, le Patrimoine libéré: 200 trésors entrés à la Bibliothèque nationale de 1789 à 1799* (Paris: Bibliothèque nationale, 1989), no. 41.

3. Jean-Louis Pailhes, "En marge des bibliothèques. L'apparition des cabinets de lecture," in *Les Bibliothèques sous l'Ancien Régime*, ed. Jolly, pp. 415-420.

4. The difficulty of access to scientific laboratories was the source of greatest frustration according to the reports written by the abbé Grégoire. For Saint-Just, see Bernard Vinot, *Saint-Just* (Paris: Fayard, 1985).

5. Leopold Delisle, *A la mémoire de Gutenberg* (Paris: Imprimerie nationale, 1900); cf. "Comment on écrivit l'histoire du livre," in Henri-Jean Martin, *Le Livre français sous l'Ancien Régime* (Paris: Promodis/Cercle de la Librairie, 1988), pp. 16-17.

6. Henri-Jean Martin, "Le sacre de Gutenberg," *Revue de synthèse* 4ème sér. (January-June 1992), pp. 15-27.

7. The fundamental work on what follows is Pierre Riberette, *Les Bibliothèques françaises pendant la Révolution (1789-1795)* (Paris: Bibliothèque nationale, 1970).

8. The Committee of Scholars served only in an advisory capacity. On the various committees and commissions that were called in, see especially *Procès-verbaux de la Commission de l'Instruction publique à l'Assemblée législative, puis de la Convention nationale*, ed. James Guillaume (Paris: Imprimerie nationale, 1891-1907; tables added 1952-1961); *Procès-verbaux de*

*la Commission des Monuments* (1790-1794), ed. Louis Tuetey, (Paris: N. Charavay, 1902-1903), 2 vols.; *Procès-verbaux de la Commission temporaire des arts*, ed. Louis Tuetey (Paris: Imprimerie nationale, 1912-1918).

9. Balayé, *La Bibliothèque nationale*, pp. 324-353.

10. Hélène Dufresne, *Erudition et esprit public au XVIIIe siècle. Le bibliothécaire H. P. Ameilhon* (Paris: Nizet, 1962).

11. This is Guillaume DeBure the Elder; cf. *Procès-verbaux de la Commission temporaire des arts*, ed. Tuetey, p. lvii.

12. See Simon Chardon La Rochette, *Notice sur la vie et les écrits de Mercier de Saint-Léger* (Paris, Year VII/1799) and dissertation in progress by Monique Esperon, Ecole des Hautes Etudes, 4ème Section.

13. *Procès-verbaux de la Commission temporaire des arts*, ed. Guillaume, p. lix. Dom Germain Poirier played a major role in the disposition of archives and monuments. Many archives were destroyed. See Léon marquis de Laborde, *Les Archives de la France, leurs vicissitudes sous la Révolution, leur régénération sous l'Empire* (Paris: Vve Renouard, 1867); Edgar Boutaric, "Le Vandalisme révolutionnaire. Les archives pendant la Révolution française, *Revue des questions historiques*, 1867, pp. 325-396.

14. Laborde, p. liv.

15. Ibid., p. lvii.

16. Dominique Coq, "Le Parangon du bibliophile français: le duc de La Vallière et sa collection," in *Les Bibliothèques sous l'Ancien Régime*, ed. Jolly, pp. 317-335.

17. Riberette, *Les Bibliothèques françaises*; Dominique Varry, "'Il faut que les Lumières arrivent par torrents': La Révolution française et la création des bibliothèques publiques: projets et réalités," *Bulletin des bibliothèques de France*, 35 (special bicentenary edition, 1990).

18. Statistics for books confiscated during the Revolution have varied greatly. Cf. Varry, "Vicissitudes et aléas des livres placés 'sous la main' de la Nation," in *Révolution française et 'vandalisme révolutionnaire': Actes du collogue de Clermont-Ferrand (December 15-17, 1998)*, ed. Simon Bernard-Griffiths, Marie-Claude Chemin, and Jean Eharard (Paris: Universitas), pp. 277-284; see also Graham Keith Barnett, *Histoire des bibliothèques publiques en France de la Révolution à 1939*, trans. Thierry Lefèvre (Paris: Promodis/Cercle de la Librairie, 1987), especially p. 50. Statistics from a 1975 study indicate that the size of the old collections of French libraries, even taking into account extensive destruction, have been greatly underestimated. The collections of the Bibliothèque nationale seem to have been purposely underreported. Cf. Françoise Blechet and Annie Charon, *Les Fonds anciens des bibliothèques françaises, résultats de l'enquête de 1975* (Paris: Institut de recherche et d'histoire des textes, 1981).

19. Balayé, *La Bibliothèque nationale*, pp. 336-338.

20. *Procès-verbaux de la Commission de l'Instruction publique à l'Assemblée législative*, ed. Guillaume, vol. 2, pp. 798-799.

21. Varry, "Vicissitudes et aléas des livres placés 'sous la main' de la Nation."

22. Michel François, "Pierre Dubrowski et les manuscrits de Saint-Germain-des-Prés à Léningrad," *Mémorial du XIVe centenaire de l'Abbay de Saint-Germain-des-Prés*, 1959, pp. 333-342. See also T. P. Voronova, "Peter P. Dubrowski, 1754-1816 and the Saint-Germain manuscripts," *Book Collector* 27 (1978); and Patricia Z. Thompson, "Biography of a Library: The Western Europe manuscript collection of Peter Dubrowski at Leningrad," *Journal of Library History, Philosophy, and Comparative Librarianship* 19, no. 4 (1984); cf. Balayé, *La Bibliothèque nationale*, pp. 347-348.

23. Varry, "Vicissitudes et aléas des livres placés 'sous la main' de la Nation." I would like to express my gratitude to Dominique Varry for having shared with me two of his papers, which were then in press. See Varry, dir. *Les Bibliothèques de la Révolution et du XIXe siecle (1789-1914)*, vol 3 of *Historie des bibliothèques français* (Paris: Cercle de la Librairie-Promodis, 1991).

24. Particularly quotable is a passage from a report by Urbain Domergue, the head of the Bibliographical Bureau:

> All the institutions of our Republic must be cast in the republican mould, and French bibliography, a prism destined to split light into its colors, ought not be pouring out over the libraries a stream of instructions for a free people, so that Cujas, d'Hozier, and Busenbaum will not pollute pure daylight with their foul exhalations. . . ; this frenzy to accumulate books has led them [i.e., the members of the Committee of Scholars] to take as much care to collect Marie Alacoque as Voltaire, the *Sinner's Guide* as *The Social Contract*, the wretched proceedings of novices against monks as the proceedings of nations against tyrants, as works that are not worth the sheet of paper on which their titles are copied.
>
> Let us take a scalpel to our huge depositories of books and amputate all the gangrenous members from the bibliographic body. Let us remove from our libraries the swelling which presages death; let us leave only the plumpness which is a sign of health. We rightly send any counter-revolutionary author or accomplice to counter-revolution to the scaffold. There are counter-revolutionaries in our libraries as well; I vote for their deportation. Let us hurl back on our enemies the poison of our books of

theology, mysticism, royalism, feudalism, and oppressive laws; and while our republican phalanxes spread death and destruction among their satellites, let us spread using our books confusion and madness; such is their blindness that they will pay dearly for this evil day. The gold of Spain, Italy, Germany, even England will come to be exchanged for the pestilential pages whose contact we fear and we will consume the loss." *Procès-verbaux du Comité d'instruction publique de la Convention,* ed. Guillaume, vol. 2, pp. 795-799.

We should point out here that Domergue requested that "one or two copies of these monuments to human stupidity" be preserved for the edification of posterity.

25. The best source on this topic is Dominique Varry, "Recherches sur le livre en Normandie: les bibliothèques de l'Eure à la fin du XVIIIe siècle d'après les saisies révolutionnaires." Thèse de 3e cycle, University of Paris-I, 1986. See also Michel Ollion, "Les Bibliothèques des nobles parisiens à la fin du XVIIIe siècle," *Positions des thèses soutenues par les élèves de la promotion de 1985.* Ecole nationale des chartes (Paris, 1985), pp. 117-124.

26. See *Procès-verbaux de la Commission temporaire des arts,* ed. Tuetey, passim.

27. Henri Grégoire, Convention nationale, Comité d'Instruction publique, *Rapports sur les destructions opérées par le vandalisme et les moyens d'y remédier.* (Paris, Year II/1799) passim. This report shows that, where books were concerned, there were few flagrant acts of vandalism, but there were countless thefts.

28. On the part played in this affair by Antoine-Augustin Renouard, see Denis Richet, "Avant Philippe Renouard: sa famille aux XVIIIe et XIXe siècles," in *Le Livre dans l'Europe de la Renaissance* (Paris: Promodis/Cercle de la Librairie, 1988), pp. 21-22.

29. *1789, le Patrimoine libéré*; Henri-Jean Martin, "Le sacre de Gutenberg."

30. Cf. Isabelle Kratz's article forthcoming in *Bulletin du bibliophile.*

31. Pierre Riberette, *Les Bibliothèques françaises,* p. 57.

32. Henri Grégoire, *Rapports de Henri Grégoire sur la bibliographie, la destruction des patois et les excès du vandalisme . . . ,* ed. E. Egger (Caen: A. Massif, 1867).

33. *Procès-verbaux de la Commission temporaire des arts,* ed. Tuetey, vol. 1, especially pp. 474, 512, 609, 610, and 618.

34. On the current state of France's book heritage, see Françoise Blechet and Annie Charon, *Les Fonds anciens des bibliothèques françaises*; Ministère de la Culture, *Le Patrimoine des bibliothèques. Rapport à Monsieur*

*le Directeur des bibliothèques par une Commission de douze membres*, 2 v. Louis Desgraves, chairman, Jean-Luc Gautier, spokesman (Paris: Ministère de la Culture, 1982).

35. Jean-Baptiste Labiche, *Notice sur les dépôts littéraires et la Révolution bibliographique* (Paris: A. Parent, 1880).

36. Ibid.

37. Varry.

38. Jean-Baptiste Labiche, *Notice sur les dépôts littéraires*.

39. One can get an idea of the state of affairs in the provinces in Graham Keith Barnett, *Histoire des bibliothèques publiques*; and the exemplary study by Guy Thuiller, *L'Histoire d'une bibliothèque. La Bibliothèque publique de Nevers de 1790 à 1940* (Nevers: Bibliothèque municipale, 1983).

40. Michel de Certeau, Dominique Julia, and Jacques Revel, *La Culture au pluriel* (Paris: Union générale d'édition, 1974), pp. 55-94.

# SOME EIGHTEENTH-CENTURY AMERICAN BOOK COLLECTORS, THEIR COLLECTIONS, AND THEIR LEGACIES

*Marcus A. McCorison*

In one of those historical coincidences that always astonishes one, three great book collectors, living in different parts of the North American continent, were active at the turn of the seventeenth and eighteenth centuries. Cotton Mather (1663-1728), dominant religious leader of Boston, William Byrd II (1674-1744), the wealthiest Virginia planter of his day, and James Logan (1674-1751), principal politician and merchant of Philadelphia, never met one another and were markedly different individuals. Still in similar ways, including the building and use of their libraries, they were agents in transforming a European culture into a distinctly American culture. Mather, Byrd, and Logan began a distinctly American tradition in library building from which sprang their successors: Thomas Prince (1687-1758), William Mackenzie (1758-1828), and Isaiah Thomas (1749-1831). These men, who came from widely varying traditions, represent the beginnings of cultural changes that found fruition at the end of the eighteenth century, so that the latter generation may be truly thought to be American, new men of a revolution.

Cotton Mather, son of the Reverend Increase Mather of Boston, was the offspring of the leading clerical families in a seventeenth-century town that was dominated by Puritan theology and the revolutionary politics that issued therefrom. Young Mather was educated for the ministry, as had been his grandfathers--Richard Mather and John Cotton--his father, his uncles on all sides, his brothers and his cousins, and his surviving son. Learned in Hebrew, Greek, and Latin in order to interpret or re-interpret the Scriptures, the Mather family acquired a great accumulation of books and pamphlets that passed between fathers and sons, brothers and cousins in a bewildering array of loans, wills, gifts, and accidental transfers. Portions of the collection, which had originated with Richard in old England, passed to family members who went from New England to Ireland and then back to England. Other portions found their way to Connecticut and Nova Scotia as the generations spread out over the northeast.

Cotton Mather inherited the largest portion of the family collection from his father, Increase, who had received a goodly portion of the library of his father Richard. The Mather collection, which at one time numbered between 7,000 and 8,000 volumes, was chiefly theological in nature as we would expect in a library of leaders of a community in which theology was the vital center of its existence. Even so, a large portion of the library dealt with contemporary English politics, including, for example, twenty-five volumes of "English Tracts" that contained hundreds of pamphlets dealing with the political and religious controversies between dissenters and the crown. A late edition of John Milton's response to Charles I's defense on the divine right of kings, *Eikonoklastes in Answer to Eikon Basilike* (London, 1690), was only one of them.[1]  In addition to theology and religious disputational works, the Mather library was rich in all the learned and practical disciplines, containing editions of the works of Descartes, Erasmus, Burnet, Aristotle, Sir Thomas More; the classics in Greek and Latin; practical books on navigation and embalming; White Kennet's *Bibliothecae Americanae Primordia*, Rycaut's history of Turkey, and *Purchas His Pilgrimes*; the pamphlets of that Quaker rabble-rouser in Philadelphia, George Keith.

Cotton Mather's use of his library was prodigious, and he made great additions to it by purchase and through the productions of his own pen. He delivered thousands of sermons and published more than 450 of them. His most famous work, *Magnalia Christi Americana* (London, 1702) constitutes his interpretation of the workings of God in the history of New England and was based upon the documents that were part of the family collection.

The works of contemporary science in the family library, stand as vivid evidence of the existence of the two contradictory worlds--religion and science--in which Cotton Mather was such an uneasy inhabitant. He used the works of Boyle, Hooke, and Sydenham and corresponded with Robert Hooke in his medical investigations which led him in 1721 to propose to Dr. Zabadiel Boylston that the population of Boston be inoculated to control an epidemic of smallpox then raging in the city. This opinion so enraged one member of the community that he threatened to kill Mather. The Royal Society of London, to which Mather had been elected a member in October 1713, published his communications entitled "Curiosa Americana." But Mather's greatest scientific work of that kind, unpublished in full until 1972, was *The Angel of Bethesda*. His manuscript is the only comprehensive medical work written during the American colonial period, and it contains Mather's best advice for the medical and religious relief of humanity's physical ills. In part pharmacopoeia, family-physician, and commonsense commentary (e.g., a recommendation to change one's stockings regularly), his book exhibits a warmly sympathetic concern for the well-being of his neighbors, a well-being that was always at risk from grossly unreliable medical knowledge and the uncontrolled whims of nature.

The library that Cotton Mather inherited and enlarged represents a guide to a man who lived intensely in the realms of mind and spirit, attempting with only partial success to find salvation between the two. It was passed to his son, Samuel, who, lacking the vigor of his father, allowed the collection to be dissipated. In all, six generations of the family contributed to its growth or dispersal before the remnants were finally deposited in the nineteenth century in libraries in Boston, Cambridge, and Worcester.

Like the library of the Mather family, the library of William Byrd II was a utilitarian one, but it was very different in content. The books in each library had been gathered to enable both collectors to pursue careers as leaders of their very different communities. Also, the Byrd library was formed by a father (William I) who passed it to his son, who passed it, alas, to the third generation who in 1766 comprised the greatest group of debtors of the bankrupt Councilors of Virginia who had "borrowed" the entire treasury of the colony to pay their personal debts.

> [July 7, 1709] I arose at 5 o'clock and read a chapter in Hebrew and some Greek in Josephus. I said my prayers and ate milk for breakfast. I danced my dance, and settled my accounts. I read some Latin. It was extremely hot. I ate stewed mutton for dinner. In the afternoon it began to rain and blow very violently so that it blew down my fence. It likewise thundered. In all the time I have been in Virginia I never heard it blow harder. I read Latin again and Greek in Homer. In the evening we took a walk in the garden. I said my prayers and had good health, good humor and good thoughts, thanks be to God Almighty.

This litany of regularity and moderation is repeated day after day throughout the extant volumes of Byrd's diary, written in shorthand. The diary reveals a life formed by a seven-year-old who was sent to the Felsted School in Essex, England, to be taught to be an English gentleman. Intended by his father to become the royal governor, he remained in England until 1705, when he returned to Virginia to take on the responsibilities of Westover, the family estate that under his administration grew to 179,000 heavily encumbered acres of Virginia land. But, although after his father's death in 1709, William succeeded to high offices in the colony, he did not become the royal governor. If Byrd failed to become an English gentleman or the governor, during the second decade of the eighteenth century he did lead the Virginia Council (planters like himself) in maintaining their financial prerogatives against Governor Alexander Spotswood.

The sample diary entry of July 1709 clearly indicates that Byrd used the books in his library to support an active, but intensely private, intellectual life. A catalog of the Westover library which then numbered 2,345 titles in 3,500 volumes was prepared about 1751, seven years after Byrd's death, perhaps in preparation for sale when the heir, William III, was in financial difficulties. The catalog was imperfectly published in 1901 by John Spencer Bassett in his edition of the Byrd's *Writings*. An unpublished version of the catalog, corrected by Edwin Wolf is in the files of the Library Company of Philadelphia. It and Wolf's excellent essay on the dispersal of the Byrd library contain the best indications of the contents of a library that was diligently and carefully selected in order to form a collection, some in vellum bindings that Byrd had especially gilded, of the works deemed to be most useful for his time and place. Classical authors were present in force and we have noted that he read from them daily. The master of a huge plantation, Byrd had books on agriculture, medicine, and all the other topics he needed to manage the place and the large numbers of free and slave people who were dependent upon his skills. The extensive collection of books on the law were useful for his service as a councilor of the colony. Substantial numbers of books on history and travel (including Rycaut's history of Turkey), divinity, and "Entertainment, Poetry, Translations &c." which included the ever-present "Turkish Spy" in seven volumes, as well as "French Books Chiefly of Entertainment" (we could hardly expect to find such a listing in the Mather library) provided a wide array of reading to absorb his varied interests. A listing of a folio volume of "Albert Durer's Drawings" suggests Byrd's love of paintings and "Perkin's Art of Witchcraft" tells us that he was not entirely free from the netherworld of spirits.

The books in the Westover library surely provided him with the examples of literary felicity that marked his narratives of running the boundary line between Virginia and North Carolina in 1728. Byrd wrote two versions of the experience *The Secret History of the Line* and *A History of the Dividing Line*, neither of which were published until 1841. These, and his other writings, reveal a person who at last had measured his life, ambitions, and style to the realities of colonial Virginia and whose life and library illuminate another regional tradition that was part of the cultural matrix of a new nation.

James Logan--man of affairs, sometime private secretary to William Penn, and the Penn family's agent and protector in Pennsylvania for nearly fifty years (1699-1747), Quaker builder of a province, scholar, and book collector--is the third exemplar whose library tells us something of the cultural life of our country, before we became a nation. The son of a respectable, middle-class Irish schoolmaster, Logan was not ridden by theological dogma, nor was he an aristocrat. His own interests revolved about secular knowledge and scientific investigation, and he was as compulsive in his way as were Cotton Mather and William Byrd in theirs. If he was not an aristocrat, he surely was not one of the commonalty, for he was the vigorous defender of the proprietor's rights against the democracy. He was disdainful of the ordinary level of learning amongst his contemporaries, but he was eager to assist the Leathern Apron crowd, Benjamin Franklin's Junto, when in 1731 they went about the establishment of the Library Company of Philadelphia by preparing a list of recommended books with which to stock their shelves.

Logan's learning included the ancient and modern languages. Arabic was his key to attaining higher mathematics. Natural history, especially botany, and civil history were amply represented in his carefully selected library. Logan, like Cotton Mather, occupied himself with original scientific research and corresponded with the Royal Society, which published his communications in their *Transactions*. His experiments on the pollination of Indian corn were warmly accepted by Linnaeus, the great Swedish founder of systematic botany, who saw to their publication. Logan's interests ranged from astronomical calculations to solving the mathematical theory of spherical aberrations to a history of mankind, the latter a project begun but finally given up, incomplete. He translated Cicero's *Cato Major*, a celebration of pleasures and advantages of old age. Its printing by Benjamin Franklin's press in 1744 resulted in an American typographical masterpiece.

Despite his duties as secretary and clerk of the provincial council on which he served from 1702 to 1747, as mayor of Philadelphia, as justice of the court of common pleas, as chief justice of the supreme court, as acting governor of the province, as land and Indian agent for the Penn family, and finally as one active in his own behalf in land speculation and the fur trade, somehow Logan kept abreast of the London book trade. His detailed, complex, and convoluted letters to long-suffering, trans-Atlantic agents were full of explicit advice on where to purchase such and such a book, in such and such an edition, and at such a price. If the agent failed him, as inevitably he must, Logan disdainfully changed his custom. To one unfortunate he wrote, "Thou may therefore well excuse me for finding fault with thee as I do when thy prices are unreasonable, who have been a buyer of Books above these fifty years and am not to be put off as a common American, as thou hast divers times served me, for I know a book well."

Toward the end of his life Logan decided to leave his splendid library (which by the way, like our other two libraries, included a copy of Paul Rycaut's history of Turkey) to the citizens of Philadelphia. Accordingly, he established an endowment and designed and built a building into which he intended his books to go. Yet, the querulous old man could not leave well enough alone and after an argument with his son-in-law, Isaac Norris, cancelled the bequest. Nevertheless, following Logan's death in October of 1751, the executors of his estate proceeded with the original plan, and the Loganian Library was finally opened in 1760 after a catalog of it had been prepared. Despite the presence in the City of Brotherly Love of such intellects as B. Franklin (who during this period spent most of his time in London) and his fellow members in the American Philosophical Society and the Library Company, it is sad to report that the then citizens of Philadelphia were as unlearned as their predecessors, for the Loganian Library was very little used. Thirty-two years later, the books were transferred to the care of the Library Company of Philadelphia, where they have since remained. An excellent catalog of the collection was published in 1974 by a latter-day librarian of that institution. It explicates with admirable detail the contents of James Logan's library, containing some 2,200 titles of the most learned and revered works of his age.

If we accept the life of the New Englander, Cotton Mather, as one dominated by the contradictions between medieval spiritual beliefs and emerging scientific thought, if we see the life of the Virginian, William Byrd, as one shaped by incompatible social and political ambitions of metropolitan London and provincial Westover, then we may view the career of the Philadelphian, James Logan, as one in which is established an alliance between the demands of incessant responsibilities for trans-Atlantic commerce and politics with an intellect that verged on modern modes of dealing with the world. Although the libraries of Mather, Byrd, and Logan contained many of the same titles, because among educated individuals there was an evident consensus of what was to be learned, each used those books within the context of differing presuppositions and ambitions. Each collector exemplifies to a remarkable degree the stereotypical images of the South, the Middle Region, and the Northeast of what was to become the United States. Each experienced a personal change that ultimately took him from the traditions rooted in the old world to new ways of dealing with the intellectual and physical requirements of a new world. If American individuals underwent profound changes by the mid-eighteenth century, so too had other fundamental conditions that were to make a new nation inevitable. The Puritan revolutions of 1640 and 1688 in England and in America assured the ascendancy of the legislative body above the king, established the middle class as a political force, and empowered religious diversity. The Virginia House of Burgesses rejected the constraints of a rigid social structure based on royal prerogative and stratification. The Quaker merchants of Philadelphia forged an independent economic structure that could withstand the impositions of a commercial system that was arranged to funnel all profits to London.

In Boston, the Mather Library maintained a reputation as a source of historical information and inspiration until the late eighteenth century. In the 1760s some parts of the library were lent to Lieutenant Governor Thomas Hutchinson when he was writing his history of Massachusetts; and when the Stamp Act mob sacked Hutchinson's mansion in 1765, they destroyed not only his own papers but also manuscripts borrowed from the Mather library, such as the diaries of the regicide, William Goffe. The Reverend Thomas Prince

(1687-1758), who became Cotton Mather's successor as the premier collector of New England historical materials, had frequent recourse to the family library then in the care of Samuel Mather.[2] Prince borrowed from the Mather library (but did not return) the history of Plymouth Plantation written by its first governor, William Bradford, and he also gathered (perhaps from the Mather collection) papers of the Winthrops, seven volumes of papers of the Mathers, those of other significant New England characters, as well as their printed works.  He bequeathed this great collection to his church, the Old South Church of Boston, where it was housed in a room at the base of the steeple.  Old South Church was the scene of some of Boston's most seditious meetings; thus, it is understandable that during the British occupation of the town in 1775-76 British troops would turn the building into a riding stable and that the library in the steeple would be badly used.  Much was scattered or destroyed.  How or when Bradford's manuscript was taken to London and deposited in Fulham Castle is not known, but it was not until 1897 that the manuscript was returned to Massachusetts by the bishop of London and Queen Victoria.  In any event, the disheveled remnants of the Prince library existed in limbo for many years until the trustees of the church placed them in the hands of the Boston Public Library, where they remain.

In Philadelphia, the successor as book collector to James Logan was the wealthy merchant, William Mackenzie (1758-1828), who, toward the end of the eighteenth century, began a collection of books that in modern terms are called "rare."  He selected his books with an eye for their beauty and significance as monuments of printing.  Thus, he had Jensen's 1470 edition of Eusebious and a copy of Pliny the Elder's *Historia Naturalis* printed in Venice on vellum, for presentation to the prince of Aragon.  It was Mackenzie who bought the manuscript catalog of the library of William Byrd II, as well as many of his books, thereby preserving the record of that remarkable Virginia collection which had found its way to Philadelphia, where it was to be dispersed over the next few decades, following the American Revolution.  Also, he bought books from Franklin's library and gathered in many American political pamphlets that remain important evidences of our national history.  Nearly all of Mackenzie's books were acquired by the Library Company or by the Loganian Library (in the Library Company) after his death at age seventy.  Thus, the Library Company of Philadelphia became the institutional home of the Loganian Library and the remnants of William Byrd's great library.  To them were added the highly sophisticated book collection of William Mackenzie, whose tastes in literature and the volumes in which those texts were housed marked a watershed between "utilitarian" book collecting and the mode of collecting we call bibliophilia.

Mackenzie's criteria for book collecting represented a significant change in the cultural nuances of our young country, as did those of his contemporary, Isaiah Thomas of Worcester.  Born in 1749 into a family without prospects, Thomas was self-educated and was bred to the art of printing by as shiftless a printer as one could possibly find in Boston.  In July of 1770 he and his former master, the feckless Zechariah Fowle, issued a new newspaper, *The Massachusetts Spy*, for which after a few months of false starts, the twenty-one-year-old newspaperman found his audience.  In his *History of Printing in America*, Thomas described the winnowing process:

> For a few weeks some communications were furnished by those who were in favor of the royal prerogative, but they were exceeded by writers on the other side; and the authors and subscribers among the tories denounced and quitted the Spy.  The publisher [Thomas himself] then devoted it to the cause of his country, supported by the whigs, under whose banners he had enlisted. . . . Common sense in common language is necessary to influence one class of citizens, as much as learning and elegance of composition are to produce an effect upon another.

So, he clothed the *Spy* in "common sense in common language" and addressed it to the common reader, thereby finding the way to wealth.  He became a publisher of a newspaper espousing the politics of revolt that was vilified by those "in favor of the royal prerogative" from North Carolina to Massachusetts.  With the help of John Hancock and the Committee of Safety, Thomas got his press out of harm's way in Boston by transporting it to Worcester just before the Battles of Lexington and Concord.  During the war his fortunes waned, but at its conclusion Thomas returned to Worcester, in time establishing partnerships that ranged from Baltimore to Walpole, New Hampshire, where Joseph Dennie and Thomas Green Fessenden enlivened the pages of the local newspaper, *The Farmer's Museum*.  The largest and most significant of Thomas's offices remained in Worcester, where during the 1790s he employed as many as 150 printers and bookbinders.  The extent of his business may be judged by the fact that between the years 1789 and 1805 he published 300,000 copies of Noah Webster's *American Spelling Book*.  He owned a partnership in a paper mill.  He bought printing types worth several thousand pounds (sterling) from English foundries, and Benjamin Franklin called him the American Baskerville in recognition of his typographical taste and skills.

In 1802 Thomas turned over much of the management of his printing business to his son, although he remained active in many financial affairs.  Despite involvement in his business interest, Thomas devoted more and more of his time to building the library he had begun in the 1780s and to historical research, resulting in 1810 in the publication of his two-volume *History of Printing in America*, a work that is still useful.  Thomas was inordinately proud of his library, from which he had gathered much of the material of the *History*. Thomas took particular care of his own publications, many of the volumes of which were elegantly bound in calf and well covered with gilt by Henry Bilson Legge and other excellent Boston craftsmen. For example, in the manuscript catalog of his library that he compiled in 1812, he listed copies of his splendid 1791 Bible thusly: in two volumes, folio, with fifty copper plate engravings, fine copy, calf, gilt, $24; two volumes in one, folio, elegantly bound in red Morocco, gilt, $22; another in two volumes, royal octavo, with forty-eight plates, calf, gilt, a fine copy, $15; and he had still other copies, plain in calf.

The catalog was divided into two sections, one for "Ancient Books, i.e., Printed previous to the Year 1700" in 57 pages, and a second devoted to "Modern Books," covering pages 59 through 217. Amongst the Bibles listed among the Ancient books was a Latin Bible, "beautifully printed with a peculiar type, on fine vellum paper at Venice 1476." After copying the colophon into the catalog, Thomas went on to write that he believed this to be the most "ancient piece of Typography to be met with in the United States." As we now know, there were other and older examples of incunabula in the libraries in Philadelphia and Boston, but we cannot now rob this collector of his pleasure at owning such a splendid book. After consulting Dibdin on values, Thomas was certain the Bible was worth $100. He owned the 1663 edition of the "Eliot Indian Bible," as well as the 1709 "Massachusetts Psalter in Indian and English," which he noted had been printed by Benjamin Green and James Printer, the latter a native American. Thomas values the Indian Bible at $5 and the Psalter at 75 cents.

The collection of ancient books was a very mixed bag. Cicero's *Rhetoric*, printed in the cursive type in Paris by the "celebrated Robert Stephens, 1544," was immediately followed by a listing for an imperfect copy of "Comical Sayings of Don Quixote" (London, 1696) which was bound up in a volume with "Old Newspapers, &c." The homilies of St. Chrysostom were followed by a volume in which three of William Hubbard's works were bound: *A Narrative of the Troubles with the Indians in New England* (Boston, 1677), *A Narrative of the Troubles with the Indians from Pascataqua to Pemmiquid* (Boston, 1676), and his 1676 election sermon, *The Happiness of a People in the Wisdom of their Rulers*. Thomas stated that these works were very scarce and valued the volume at all of $2. A Latin history of the popes printed in Cologne in 1500 was valued at $4, as was his copy, sadly lacking the title and errata pages, of "Psalms in Metre, printed at Cambridge, New-England, 1639." Not knowing of the five copies of the *Whole Booke of Psalms*, the Bay Psalm Book of 1640, that lay neglected in the Prince Library in Boston, Isaiah Thomas believed that his copy of "the first Book printed in British America (now the United States)" probably was "the only copy in being, and is therefore very valuable," for after advertising for it throughout New England, he had been unable to even hear of another. Thomas listed the contents of bound-up tract volumes on sixteen pages. They included pamphlets on the Glorious Revolution of 1688, the controversies with George Keith, many seventeenth-century Boston imprints, and a copy of Moxon's *Mechanick Dyalling*, but not his *Mechanick Exercises*.

Thomas's listing of "Modern Books" began with the entry for "Account of the New Invented Fire-Places, (Franklin's)" and ended with "Zenger, John Peter, printer of New-york, Narrative of his Case and Trial, for a Libel, . . . Newyork Reprinted 1770." Between those extremes were entries for a poem printed in 1770 in Charleston, South Carolina, by Mr. Timothy; and facing pages 90 and 91 began with a mock epic, M'Fingal, by John Trumball. Also included were listings of five sermons by Increase Mather and two works of Hannah More; the section is finished up with a copy of a *Miss in her Teens; or The Medley of Lovers, a farce* and *Mother Midnight's Comical Pocket Book*.

Thomas went on to list classified books--Dictionaries, Indian (native language imprints), Physic and Surgery, Printing (a two-page account that included 21 type specimens and Fournier's *Manuel Typographique*), Trials, 33 pages of Books printed by Isaiah Thomas, Music, Pamphlets, Books for Children, and Books printed by Isaiah Thomas, Jr. Periodicals and Newspapers covered 14 pages and included 15 complete volumes of the first American newspaper, the *Boston News-Letter* from issue number one, April 24, 1704; seven volumes of Andrew Bradford's *American Mercury*, 1719-46 (the first Philadelphia newspaper); and the *Halifax Gazette*, 1765-66, a newspaper that Thomas had worked on as a wild youth. The catalog ends with three pages of registers and Almanacks. Thomas's earliest almanac was dated Boston, 1656. He had eighteen published prior to 1701.

All these books and papers Isaiah Thomas gave to establish the American Antiquarian Society in 1812. He cast up its value at $5,000, but not to appear to be too vain, he deducted 20 percent and placed its worth at $4,000 when title was passed for $1. Thomas's collection was unique. It was based on common sense in common language for common people, not a collection of classical and European books. He was indefatigable in his efforts to improve the collections. In 1813 he visited a printer's office in Boston where he bought copies of popular ballads that he bound up in three volumes in order to show what was current among the "vulgar." The next year he bought the remnants of the Mather library from Cotton Mather's granddaughter, Hannah Crocker. In 1820, after he had built the Society's library building, he gave books worth another $5,000. Thomas knew that his generation had taken part in a great event, the American Revolution, and he set out to preserve the materials used by, read from, or worked upon by the citizens of the new American republic. He and his colleagues took as their charge the collection of all the antiquities of the Western Hemisphere--literary, natural, man-made--

an ambition that immediately proved to be far beyond the capabilities of the institution. Nevertheless, collections were built and in 1820 were placed in Antiquarian Hall, where they were opened to the public and have been ever since. To this day the course that Isaiah Thomas set remains the direction for adding to the Society's collections.

It is revealing to realize that the three great libraries that originated in seventeenth-century Massachusetts, Pennsylvania, and Virginia are now vital parts of twentieth-century libraries, institutions that are now formal institutions of higher learning. Portions of the Mather library passed through the hands of Thomas Prince and found their way, finally, to the Boston Public Library. The largest single group of Mather books was purchased not for Harvard College, but for the American Antiquarian Society. James Logan's library was incorporated into the holdings of the Library Company in Philadelphia, the city's earlier "public" library. In his day, William Mackenzie of that city was instrumental in gathering into the Library Company not only the catalog of the Byrd family library but a number of the volumes still remaining in the hands of the local booksellers. The disposition of these libraries into secular, non-academic institutions is significant and tells us something about the cultural change that occurred following the American Revolution. A portion, at least, of our forebears believed that books and learning belonged to the public and put that belief into action.

Access to knowledge is part and parcel of the democratic ideal, in which is embodied the notion of the perfectibility of man. Progress is to be gained through one's own efforts, a notion linked to expectations of both spiritual and worldly rewards. For example, the American Antiquarian Society, modeled on English and Irish institutions, was founded to provide the sources of and opportunities for self-improvement, self-knowledge, and wisdom to any citizen of the Republic who desired to make use of them. Through its collections, the new institution would preserve the proofs of a social ideal that, for its adherents, balanced personal freedom with self-control and communal responsibility and would open channels to historical knowledge and opinion in an arena from which truth would surely emerge.

The sources for these investigations were to be worthy of a new Republic. They were not the classical antiquities of Europe, but the evidences of the origins of the New World. Americans would excavate the remains not of ancient Greece, or Rome, but those of the Mississippi Valley or Peru. The collections would not be filled with volumes of classical learning but with the public prints, pamphlets, books, and broadsides produced in the Western Hemisphere. Participants in political revolution, the founders would establish a library on revolutionary principles, one that preserves democratic literature and the written materials of a culture in which all kinds of ideas freely circulate and from which precipitate new ideas of the true and the beautiful.

This plan was revolutionary, because even the libraries that passed in 1812 as public still were given over to a reasonably stable body of literature, that is, the classics in the original and translation; basic works of religious commentary; volumes on ancient history; some mathematical, scientific, and practical works; and a handful of belles lettres. A review of the catalogs of the collections discussed above or those of the Redwood Library of Newport, Rhode Island, or the Harvard College Library demonstrates remarkable congruence on what constituted an acceptable stock of books in collegiate or social libraries. Nevertheless, students were not expected to use the books in their library because the collegiate curricula were still constructed on sixteenth-century principles. Thus, the library and field of inquiry established in Worcester constituted real departure from the norm and reflected Thomas's own essentially secular, non-academic, and proletarian background.

During the early years of the nineteenth century the old learned societies such as the American Philosophical Society, the Massachusetts Historical Society, and the American Antiquarian Society were centers for the encouragement of learning. Our national government was notoriously slow to assume such a task, taking a decade before accepting the opportunity to establish the Smithsonian Institution, offered through the 1836 bequest of the Englishman, James Smithson. College faculties tended to transmit received knowledge rather than attempting to enlarge its corpus. The learned societies encouraged and published the results of the investigations of their members who were amateurs of learning or who were of the learned professions--theology, medicine, law. They met on equal footing then and now, two centuries later, the old learned societies still cling (with varying degrees of effectiveness) to the tradition of the open republic of letters. The interaction of laypeople and members of the professions resulted in a "multiplicity of thriving new worlds of learning," rather than encouraging a separation between professional scholars and their unwashed brethren. The nineteenth-century learned society was an example of that free state in which the growth of polite arts and learning was the natural result.

## SOURCES

Bassett, John Spencer. *The Writings of "Colonel William Byrd, of Westover in Virginia, Esqr."* (New York: Doubleday, 1901), Appendix A, "A catalogue of the books in the library at Westover belonging to William Byrd Esqr.", pp. 413-443.
Cannon, Carl L. *American Book Collectors and Collecting from Colonial Times to the Present* (New York: H. W. Wilson, 1941).
Hall, Michael G. *The Last American Puritan, the Life of Increase Mather, 1639-1723* (Middletown, Conn.: Wesleyan University Press, 1988).

Korey, Marie Elena. "Three Early Philadelphia Collectors," in *American Book Collector*, n.s. Vol. 2, no. 6, Nov.-Dec. 1981, pp. 2-13.

Library Company of Philadelphia. *A Catalogue of Books Belonging to the Library Company of Philadelphia*, Intro. by Edwin Wolf, 2d ed. (Philadelphia: Library Company of Philadelphia, 1956).

Lockridge, Kenneth A. *The Diary and Life, of William Byrd II of Virginia, 1674-1744* (Chapel Hill: University of North Carolina Press for the Institute of Early American History and Culture, 1987).

McCorison, Marcus A. *Isaiah Thomas, the American Antiquarian Society, and the Future* (Worcester, Mass.: American Antiquarian Society, 1981), pp. 27-37. Reprinted from the *Proceedings of the American Antiquarian Society*, April 1981.

McCorison, Marcus A. "Three New England Patriot Printers of the American Revolution." 46 pp., unpublished paper, 1976.

Redwood Library and Athenaeum. Newport, R.I. *The 1764 Catalogue of the Redwood Library Company at Newport, Rhode Island*, ed. Marcus A. McCorison (New Haven, Conn.: Yale University Press, 1965).

Silverman, Kenneth. *The Life and Times of Cotton Mather* (New York: Harper & Row, 1984).

Shipton, Clifford K. *Isaiah Thomas: Printer, Patriot and Philanthropist, 1749-1831* (Rochester, N.Y.: Printing House of Leo Hart, 1948).

Thomas, Isaiah. "Catalogue of The Private Library of Isaiah Thomas, Senior, of Worcester, Massachusetts taken in March in the Year 1812." MS, 217 pp., at the American Antiquarian Society, Isaiah Thomas Papers.

Tolles, Frederick B. *James Logan and the Culture of Provincial America* (Boston: Little, Brown, 1957).

Tuttle, Julius Herbert. *The Libraries of the Mathers* (Worcester, Mass.: American Antiquarian Society, 1910), 90 pp., interleaved copy at AAS. Reprinted from the *Proceedings of the American Antiquarian Society*, April 1910.

Winship, George Parker. *The John Carter Brown Library, a history* (Providence, 1914).

Whitmore, William H. *Catalogue of the American Portion of the Library of the Rev. Thomas Prince* (Boston: J. K. Wiggin & Wm. Parsons Lunt, 1868).

Wolf, Edwin, II. *The Dispersal of the Library of William Byrd of Westover* (Worcester, Mass.: American Antiquarian Society, 1958), pp. 18-106. Reprinted from the *Proceedings of the American Antiquarian Society*, April 1958.

Wolf, Edwin, II. *The Library of James Logan of Philadelphia, 1674-1751*, (Philadelphia: Library Company of Philadelphia, 1974).

NOTES

1. Although the Mather family was separated from Great Britain by an ocean, members of it were participants in the Puritan Revolution that dethroned Charles and led to his beheading in 1649. Following the Restoration of James II to the throne in 1660, the Mathers arranged safe haven in New England for two of Charles's Regicides, and the diaries of one of them, William Goffe, were once part of the Mather collection. Increase Mather, who had spent the first seven years of his ministry in England, returned to England from 1688 until 1691 in a successful effort to nullify James II's royal charter of 1684 that had replaced the original charter of the Massachusetts Bay Company, and to secure the new charter from William and Mary that restored many former privileges. And, following the Glorious Revolution of 1688, it was Cotton Mather who led the citizens of Boston in the arrest of the Royal Governor, Sir Edmund Andros, who was then shipped off to England as a political prisoner.

2. Hannah Mather Crocker, Samuel's daughter and Cotton's granddaughter, recalled that Prince one time came to the house in the morning to consult something in the collection. At dinner time the family discovered that Prince was still at work in the library, so he was asked to eat with them. Suppertime came and the Mather family realized that the reverend scholar was still in the library. When apprised of that news, Prince profusely apologized and "roused himself from the litter in front of him and departed for home with the manuscripts under his arm."

# SELECT BIBLIOGRAPHY

Bailyn, Bernard, and John Hench, eds. *The Press and the American Revolution.* Worcester, Mass.: American Antiquarian Society, 1980.

Carpenter, Kenneth E., ed. *Books and Society in History.* New York: Bowker, 1983.

Censer, Jack R., and Jeremy D. Popkin, eds. *Press and Politics in Prerevolutionary France.* Berkeley and Los Angeles: University of California Press, 1987.

Chartier, Roger. *Frenchness in the History of the Book: From the History of Publishing to the History of Reading.* James Russell Wiggins Lecture. Worcester, Mass.: American Antiquarian Society, 1989.

Darnton, Robert. *The Business of Enlightenment: A Publishing History of the 'Encyclopédie,' 1775-1800.* Cambridge, Mass.: Harvard University Press, 1979.

---, and Daniel Roche, eds. *Revolution in Print: The Press in France, 1775-1800.* Berkeley: University of California Press in collaboration with the New York Public Library, 1989.

Davidson, Cathy. *Revolution and the Word: The Rise of the Novel in America.* New York: Oxford University Press, 1986.

---, ed. *Reading in America: Literature & Social History.* Baltimore: Johns Hopkins University Press, 1989.

Davis, Donald G., ed. *Libraries, Books, and Culture.* Austin: Graduate School of Library and Information Science, University of Texas at Austin, 1986.

---, and John Mark Tucker. *American Library History.* Santa Barbara, Calif: ABC-CLIO, 1989.

Eisenstein, Elizabeth. *The Printing Press as an Agent of Change.* Cambridge: New York: Cambridge University Press, 1979.

Feather, John P. and David McKitterick. *The History of Books and Libraries*: Two Views. Washington: Library of Congress, 1986.

Febvre, Lucien, and Henri-Jean Martin. *L'Apparition du livre.* Paris: Albin Michel, 1958; *The Coming of the Book*, Trans. David Gerard. London: N.L.B., 1976; rpt. 1990.

Hall, David D. *On Native Ground: From the History of Printing to the History of the Book.* James Russell Wiggins Lecture. Worcester, Mass.: American Antiquarian Society, 1984.

---, and John B. Hench, eds., *Needs and Opportunities in the History of the Book: America, 1639-1876*. Worcester, Mass.: American Antiquarian Society, 1987.

Hesse, Carla. *Publishing and Cultural Politics in Revolutionary Paris, 1789-1810*. Berkeley and Los Angeles: University of California Press, 1991.

*Histoire de l'édition française*. 4 vols. Ed. Henri-Jean Martin, Roger Chartier, and Jean-Pierre Vivet. Paris: Promodis, 1983-1986.

*Histoire des bibliothèques françaises*. 4 vols. Dir. André Vernet. Paris: Promodis-Cercle de la Librairie, 1988-1992.

Joyce, William, et al., eds. *Printing and Society in Early America*. Worcester, Mass.: American Antiquarian Society, 1983.

Martin, Henri-Jean. *Livre, pouvoirs et société à Paris au XVIIe siècle (1598-1701)*. (1969; *Print, Power, and People in 17th-Century France*. Trans. David Gerard. Metuchen, N.J.: Scarecrow Press, 1992.).

Popkin, Jeremy D. *Revolutionary News: The Press in France, 1789-1799.*. Durham, N. C.: Duke University Press, 1990.

Smith, Jeffery Alan. *Printers and Press Freedom: The Ideology of Early American Journalism*. New York: Oxford University Press, 1988.

Tanselle, G. T. *Copyright Records and the Bibliographer*. Charlottesville, Va: Bibliographical Society of the University of Virginia, 1969.

---. *A Description of Descriptive Bibliography*. Washington: Library of Congress, 1992.

Warner, Michael. *The Letters of the Republic: Publication and the Public Sphere in Eighteenth-Century America*. Cambridge, Mass.: Harvard University Press, 1990.

Ziff, Larzer. *Upon What Pretext?: The Book and Literary History*. James Russell Wiggins Lecture. Worcester, Mass.: American Antiquarian Society.

---. *Writing in the New Nation: Prose, Print, and Politics in the Early United States*. New Haven, Conn.: Yale University Press, 1991.

# ABOUT THE CONTRIBUTORS

CAROL ARMBRUSTER is French/Italian area specialist in the European Division at the Library of Congress. She writes primarily on Western European publishing and research trends as they relate to American libraries and American information and research interests.

ROGER CHARTIER is a director of studies at the Ecole des Hautes Etudes en Sciences Sociales. His publications include *Lectures et lecteurs dans la France d'Ancien Régime* (1987; Trans. *The Cultural Uses of Print in Early Modern France*, 1987); *Les Usages de l'imprimé (XVe-XIXe siècle)* (1987; Trans. *The Culture of Print: Power and the Uses of Print in Early Modern Europe*, 1989); *Les Origines culturelles de la Révolution française* (1990; Trans. *The Cultural Origins of the French Revolution*, 1991), and the 4-volume *Histoire de l'édition française*, co-editor with Henri-Jean Martin (1983-1986).

ROBERT DARNTON is Shelby Cullom Davis Professor of European History at Princeton University. His publications include *The Business of Enlightenment: a Publishing History of the Encyclopédie, 1775-1800* (1979), *The Literary Underground of the Old Regime* (1982), *Revolution in Print: the Press in France, 1775-1800*, co-editor with Daniel Roche (1989), *Révolution et séduction: l'univers de la littérature clandestine* (1991).

JAMES GILREATH is American History Specialist in the Rare Book and Special Collections Division at the Library of Congress. His publications include *Federal Copyright Records, 1790-1800*, introduction (1987); *Thomas Jefferson's Library: A Catalog with the Entries in His Original Order*, co-author with Douglas Wilson 1989); and *The Judgment of Experts: Essays and Documents about the Forging of the Oath of a Freeman*, editor (1991).

JANE C. GINSBURG is Morton L. Janklow Professor of Literary and Artistic Property Law at Columbia University School of Law. She is a co-author of two law school casebooks, *Copyright for the Nineties* and *Trademark and Unfair Competition Law*, and has published many articles on French and American copyright issues. She is a member of the editorial or advisory boards of the *Columbia-VLA Journal of Law and the Arts*, the *Revue du droit de la propriété intellectuelle* (Paris) and the *Entertainment Law Review*

(London). She also serves on the international Executive Committee of the *Association Littéraire et Artistique Internationale.*

DAVID HALL is Professor of American Religious History at Harvard Divinity School. He chairs the American Antiquarian Society's Program in the History of the Book in American Culture. His publications include *On Native Ground: From the History of Printing to the History of the Book* (1984) and *Worlds of Wonder, Days of Judgment: Popular Religious Belief in Early New England* (1989).

CARLA HESSE is associate professor of history at the University of California - Berkeley. She is the author of *Publishing and Cultural Politics in Revolutionary Paris, 1789-1810* (1991), co-compiler with Laura Mason of *Pamphlets, Periodicals, and Songs of the French Revolutionary Era in the Princeton University Library* (1989), and was the research curator for The New York Public Library's exhibition "Revolution in Print: France, 1789."

LYNN HUNT is Annenberg Professor of History at the University of Pennsylvania. Her publications include *Revolution and Urban Politics in Provincial France* (1978); *The New Cultural History*, editor and introduction (1989); *Politics, Culture, and Class in the French Revolution* (1984); *Eroticism and the Body Politic*, editor (1991); and *The Family Romance of the French Revolution* (1992).

HENRI-JEAN MARTIN is professor at the Ecole Nationale des Chartes. His publications include *L'Apparition du livre* (1958; Trans. *The Coming of the Book, 1976); Livre, pouvoirs et société à Paris au XVIIe siècle (1598-1701)* (1969; Trans. *Print, Power, and People in 17th. Century France*, 1992); *Le Livre français sous l'Ancien Régime* (1987); *Histoire et pouvoirs de l'écrit* (1988); and the 4-volume *Histoire de l'édition française*, co-editor with Roger Chartier (1983-1986). He is also formerly the director of the Bibliothèque de la Ville de Lyon.

MARCUS A. MCCORISON is president emeritus of the American Antiquarian Society. He speaks frequently on the history of the book in early America. His publications include *The History of Printing in America by Isaiah Thomas*, editor (1970); *Vermont Imprints, 1778-1820*, compiler (1963); *The 1764 Catalogue of the Redwood Library Company at Newport, Rhode Island*, editor (1965).

DANIEL ROCHE is professor of modern European history at the Université de Paris I, Directeur de l'Institut d'Histoire Moderne et Contemporaine (CNRS). His publications include *Le Siècle des Lumières en province* (1978);

*Le Peuple de Paris* (1981; Trans. *The People of Paris*, 1987); *Le Journal de ma vie: Jacques-Louis Ménétra* (1982; Trans. *Journal of My Life by Jacques-Louis Ménétra*, 1986); *Les Républicains des lettres* (1988); *La Culture des apparences* (1989); and co-edited with Robert Darnton *Revolution in Print: the Press in France, 1775-1800* (1989).

MICHAEL WARNER is associate professor of English at Rutgers University. He is co-editor with Gerald Graff of *The Origins of Literary Studies in America* (1989) and the author of *The Letters of the Republic: Publication and the Public Sphere in Eighteenth-Century America* (1990).

LARZER ZIFF is Caroline Donovan Professor of English at Johns Hopkins University. His publications include *The American 1890s* (1968; Christian Gauss Award), *Puritanism in America* (1973; National Book Award Nominee), *Literary Democracy* (1981), and *Writing in the New Nation* (1991) in preparation for which he prepared the paper included in this volume.

# INDEX